K

Pose-Invariant Face Recognition

Kazunori Okada

Pose-Invariant Face Recognition

Analysis, Synthesis, Identification of Human Faces with Pose Variations

VDM Verlag Dr. Müller

Impressum/Imprint (nur für Deutschland/ only for Germany)
Bibliografische Information der Deutschen Nationalbibliothek: Die Deutsche Nationalbibliothek
verzeichnet diese Publikation in der Deutschen Nationalbibliografie; detaillierte bibliografische
Daten sind im Internet über http://dnb.d-nb.de abrufbar.
 Alle in diesem Buch genannten Marken und Produktnamen unterliegen warenzeichen-, marken-
oder patentrechtlichem Schutz bzw. sind Warenzeichen oder eingetragene Warenzeichen der
jeweiligen Inhaber. Die Wiedergabe von Marken, Produktnamen, Gebrauchsnamen,
Handelsnamen, Warenbezeichnungen u.s.w. in diesem Werk berechtigt auch ohne besondere
Kennzeichnung nicht zu der Annahme, dass solche Namen im Sinne der Warenzeichen- und
Markenschutzgesetzgebung als frei zu betrachten wären und daher von jedermann benutzt
werden dürften.

Coverbild: www.ingimage.com

Verlag: VDM Verlag Dr. Müller Aktiengesellschaft & Co. KG
Dudweiler Landstr. 99, 66123 Saarbrücken, Deutschland
Telefon +49 681 9100-698, Telefax +49 681 9100-988
Email: info@vdm-verlag.de
Zugl.: Los Angeles, University of Southern California, Diss., 2001

Herstellung in Deutschland:
Schaltungsdienst Lange o.H.G., Berlin
Books on Demand GmbH, Norderstedt
Reha GmbH, Saarbrücken
Amazon Distribution GmbH, Leipzig
ISBN: 978-3-639-29053-0

Imprint (only for USA, GB)
Bibliographic information published by the Deutsche Nationalbibliothek: The Deutsche
Nationalbibliothek lists this publication in the Deutsche Nationalbibliografie; detailed
bibliographic data are available in the Internet at http://dnb.d-nb.de.
 Any brand names and product names mentioned in this book are subject to trademark, brand
or patent protection and are trademarks or registered trademarks of their respective holders. The
use of brand names, product names, common names, trade names, product descriptions etc.
even without a particular marking in this works is in no way to be construed to mean that such
names may be regarded as unrestricted in respect of trademark and brand protection legislation
and could thus be used by anyone.

Cover image: www.ingimage.com

Publisher: VDM Verlag Dr. Müller Aktiengesellschaft & Co. KG
Dudweiler Landstr. 99, 66123 Saarbrücken, Germany
Phone +49 681 9100-698, Fax +49 681 9100-988
Email: info@vdm-publishing.com

Printed in the U.S.A.
Printed in the U.K. by (see last page)
ISBN: 978-3-639-29053-0

To Eve, Michiyo and Hiromasa.

Acknowledgments

We have an unknown distance yet to run, an unknown river to explore.
What falls there are, we know not; what rocks beset the channel, we
know not; what walls rise over the river, we know not. ... John W.
Powell

This thesis is a result of my five-year doctorate study at University of Southern California. I thank my Ph.D. advisor *Christoph von der Malsburg* and committee members *Irving Biederman, Gerard Medioni*, and *Antonio Ortega* for their mentorship, stimulating discussion, and encouragement. Prior to this Ph.D. period, the idea of studying automatic face recognition was planted in my mind when I was just entering into my first graduate study in Nagoya University. I received from various people much training as a scientist and encouragement for studying abroad. I am forever indebted to *Peter High, Kiyoshi Minemura, Hirofumi Saito, Kazuo Takatsuka, Takashi Watanabe, Hajime Yokosawa, Satoru Kuroda, Naoyuki Hashimoto*, and *Zhong Yuan*. At USC, I was extremely fortunate to have met excellent colleagues who have made my time so stimulating, enjoyable, and memorable. Without their tremendous help, my study would have never reached its completion. I wish to thank all the fellow students of the von der Malsburg's group both at USC and at Ruhr-Universität Bochum. Especially for this thesis, I want to thank *Jan Wieghardt* and *Junmei Zhu* for their fruitful discussion, *Hartmut Loos* for proof-reading an abstract, and *Thomas Maurer* for helping me to prepare the facial image sequences. In 1999, I had an opportunity to visit ATR in Kyoto. This experience gave me the chance to further my doctorate study in a supportive and stimulating environment and to interact with so many different talents. I wish to thank my friends and colleagues at ATR for making my stay such a productive and memorable one. My special gratitude goes to *Shigeru Akamatsu* for giving me this opportunity, *Hiromi Mochizuki* for making my visit care-free, and *Katsunori Isono* for providing the 3D facial data and software. *Ken Ehrlich, Doug Fidaleo*, and *Eve Luckring* copy-edited my drafts. I thank their patience. Finally, I express my at most gratitude to people who stood right beside me during many difficult times of this long journey. I dedicate this work to my family *Eve, Michiyo*, and *Hiromasa* and to those special friends *Jean-Marie Bouteiller, Choi Choi, Reyes Enciso, Behrend Freese, Edith Götzen, Alex Guazzelli, Masayoshi Higuchi, Shingo Honda, Markus Karner, Laurence Lamarcq, Eve Luckring, Pierre Ray, Mady Schutzman, Barnabas Takacs*, and *Vijay Uttam*.

Contents

List of Tables

List of Figures

9

Chapter 1

Introduction

1.1 Background

Visual information plays an extensive and crucial role in all aspects of human behavior. A large part of the sensory information our brain processes is visual. Moreover, visual analysis of our surroundings enables us to interact with fine details of the outside environment. Perhaps one of the most important factors in this realm is the recognition of objects. Without this capability, the flexibility of interaction would be drastically reduced. The field of object recognition stems from this observation and has been, for decades, an active field including the disciplines of computer vision, psychology, and neuroscience.

Two key questions in this field are the nature of the **internal representation** of objects, how objects are represented in our mind and how they should be encoded in computer systems, and the **information process** of the representations, how these internal representations are processed to solve complex cognitive tasks, as questioned by Marr [123]. We are concerned with two issues with regard to these questions. One is the mechanism of generalization. Images of objects vary in appearance due to changes in image projection settings (e.g., shift of view direction), outside environment (e.g., change of illumination), and the object itself (e.g., rotation of objects, deformation of shape, change of surface properties). One simple way to represent an object is to store an enormous number of views which cover all possible appearances of the object in the environment. This simple-minded strategy can be easily rejected for both artificial and biological systems due to the lack of resources for storage. Also its ability for generalization is intrinsically limited because of its view-based nature. Therefore, in order to cover all image variations, we need a process which can generalize over all possible appearances of an object from a limited number of views.

The second issue is whether the representation should be 3D (structure) based or 2D (image) based. It is most likely that representation is not based solely on 3D structures or 2D images. Biederman [20] indeed proposed that two types of representation are used for different classes of objects in human visual systems. The theory of stereo vision has shown that the 3D structure of an object can be reconstructed from two or three images of the object (e.g., Horn [94], and Havaldar and Medioni [88]). This suggests that a set of 2D images of an object implicitly contains structural information of the object. It should thus be possible to represent structural aspects of an object by a combination of 2D images.

Our long-term goal is to find a computational theory which answers these questions for all classes of objects considering all possible variation sources. In this dissertation, we describe our investigation which seeks a solution of the **generalization process** based on a combination of **2D** images. More details of our approach and the specific problem of our focus are described in the following sections.

1.2 Our Approach: A Compact, Generalizable, Data-Driven, Flexible and Parametric Representation Model

As described earlier, images of objects change in appearance due to many variation sources. The fact that these variations are entangled with each other and encoded **implicitly** in the image makes the task of object recognition difficult since it becomes very hard to distinguish each source of variation and to estimate the magnitude of each variation. Only after we extract these variations from the image, can we analyze the innate characteristics of the object. Therefore, our goal must be to make these encoded variations **explicit**.

The representation of objects has to be 1) **compact**, but at the same time 2) able to generalize all possible appearances of the object (**generalizable**). Observations from two extreme cases will help to illustrate these two requirements. In one case, each object is represented by a single image, and in the other case, by a set of images of all possible appearances of the object. The former severely limits the amount of information; thus it inevitably has a poor ability for generalization. The latter will be faced by *combinatory explosions* of the number of required images, which causes problems due to resource limitation. Furthermore, in many cases, different images of an object share local information. The latter case is not economical since these redundancies in local information are not compressed.

Let us call a computational unit which includes a specific format of object representation, as well as algorithms of the processes for the representations, a **representation model**. Inherently, the representation model needs to meet the two requirements above.

How can we then use the representation model to make the entangled variations explicit? This problem could be solved by **parameterizing** the representation model by the actual physical variations. A parameterized representation model is one that can be controlled by a set of parameters, **model parameters**. These model parameters are used to **analyze** the input image by fitting a model to the input, and to **synthesize** the appearance of the object controlled by different values of the model parameters within their parameter space. An explicit parameterization would make the model parameters coincide with the physical variations. This coincidence then allows for both the analysis of the physical variations of an object image and the synthesis of the object image with a specific physical variation. In other words, image variations could be explicitly interpreted only if model parameters were directly associated with physical variations. The construction of such a model, however, poses the difficult problem of learning transformation between the spaces of object representations and physical variations. In many cases, this transformation is complex and hard to learn.

We set two further requirements for the representation model: we want it to be **data-driven** and **flexible** (as opposed to **hand-crafted** and **rigid**). A data-driven model is strictly based on the statistics of training samples, whereas a hand-crafted model relies on *a priori* knowledge of the task provided by the designer of the model. In order to address all the possible image variations within a single framework, a representation model must be data-driven; it needs to be learned rather than constructed. A model utilizing an analytical description of a specific image variation may satisfactorily process the variation but it may not be applicable to other types of variation. This is similar to the situation that *traditional artificial intelligence* fell into; a zoology of highly specialized *expert systems* were developed to solve specific problems very well, but none of them could account for the whole *intelligence*. In order to achieve our goal of realizing a general framework, we must avoid this pitfall. Moreover, data-driven models help to automate the procedure of training sample collection, eliminating the need for operator assistance and collaboration from subjects.

The difference between a flexible and a rigid model comes from the nature of the generalization in the parameter space. A flexible model implies that the model smoothly and continuously covers the parameter space by virtue of its generalization, whereas the rigid model covers the space only discretely, at specific sampling points. As we consider more image variations in a single framework, the parameter space naturally becomes high-dimensional. Learning transformation between the spaces of representations and variation parameters becomes increasingly difficult in a higher-dimensional space because of a problem called the **curse of dimensionality**, namely the number of training samples required to learn the transformation increases exponentially as the dimensionality of a parameter space is increased. Our representation model must be flexible because it is practically impossible for a rigid model to cover the whole parameter space due to this problem.

The objective of our investigation is then to propose a compact, generalizable, data-driven, and flexible representation model with model parameters that can be interpreted explicitly in terms of physical variations. In order to reach this objective, we need to provide answers to the following questions:

1. What is the optimal functional form of the representation model for realizing a compact, generalizable and flexible transformation between object representations and physical variations?

2. How to learn the transformation from a set of training samples?

1.3 Our Focus:
Pose Variations in 2D Facial Images

In this study, we choose faces as the target of our investigation. In the field of computer vision, face recognition has been one of the most challenging tasks. Innate characteristics of the face, which distinguish one face from another, do not vary greatly from individual to individual. Moreover, magnitudes of the variations of the innate characteristics are often much smaller than magnitudes of common variations (i.e., head rotation, change of illumination, facial expression, etc.). Therefore, extraction of the innate characteristics from a facial image becomes a very difficult task. Faces are also one of the most studied class of objects (see surveys: Samal and Iyengar [173], Valentin et al. [199], and Chellappa et al. [38]). This is due to its extensive use in human communication, availability of data, and keen interest for a wide range of applications.

Our investigation also focuses on **head pose variation** among the many other types of variation. In general, head pose variation is very common since humans can move freely in the environment. Therefore, successful handling of pose variation is one of the most important factors for realizing systems for facial processing in virtually any realistic and practical scenario. Favorably, the pose variation is relatively tractable. The number of degrees of freedom for this variation is limited to three, which is much smaller than for other types of variation. Moreover, the pose variation can be understood by simple 3D Euclidean geometry, while such analytical knowledge is not available for other variations. There are a number of previous studies which have attempted to solve the problems of analysis, synthesis, and recognition of human faces with pose variations. However, despite its tractability, a number of important theoretical and practical issues in these tasks remained unresolved. Furthermore, these problems are often addressed independently and studied in different contexts. There have been very few efforts to address these problems in an unified framework. Note, however, that our motivation is not limited only to the pose variation. As mentioned earlier, our long-term goal is to realize a representation model which covers all possible variation sources. Towards this goal, this study aims to solve the pose problem, for which there is the aforementioned analytical solution, with methodology that can also be used for other types of variation, for which there are no such solutions.

For the analysis of head pose in 2D views (**pose estimation**), approaches in previous studies can be roughly categorized into two groups: shape-based geometrical analysis (e.g., Brunelli [30], Maurer and von der Malsburg [127], Heinzmann and Zelinsky [89], Chen et al. [39], and Xu and Akatsuka [220]) and texture-based template matching (e.g., Bichsel and Pentland [18], Tsukamoto et al. [194], Kruger et al. [108], McKenna and Gong [128], and Elagin et al. [64]). The former approach for pose estimation deduces the head poses analytically from geometric information of faces such as configuration of facial landmarks. The latter, on the other hand, is based on a nearest-neighbor classification with a set of texture-based (gray-level) templates, each of which is associated with a specific head pose. Most of these previous approaches, however, did not achieve high estimation accuracy. Moreover, they often restricted their systems to only one or two dimensions of 3D head rotations (see section 2.2.1 for details).

For the synthesis of facial appearances of specific poses (**pose transformation**), several studies have successfully demonstrated synthesizing a new pose from a single input view by applying a transformation function learned from training samples. Beymer and Poggio [16] proposed an algorithm based on an optical flow technique to find pixel-wise correspondences between facial images in two different poses. Maurer and von der Malsburg [126] also demonstrated an approach combining affine transformation of feature descriptors (jets), sampled at two different poses, with knowledge of 3D surface normals. Note that both approaches are rigid: their transformations are defined as an explicit mapping from one pose to another and learned from training samples with *fixed* poses. Therefore, a prohibitively large number of transformations have to be learned in order to continuously cover the complete viewing sphere. Furthermore, operator assistance and subject collaboration are required to collect the training samples of the fixed poses (see section 2.2.2 for details).

For the task of recognizing faces for identifications, a number of approaches have been proposed for improving recognition performance against pose variations. (**pose-invariant face recognition**). [1] They include studies by Beymer [15],

---

[1] The term, pose-invariant, is used loosely here. This term is used even for non-invariant systems for the sake of maintaining a consistency with the face recognition literature.

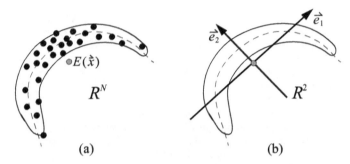

(a)   (b)

Figure 1.1: 2D Sketches of a Non-linear Sample Distribution in a N-dimensional Vector Space

Maurer and von der Malsburg [126], Pentland et al. [149], Graham and Allinson [80], Lando and Edelman [112], and Duvedevani-Bar et al. [57]. Again, most systems developed in these studies are rigid: continuous pose variation is very crudely discretized only along one to two rotation axes. Due to this, the scalability of their systems suffers immensely. When applying these systems to more realistic scenarios which require full continuous coverage of the pose variation, they are confronted by the curse of dimensionality problem described in the previous section (see also section 2.2.3 for details).

To summarize, rough discrete treatment of continuous pose variations was one of the shortcomings of the previous studies about processing human faces with pose variations. Our approach attempts to resolve this issue by using a flexible representation model.

1.4   Non-linear Sample Distribution and Low-Dimensional Subspaces

Before we proceed further, let us introduce some basic terminologies and concepts used throughout this dissertation. Figure 1.1(a) illustrates a number of training samples in a N-dimensional space R^N. Suppose that a sample consisting of N variables (e.g., an image with N pixels) is numerically represented by a 1D N-component vector $\vec{x}$ (**sample vector**). Such a sample vector forms a point in a N-dimensional **vector space** spanned by N orthogonal vectors. We call this vector space a **representation space**. An expectation (mean) of the sample vectors $E(\vec{x})$ is denoted by a shaded point in the figure. Suppose also that the set of samples are drawn from views of a single object undergoing a certain **data variation** described

16

in section 1.1 as **image variation**. Due to the innate similarity across different views of an object, a distribution of points (**sample distribution**) forms a cluster which we call a **data-cloud**. The shape and density of a data-cloud vary depending on the characteristics of the data variation. Figure 1.1(a) schematizes a curved data-cloud by a banana-shaped oval. A dotted line in the figure represents a main **axis** of the data-cloud which corresponds to a main direction of the data variation. The curve of the axis indicates that the data variation is **non-linear**.

Assume next that a data-cloud in figure 1.1(a) is distributed under a data variation which restricts samples to be only on a surface of a 2D figure plane in R^N. In fact, the degrees of freedom (**DOF**) of data variation (e.g., 3 for 3D rotation variation) are often much lower than a dimensionality of the representation space (e.g., N in this case). In such a case, a high-dimensional sample distribution becomes embedded in a low-dimensional **subspace** of the representation space. In this figure, the data-cloud is embedded in a 2D subspace.

Figure 1.1(b) illustrates a coordinate frame of a 2D linear subspace R^2. The subspace is spanned by two **component vectors** $\vec{e_1}$ and $\vec{e_2}$ which collectively form a **basis** of the subspace. An arbitrary N-dimensional sample is then parameterized by two coordinate values in this 2D reference frame. These component vectors can be manually constructed (see section 2.1.2 for details) or learned from training samples (see section 2.1.2 for details). Note that the component vectors shown in the figure are **linear**, while the sample distribution is non-linear. Although the two coordinate values in the linear frame unambiguously determine a point in R^2 describing an arbitrary sample, such coordinate values do not accurately describe the non-linear variation (**non-linearity problem**).

A linear subspace illustrated in figure 1.1(b) can be utilized as a representation model. We call such a model the **linear subspace model** or **subspace method** following a convention in the pattern recognition literature. A technique of learning component vectors using an unsupervised statistical learning method called **principal component analysis (PCA)** is commonly called an **eigenspace method** or **eigenface** specifically for faces (e.g., Shirovich and Kirby [182], and Turk and Pentland [195]). This technique will be described further in section 2.1.2.

Figure 1.2 illustrates the concept of the subspace model with facial images as an example. A subspace model describes an arbitrary face $\vec{x}$ by a **linear combination** of weighted component vectors $w_1\vec{e_1}, .., w_p\vec{e_p}$ and a mean face $E(\vec{x})$. The component vectors $\vec{e_1}, .., \vec{e_p}$ displaying facial patterns correspond to those displaying 2D arrows in figure 1.1(b). Note that a vector of the weights $(w_1, .., w_p)$ is equivalent to the *model parameters* and *coordinate values* described earlier. Compactness of a subspace model is achieved by reducing the dimensionality p of the subspace, resulting in only a few parameters for describing a sample. A subspace model learned by PCA is an example of a compact, generalizable, data-driven, flexible, and parametric representation model. However, its model parameters

17

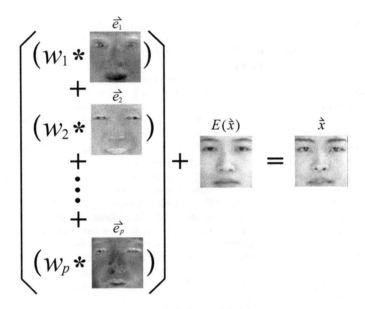

Figure 1.2: Subspace Model

cannot always be interpreted explicitly due to the non-linearity problem described above.

1.5 Our Solution: The LPCMAP Model

Now let us go back to the two questions raised at the end of the section 1.2. They concern how to implement the representation model that meets the criterion; *compactness, generalizability, data-drivenness*, and *flexibility*. The data-drivenness and flexibility are assured by learning transformation or mapping between object representations and physical variations from a set of training samples. So the remaining problem is the choice of functional form and learning algorithms to achieve compactness and generalizability in the transformation.

This dissertation presents the **LPCMAP model** (Okada et al. [140]) as our solution to this problem. The LPCMAP (Linear Principal Components MAPping functions) model consists of a combination of two linear systems: 1) PC-based

18

linear subspace models and 2) linear mapping functions between different parameter spaces. Representations derived from training samples are first subjected to principal component analysis (PCA) in order to generate a compact flexible parameterized linear model. Then we explicitly relate the model parameters and head pose variations by a linear mapping function which is also learned from the training samples. This model's data-drivenness facilitates its applicability to other types of image variation, while its flexibility mitigates the curse of dimensionality problem. These two linear systems will be described further in chapter 2.

Note that we choose to *linearly* approximate the representation-to-parameter mapping, although it is obvious that the mapping is *non-linear* Our main argument for this choice is to emphasize the model's generalizability and simplicity. The small number of degrees of freedom (DOF) of our linear mapping function (in comparison with non-linear functions with higher-order terms) decreases functional complexity thus avoids overfitting which would directly inhibit the model's generalizability. It also helps to mitigate the difficulty of learning. Learning a linear system can be reduced to solving a set of multivariate linear equations for which stable analytical solutions exist, while learning a non-linear system often requires time-consuming iterative optimization algorithm, which can be numerically unstable. The above arguments favoring a linear system are an example of **Occam's Razor**. It implies that the *simplicity* of our model is preferred to the *inherent complexity* of a non-linear functional approximation. Non-linear systems also often suffer from ad-hoc and exhaustive searches (**model selection**) for finding the optimal non-linear functional form of unknown mappings.

The LPCMAP model also employs separate representations for shape and texture information within a single facial image. Geometrical information of facial shape is represented by 2D locations of a set of facial landmarks (**shape representation**) and pictorial information of facial texture is represented by a set of 2D Gabor jets (**texture representation**) which describe contrast gradients of local gray-level distribution (Lades et al. [111]). Both types of representation are parameterized by linear subspace models learned from training samples (**shape parameters** and **texture parameters**). Head pose variation is quantized by continuous 3D rotation angles of a face from its frontal pose (**pose parameters**). [2]

The LPCMAP model unifies the processes of analysis, synthesis, and recognition within a single **simple** and **general** framework. The analysis process is realized by relating the pose and shape parameters so that it is based solely on shape information. This is a natural design since pose estimation can be formally reduced to a geometric problem. The synthesis process consists of synthesizing

---

[2]Pose parameters can be constructed by filtering the 3D rotation angles with non-linear trigonometric functions in order to improve the mapping's accuracy. Such possibility is explored in chapter 3.

both shape and texture. Shape is first synthesized by a pose-to-shape mapping (a mapping inverse to the one for the analysis process). Texture is then synthesized by a shape-to-texture mapping which linearly relates shape and texture parameters, modeling a correlation between them. Furthermore, by using an output of the analysis as an input of the synthesis (**analysis-synthesis chain**), a sequential application of the analysis and synthesis processes provides a model view whose pose is aligned to an input (**model matching**). This head pose alignment of model views to arbitrary inputs gives a basis for our pose-invariant face recognition system (Okada et al. [143]).

The LPCMAP model provides continuous coverage of the pose variations which improves performance of previous *rigid* systems. Its generalization capability for different poses enables the model to learn from a small number of training samples. The explicit interface of our model with 3D head angles provides practical advantages for a number of application scenarios such as low-bandwidth communication (transmitting only pose information instead of images), tele-conferencing (adjusting head poses in a virtual space for creating eye contact), facial identification (aligning head poses of inputs and models). More details of the LPCMAP model are described in chapter 3.

Our model is related to a number of previously proposed models. These models address the issue of the continuous coverage of the pose variations which is one of our main goals. A **parametric eigenspace** system proposed by Murase and Nayar [133] realized pose-invariant object recognition based on a representation which utilizes a compact and continuous **manifold** of model parameters interpolated by cubic-splines in linear subspaces. A facial representation scheme proposed by Lanitis et al. [115] combined separate shape and texture flexible models of facial images using PC-based linear subspace models. An RBF network-based system proposed by Beymer et al. [17] realized continuous pose estimation and transformation by learning a mapping which directly and continuously associates image-based representations to the pose variations using a non-linear neural network. These studies, however, do not fully address the issue of generalization to unknown poses by considering only a subset of the 3D rotation. These model's ability for this generalization is questionable because of their use of the non-linear systems. Our study, instead, emphasizes this generalization capability by constructing our model with linear systems and by evaluating its performance with a full 3D rotations. See section 2.3.4 for more detailed comparisons of these systems.

1.6 Extending the LPCMAP Model by Piecewise Linear Model Approach

In the previous section, we have argued the advantages of linear approximation as a functional form of our representation model. There is, however, a common pitfall of linear approximation which sacrifices fitting accuracy. The **bias-variance dilemma** by Geman et al. [72] discusses this disadvantage. It describes a trade-off between oversmoothing (bias) and overfitting (variance) in the function approximation problem. The trade-off depends on a balance between the model's internal degrees of freedom (DOF) and the intrinsic dimensionality of data to be fitted. When the number of the model's DOF is smaller than the intrinsic dimensionality, the model tends to oversmooth the data, decreasing the accuracy of the model's fit. Experimental results in chapter 4 show that our linear model is accurate only within a limited range (ca. ± 15 degrees) of pose variation, although the model was highly accurate and capable of generalizing to unknown poses within this range. This is a natural property of linearity, but it raises a serious problem that disables our model from covering the full range of the pose parameter space.

This dissertation proposes a solution to this problem by using a **piecewise linear model approach**. As we will illustrate in figures 6.1 and 6.2, the idea is to cover a wide range of the pose parameter space by a number of localized linear models. In this framework, the LPCMAP model described in the previous section serves as a linear model localized in the parameter space. In order to piece together a number of localized models, we utilize weighted averaging of outputs of localized models. A similar idea has been exploited for approximating a non-linear function by localized linear functions in a broad range of fields (e.g., Brailovsky and Kempner [25], Fritzke [69], Mael [121], Venkataraman and Poston [201], and Schaal and Atkeson [176]). Our experimental results will successfully show that this extension of the LPCMAP model greatly expands the range of pose variations in which high accuracy is maintained.

This dissertation also addresses the missing data problem due to self-occlusion of facial landmarks. By considering a wide range of head pose variations, some facial landmarks naturally become invisible because they are hidden behind other parts of the face. This problem is called **self-occlusion of landmarks**. Since our shape representation consists of 2D coordinates of the landmarks, the self-occlusion creates uncertainty for some variables in shape samples. In the field of statistics, this problem is known as the **missing data problem** (e.g., Little and Rubin [120]). Common statistical analyses of data, such as national surveys, can be biased due to this problem. In our case, the learning process of a shape linear model becomes problematic since PCA used for the process is vulnerable to this problem. We test a number of approaches to solve this problem. Our experimental results will show that they effectively solve this problem.

Another interesting issue for processing human faces is **interpersonal generalization**. This dissertation proposes two novel methods for estimating head pose of arbitrary persons, which further extend the piecewise linear model approach. In the previous sections, we have discussed our model's generalization capability for different *poses*. In this case, a model is constructed for a single person but generalizable to different views of the person. This is simply done by learning a LPCMAP model with samples derived from a single person. This approach is appropriate for a synthesis process where each model should be able to capture a peculiar appearance of a single individual's face. However, for the analysis process or pose estimation, learning a model for the generic object class of human faces can be natural and beneficial. Pose estimation generalized over different individuals is supported by our common sense: humans can easily tell which direction a person is looking without knowing who she or he is. It should also be computationally tractable because of the relative proximity of facial shapes over different individuals. Our experimental results will successfully show effectiveness of the two proposed methods.

1.7 Organization of Manuscript

This dissertation consists of nine chapters. This chapter introduces the framework of our investigation. In chapter 2, the most relevant literature including the state-of-the-art systems of our focus is reviewed in order to clarify open problems of our interests. We also discuss how our approach could help to solve some of the problems. In chapter 3, we describe the LPCMAP model in both formal and informal manners. In chapter 4, we empirically assess feasibility of the LPCMAP model by a series of numerical experiments. Analyses with artificial and real data are conducted in order to show the model's feasibility for the tasks of pose estimation and transformation. We show that our model can perform successfully within a limited range of pose variations. In chapter 5, we propose and empirically evaluate a novel framework of a face recognition system using the LPCMAP model as a representation unit. In chapter 6, we introduce strategies to remove the pose range limitation encountered in our previous experiments. We propose a PWLM system, an extension of the LPCMAP model by using the piecewise linear model approach, as a solution to this limitation problem. This chapter also addresses a strategy to overcome a problem of the self-occlusion which is inevitable for covering a wide range of pose variations. In chapter 7, we empirically show that the PWLM system is effective for a much wider range of pose variations than those a single LPCMAP model can cover. In chapter 8, our investigation towards interpersonal generalization of pose estimation in this framework is presented. Finally, in chapter 9, we conclude by summarizing contributions of our investigation, discussing relationship of our systems to their biological counterparts, and presenting our ideas for future work.

Chapter 2

Literature Review

As discussed in the introduction, our investigation is concerned about two questions: **1) how to represent faces with pose variations** and **2) how to process (analyze, synthesize, and recognize) faces with pose variations.** In this chapter, we attempt to assess strategies that give solutions to these questions based on past literature. The first section of this chapter addresses the first question. Its purpose is to provide an overview of the most relevant fundamental representation methods for faces and objects. However, literature in generic object recognition is numerous. Thus it is out of our scope to provide a complete review. This section should, instead, provide a sufficient background for further discussion of specific techniques in the following sections. The second section reviews studies specifically about processing faces with pose variations. The process of pose information involves two sub-processes: analysis and synthesis. They correspond to the task of pose estimation and transformation, respectively. Another important aspect of processing faces with pose variations is to recognize faces with arbitrary poses: the task of pose-invariant face recognition. We provide a thorough review of studies which address these three tasks. At the end of both sections, the findings are summarized and discussed. Finally, in the third section, we discuss how our approach can help to solve some open problems found in this review.

2.1 Representing Faces with Pose Variations

The problem of how to represent objects from physical measurements such as digital images has been a key question in computer vision. Such an object representation needs to account for a variety of views of a single object caused by pose variation, illumination variation, and shape deformation etc. On the other hand, the number of possible views of a single object is prohibitively large so that they cannot be simply stored for each single object. One solution to this problem is to represent the variety of views by an economical representation model based on a few sample views of the object. In this section, we first provide an overview of the broad range of representation methods. Next, literature concerning the model-based representation is reviewed and discussed in depth. Furthermore, we review a number of studies which concern relationships between shape and texture information within facial images. Finally, this section concludes with a summary of these methods.

2.1.1   Overview of Relevant Representation Methods

Many object representation methods which have been proposed in past years can be roughly categorized into **single-view representation** and **multiple-view representation** by differences in their purposes. The following provides an overview of some examples from these two categories.

Single-View Representation

Single-view representation describes objects by information based only on a single-view of an object captured in 2D intensity data such as digital images. This type of representation scheme has long been studied because of availability of the raw data. Many methods have been proposed for extracting meaningful **features** from 2D images in the past. Such features are designed to represent the innate characteristics of the faces under many types of variation. These features can be categorized into two types: **geometric** and **pictorial**.

2.1.1(a)   Geometric Features   Geometric features are based on geometrical or topological characteristics of distinctive facial features such as eyes, nose, mouth, and chin. In his pioneering work towards the first automated face recognition system, Kanade [171, 172] utilized a set of 16 geometrical features based on the size and position of eyes, nose, mouth and chin as representation of faces. Similar approach was also taken by Brunelli and Poggio [31, 32, 33], by Gordon [76] with additional depth and curvature features derived from a 3D depth map of a face, and by Fellous [67] towards gender analysis.

Recently, two new approaches have been proposed and widely used by a number of studies. The first approach represents faces by a number of points or facial landmarks distributed over faces (e.g., Craw and Cameron 1992 [47], Cootes et al. 1994 [43, 113]). They typically use more feature points than the previous methods and these landmarks are not necessarily located at the distinctive facial parts. Statistical analysis of this **point-distribution** (e.g., Lanitis et al. 1997 [115], Craw et al. 1997 [48]) provided information of facial shape structure reliably. The second approach uses a dense vector field of pixel-wise correspondences between a target and a reference face (e.g., Beymer and Poggio 1995 [16], Vetter and Poggio 1997 [204]). We further discuss the details of these two approaches in sections 2.1.3 and 2.2.2.

2.1.1(b) Pictorial Features Pictorial features are based on a local distribution of image intensities which is a function of the surface reflectance properties. The most simple way to represent texture is to use the image intensity itself. Brunelli and Poggio [34] and Gordon [77] used a set of local image regions (local templates), each of which includes a distinctive facial part, in order to represent faces. Since the intensity of raw images is very sensitive to illumination variations, a number of preprocessing steps, such as histogram equalization, gradient operator, or Laplacian operator, are often applied to the raw images in order to mitigate the illumination influence [34].

An interesting class of representation schemes that has been inspired from the visual system of higher vertebrates (Jones and Palmer [103]) has become popular in recent years. These approaches are based on integral transformation with a family of localized filters. 2D Gabor wavelets is a family of sinusoidal plane waves enveloped by Gaussian windows, which is parameterized by wave lengths and orientations. Filtering with a bank of these Gabor wavelets at an image position provides a complex-valued feature vector or **jet**, which represents a local edge structure around the position. It was Daugman [50, 51] who first pushed the idea that receptive fields in the primary visual cortical areas are most appropriately described as two-dimensional Gabor filters. It is tempting to liken simple cells (Huebel and Wiesel [97]) to the sine and cosine components of wavelets and complex cells [97] to the magnitudes of the complex components. Von der Malsburg and his associates (Lades [110], Wurtz [218], Wiskott [211]) further extended this idea using Dynamic Link Matching (DLM), a dynamical solution to the correspondence-finding-problem. They proposed object representation schemes with jet-labeled rectangular grids (Lades et al. [111]) and jet-labeled flexible graphs whose nodes are located at fiducial points of faces (Wiskott et al. [213, 214, 215]). This Gabor wavelet-based representation method together with elastic graph matching [214], an algorithmic version of the DLM, has been successfully applied to face recognition (Okada et al. [141]) and related applications (Steffens et al. [184], Hong et al. [93], Okada and von der Malsburg [142]).

Another example by Edelman and his associates [61] modeled receptive fields (RFs) by convolution of a set of Gaussian filters with various sizes and locations in an input space. Activities of these filters can be used as inputs to a radial basis function (RBF) network (Poggio and Girosi [161]) for interpolating multivariate non-linear functions. This RBF network based on RF representations of 2D images was applied to recognizing generic objects (Edelman and Poggio [60]) and faces (Edelman et al. [61]). This example in the context of functional approximation will be revisited in section 2.1.2.

2.1.1(c)   Comparison of the Features   One of the advantages of using geometric features as single-view representation is its illumination invariance; geometrical information of faces is not influenced by the illumination variations. However automatic detection of these features often relies on texture information which is sensitive to illumination variations. Therefore it is difficult to automatically locate these geometrical features precisely. Moreover, the geometric features are suitable for tasks which could be reduced to geometrical problems such as head pose estimation (see section 2.2.1) and facial expression recognition (e.g., Matsuno and Tsuji [124], Yacoob et al [221], Black and Yacoob [23], Essa and Pentland [65]).

On the other hand, the pictorial features seem to capture information which is crucial to a process of facial identification. Poggio [33] and Craw [49] both showed that facial identification performance was better by a system with pictorial features than by a system with geometric features. The disadvantages of pictorial features include that they tend to have much higher-dimensionality than the geometric features and that they are inherently sensitive to physical variations such as illumination and pose.

Multiple-View Representation

A multiple-view representation describes the complete appearance of an object as a whole. Unlike the single-view representation which contains only limited information of the target object, the multiple-view representation attempts to capture a spectrum of all possible views. Related to this type of representation, there is a class of representation methods which is based on explicit knowledge of 3D shape information of objects. We call this type of representation the **3D model-based approach**. Our study, however, focuses on a type of representation which represents 3D objects by a number of 2D views without explicit 3D shape knowledge. We categorize these 2D methods into two approaches: the **2D template-based approach** and the **2D model-based approach**. The difference of the two approaches lies on whether it learns a strategy of information process from samples or not. The former consists of a set of single-view representations or templates which are simply *stored*. Its information process is fixed to the nearest-neighbor algorithm or its variations which do not involve learning. On the other hand, the latter statistically learns the information process or part of it from a set of training views. A set of single-views are utilized for the *learning*, instead of *stored*, in this case. The following provides an overview of these approaches.

27

2.1.1(a) 3D Model-Based Approach In this approach, a face of a person is represented by a model of 3D shape structure. A 3D shape model consists of a 3D structure of facial surface represented as a depth map, a set of 3D triangular patches, or a set of 3D curvatures. The 3D shape model could be also associated with its corresponding texture in order to synthesize 2D views. In computer graphics, the majority of algorithms utilize this type of 3D shape model for realistic facial animations (e.g., Parke [147], Günter et al. [83], Pighin et al. [158]). A number of algorithms have also successfully demonstrated matching such a 3D shape model to 2D input images in order to estimate geometrical structures of the 2D inputs (e.g., Aizawa et al. [3], Huttenlocher and Ullman [98], Choi et al. [41], Heinzmann and Zelinsky [89], Shimizu et al. [181]). This technique will be revisited in the context of pose estimation in section 2.2.1. Advantages of this approach are that 1) it is invariant against pose (or view-point) variations, 2) it helps to analyze illumination variations because the geometrical structure (e.g., surface normal) of the face is known, and 3) the size of the representation can be compact in comparison to the simple 2D template-based approach described in the next section. The first and second advantages are very attractive; the analysis of pose variations can be reduced to a simple geometrical problem in theory and once the pose is known, a new view of the face can be easily synthesized by geometrical projection followed by a texture mapping. The third advantage does not always hold, depending on the data structure chosen; a 2D model-based approach which will be described later could be a better solution for reducing the size of representations. The most significant disadvantage of this approach is the potential difficulty for constructing the 3D model. It requires either specific hardware such as a range finder (e.g., Sato and Otsuki [175], Okada [139], Proesmans and Gool [165]) and a Cyberware scanner (e.g., Vetter and Blanz [202, 24], Günter et al. [83], Isono et al. [102]) or computationally unstable algorithmic solutions for reconstructing depth information from a number of 2D views such as stereo methods (e.g., Havaldar and Medioni [88], Lengagne et al. [118], Neumann et al. [134]) and structure from motion (e.g., Horn [94], Tomasi and Kanade [190], Fua [70]).

2.1.1(b) 2D Template-Based Approach Without constructing an explicit model of 3D objects, the most naive way to represent the 3D nature of an object is to describe the object by a collection of all possible views. We call this type of representation method 2D template-based approach. Each object can be represented by a set of single-view representations described in section 2.1.1. An unseen input view can be approximated by a nearest-neighbor algorithm with the stored views. What characterize different methods in this approach are the types of single-view representation used for each template and the types of similarity

28

metric used for the nearest-neighbor algorithm.

The notion of **object class** has been commonly used in both the psychology and computer vision literature. Distinguishing two hierarchical levels in this object class, **basic-level** and **subordinate-level**, has helped to describe nature of object recognition (e.g., Rosch et al. [168], Bruce and Humphreys [28], Biederman [19], Basri [11]).

In the case of faces, the subordinate-level corresponds to a single person's face, whereas the basic-level corresponds to the generic class of faces including different persons (Bruce and Young [29], Biederman and Kalocsai [20, 21]). The knowledge of basic-level classes is often used to detect faces among other types of object such as desk, cup and banana, whereas the knowledge of subordinate-level classes is required for identifying individuals. The 2D template-based approach has been used for describing the knowledge of both levels of classes. For the basic-level, many algorithms for detecting faces from 2D images exploit a general knowledge of faces in the form of this approach, including views of multiple individuals under various conditions. For example, a technique of **template matching** uses this approach with 2D gray-level images as single-view representation and with a correlation coefficient as a similarity metric (e.g., Brunelli and Poggio [33, 34], Kwon and Lobo [109]). Wiskott et al. [214, 215] exploited a 2D template-based approach (general face knowledge or GFK) with a single-view representation based on Gabor jets and with, as a similarity metric, the normalized dot-product of corresponding jets averaged over graph nodes. This GFK was used for automatically locating facial features in input images, as well as analyzing facial attributes such as the presence of a beard or eye-glasses (Wiskott [212]). For the subordinate-level, each person in a database of known people can be represented by a set of single-view representations. Gordon [77] reported a face recognition system, in which each person was represented by both frontal and profile views. With these two views per person, it attempts to capture depth information of a face explicitly. In Beymer's earlier work [15], 15 views of different head poses covering a range of the viewing sphere were used to represent each individual in a database. A recognition system based on template correlation as a similarity metric demonstrated reliable performance against head pose variations.

The 2D template-based approach provides a simple framework to represent a spectrum of possible views of objects. An inherent problem, however, is that it covers continuously varying object appearances only by discrete samples. For continuous coverage of all possible views, it often requires an prohibitively large number of templates. Furthermore, these types of method lack the ability to determine 1) what and 2) how many templates should be used. Thus the choice of the templates has often been manual and subjective.

29

2.1.1(c)   2D Model-Based Approach   The 2D model-based approach aims to solve the disadvantage of the 2D template-based approach by providing a continuous and compact representation model learned from a set of training 2D views. As described in section 1.4, **subspace method** is one of the most common frameworks in this approach. In this method, each 2D view representation is considered to be a point in a high-dimensional vector space spanned by variables of the chosen single-view representation (**representation space**). A set of training samples then forms a cloud of data points in this space. The subspace method models the characteristics of the data-cloud by finding a **basis** (a set of **component vectors**) which forms a relatively low-dimensional subspace of the representation space. Unlike the 2D template-based approach which only uses discrete samples of continuous variation, this approach provides a mean for smoothly modeling different appearances of objects. Later in this chapter, we will show that this is our choice of data representation. We review literature related to this approach in more detail in the next section.

2.1.2   Methods for the 2D Model-Based Approach

The 2D model-based approach is a multiple-view representation model based on a continuous and compact representation model learned from a set of training 2D views. The subspace method described in sections 1.4 and 2.1.1(c) provides a simple framework for this approach by describing the innate characteristics of an object in a low-dimensional subspace of a representation space. The subspace is spanned by a set of component vectors derived from training samples. We call a representation model created by a subspace method a **subspace model**. An arbitrary input can be approximated by a **linear combination** of the component vectors. This can be seen as parameterization of the input by a subspace model. We call the weights of this linear combination **model parameters**. A number of different models exist which differ in the way of finding the component vectors and of constructing a subspace. The following provides reviews of four types of model, **template-based linear subspace models**, **PC-based linear subspace models**, **non-linear subspace models**, and **transformation models**.

Template-Based Linear Subspace Models

This type of method constructs a *linear* subspace model using prototypical templates as component vectors. This is the simplest implementation of the 2D model-based approach since no computation is required to generate the basis of a subspace.

Ullman and Basri [197] pioneered an approach using this 2D template-based linear subspace model for representing geometric line drawings of generic objects. They showed that line drawings of an object can be expressed as linear combinations of just three views of the *same* object under the assumptions that 1) the object is rigid and 2) the views correspond to rigid 3D transformations followed by weak-perspective (orthographic) projection. They proved that only 6 different views of an object are usually sufficient to express all the possible views of smooth objects. A novel view of an object can be parameterized by finding optimal model parameters that give the linear combination most similar to the input view. These parameters can be determined by aligning the linear combination to the input view. This alignment is realized by either 1) solving a set of linear equations derived from more than 3 corresponding control points between an input view and model (alignment method by Huttenlocher and Ullman [98]) or 2) performing an exhaustive search in the parameter space. This method provides a framework for a 2D linear subspace model for a single object at the subordinate level. Recently, Peters and von der Malsburg [151] experimentally showed that a similar interpolation of novel views from only 2 to 3 stored views in gray-level images is possible using the Gabor jet-based single-view representation described in section 2.1.1(b).

Poggio and Vetter [162] extended the above idea to represent a class of objects in their **linear class theory**. In this approach, a new view of an object is created by linear combination of prototypical views of *different* objects of the same class. Therefore their 2D linear subspace model works for basic-level objects. They demonstrated this basic-level model for line drawings of generic objects [162] and 2D gray-level images of faces (Vetter and Poggio [204]).

This basic-level model can be applied to create new views from a single prototypical view of an object using a **class-specific transformation** which may be known *a priori* or pre-learned from a set of models. For example, a single-view of an object with pose-A can be rotated to pose-B by 1) estimating model parameters of the linear class model for pose-A, 2) transforming the parameters of the linear class model for pose-A to ones for pose-B, and 3) generating a new view by a linear combination of the linear class model for pose-B with the transformed parameters. Given the prototypical views at both pose-A and -B *a priori*, the transformation can be pre-computed. This technique will be revisited in the context of pose transformation in section 2.2.2.

The general difficulty of these methods lies in finding corresponding control points across different views, especially in gray-level images. Vetter and Poggio [204] used a coarse-to-fine gradient-based optical flow algorithm to find pixel-level correspondences between two images in the same pose. It is, however, still difficult to automatically locate these points precisely and reliably because of the effects of illumination on the pictorial features used for their algorithm. Furthermore, an inherent problem of this type of method is their inability to determine 1) what and 2) how many templates should be used as the basis. The 2D template-based approach described in section 2.1.1(b) shares the same problems, however it could only cover the continuous variations discretely, whereas this approach provides a model which continuously covers the variations. These studies [197, 98, 162, 204, 151] described in this section did not address these two problems and the component vectors (template views) of the linear model were chosen manually.

PC-Based Linear Subspace Models

The template-based linear subspace method described in the previous section offers a framework for modeling 3D objects by the linear combination of a small number of 2D template views. However these methods require construction of the subspace model manually. As mentioned in section 1.4, one solution to this problem is to learn the component vectors from the statistics of training data.

Principal component analysis (PCA) is a statistical method (also known as Karhunen-Loeve expansion in the pattern recognition literature) to derive, from a set of samples, a compact set of linearly independent component vectors which describe modes of the sample distribution (e.g., Press et al. [164], Duda and Hart [55]). The analysis is based on an eigen decomposition of a centered covariance matrix derived from the samples, resulting in eigenvectors with associated eigenvalues. These eigenvectors are called principal components (PCs) and form an orthonormal basis. Each eigenvalue represents the variance in the training samples along a direction of the corresponding eigenvector in the representation space. An image can be represented by a vector of orthographic projection coefficients of the image to a space spanned by the PCs. This representation scheme is optimal in that it minimizes the reconstruction error in the least-square sense. Furthermore, when the data is normally distributed, forming a dense convex data-cloud (in the best case an ellipsoid), a subspace spanned by only a few PCs which represent the most significant variations of the data can be used as a compact linear model; dimensionality of the representation can be greatly reduced which results in data-compression. See also figures 1.1 and 1.2 for visual examples of these concepts.

Sirovich and Kirby [182] first applied this PCA-based representation to an ensemble of facial images, demonstrating a low-dimensional linear model and its reconstruction performance. Pentland and his associates [195, 131] and others (Shackleton and Welsh [179], Craw and Cameron [47]) extended this technique to automatic face recognition systems. This technique has been widely used and is known as **eigenface systems**. Statistical techniques such as Linear and Fisher Discriminant Analysis (e.g., Zhao et al. [224], Moghaddam et al. [132], Kalocsai et al. [106]) for learning an optimal classification boundary have been recently used to improve this type of recognition system. Related to these analytical for-

32

mulations of the problem, PCA can be also expressed as a learning task of an auto-associative neural network. Kohonen [107] was the first to use an auto-associative network as a representation scheme for storing and retrieving an ensemble of facial images. In this approach, the network learns associations from training facial samples to themselves by the delta rule, resulting in a weight matrix which approximates a set of PCs (O'Toole and associates. [145, 198, 1], Cottrell and Munro [45]). Oja [136] pioneered another type of approach using 2-layer feedforward networks with constrained Hebbian learning for finding a subspace spanned by PCs. See a survey paper by Baldi and Hornik [7] which gives a good overview of this type of method. These connectionist solutions have an advantage when the dimensionality of the representation space is so large that the analytical solution can not be computed in a reasonable time and when incremental learning is asked for (e.g., Oja and Karhunen [138]).

The studies described above were based on a **global representation** which captures a whole facial region as a data unit. This type of representation scheme requires precise alignment of images across different views. Because of the shape variations across different people and the non-rigidness of faces, this alignment becomes a non-trivial task. The above studies have dealt with this alignment problem by normalizing the shape of each face using a few anchor points, however the precision of the alignment was often poor. A more complete solution to this alignment problem was given by techniques based on image warping (e.g., Vetter and Troje [205], Lanitis et al. [116], Craw et al. [49]), which registers a facial image to a fixed reference shape by finding pixel-wise correspondences between them. The resulting shape-normalized facial images were called **shape-free texture representations** and subjected to PCA. These studies will be revisited in section 2.1.3 when we discuss the use of both shape and texture information.

A **local representation** which describes a face by a set of local features serves as another solution to the alignment problem, if the location of the landmarks can be found precisely. It is preferred to a global representation because of its robustness for partial occlusions and its flexibility to non-rigid shape transformation. Pentland et al. [149] proposed an approach which represented a face by a set of local PCA models (eigen features) located on four distinctive facial regions (i.e. eyes, nose and mouth) and showed that a recognition system based on these local eigen features outperformed one with the global eigenfaces. Penev and Atick [148] also proposed Local Feature Analysis (LFA) which analytically constructs a spatially dense set of local topographic filters from global PCA modes. These local filters are defined at each pixel of the image coordinates, different from each other, and optimally matched to the input ensemble, by decorrelating the outputs from these filters as much as possible. This topographic LFA representation maintains the same best reconstruction property of the global PCA. A technique to *sparsify* the spatial allocation of the filters using residual correlation

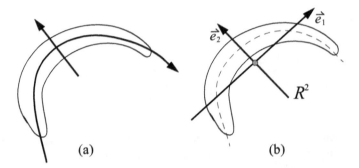

Figure 2.1: Non-linear Components

as a lateral inhibition was proposed to reduce the dimensionality of the representation.

An advantage of these PC-based linear subspace models is that their component vectors are learned from examples rather than picked manually. Furthermore, the linearity of the PCs simplifies the matching process of a subspace model to an arbitrary input (or the estimation of model parameters which give the most similar linear combination to the input). The parameters could be simply computed as a dot-product of the input and each PC (or orthographic projection of the input to the basis). The orthogonality of the PCs also simplifies the model processes because it coincides a basis for the linear combination and filters for the matching process within a single subspace model. However, these two properties of PCs also impose a disadvantage. Due to them, PCs cannot capture variations that are non-linear. Therefore, PCs computed from samples undergoing strong non-linear variation will fail to account for the variation.

Non-Linear Subspace Models

As pointed out in the previous section, a PCA cannot perfectly capture non-linear variations because of its restrictions to linearity and orthogonality. Within the framework of the subspace model, it is of obvious interest to extend the approach such as to capture the non-linear variations. This idea is illustrated in figure 2.1. The right figure 2.1(b) schematizes a N-dimensional data-cloud embedded in a two-dimensional linear PC subspace as also shown in figure 1.1. Because of non-linearity indicated by a curved axis, the PC-spanned linear basis cannot describe the non-linear variation accurately. The left figure 2.1(a) shows a **non-linear component approach** which allows the component vectors to be non-linear such that

34

the components coincide with the non-linear variation axis. [1] Therefore, this approach intrinsically solves the non-linearity problem in subspace methods.

Independent component analysis (ICA; e.g., Common [42], Oja [99]) is a generalization of PCA, which decorrelates higher-order moments of the input ensemble, while PCA addresses only second-order moments of the input. Bell and Sejnowski [13] and Amari et al. [4] proposed an unsupervised learning algorithm to derive statistically independent components (ICs) by maximizing the mutual information between the input and output of a non-linear transformation. Applications of such ICA include a blind separation problem of various kinds of signals (e.g., Makeig et al. [122]). This technique has also been applied for representing facial images by Bartlett et al. [10, 9, 8], Donato et al. [54], and Futamura et al. [71]. These studies have successfully showed that the ICA-based representation improves the performance of face recognition over one based on PCA representations. Similar to LFA by Penev and Atick [148], ICA tends to produce local feature-like filters (e.g., Bell and Sejnowski [14]) and also provides non-orthogonal components (Futamura et al. [71]). Note, however, that ICA provides only linear basis, not non-linear one, although its learning process incorporates non-linearity. Therefore, a basis spanned by ICs still fails to capture curve-linear variations (Futamura et al. [71]).

Another approach is to combine an explicit non-linear transformation and the orthodox PCA technique for extracting actual non-linear components. For example, Kernel PCA (e.g., Schölkoph et al. [177], Mika et al. [129]) computes PCs in high-dimensional feature spaces which are derived from an input representation space by a non-linear mapping. They substitute kernel functions, which satisfy Mercer's condition [200] and are chosen *a priori*, for computing dot-products of samples in the feature space transformed by an implicit non-linear mapping, providing a way to account for higher-order statistics of inputs without a combinatorial explosion of time complexity for explicitly evaluating the non-linear mapping. Although this method provides a simple algorithm to construct non-linear (or curve-linear) basis, it complicates the synthesis process of a subspace model; a point in the high-dimensional feature space, representing a linear combination of these non-linear components, might not have a mapping point in the low-dimensional input representation space. This prevents the method from synthesizing a model view directly from arbitrary parameters. Furthermore, there is no simple standard rule to choose the appropriate kernel functions for a given problem.

Other approaches for learning non-linear component vectors include principal curve (Hastie and Stuetzle [87]), curvilinear component analysis using a self-

---

[1] Such a non-linear component becomes a function instead of a vector, therefore it is called *components* instead of *component vectors*.

organizing neural network (Demartines and Herault [52]), and mixtures of probabilistic principal component analyzers for statistically combining localized linear subspaces (Tipping and Bishop [189]).

Transformation Models

In the previous sections 2.1.2, 2.1.2, and 2.1.2, we gave extensive reviews of methods within the paradigm of the subspace model with linear or non-linear component vectors. As another approach, one can try to explicitly address a mapping function between a representation space of objects and a parameter space of their physical variations (e.g., 3D head pose angles). We call a model which consists of such a mapping function a transformation model. The advantage of this approach is that it makes the variations explicit and directly available to other components of a perceptual system. This task can be solved by a general supervised learning algorithm as a task of **multivariate function approximation**.

The simplest form of this model is to linearly approximate a mapping function. In this case, a mapping function is defined as a matrix whose size is determined by dimensionalities of both spaces (**transfer matrix**). In the field of statistics, this problem is also known as **multivariate regression** [22]. With a sufficient number of training samples, this transfer matrix or regression function can be computed by solving an overcomplete set of linear equations by standard algorithms such as singular value decomposition (SVD; e.g., Press et al. [164]).

In reality, the mapping function is non-linear for most types of variation. Thus non-linear learning algorithms are often applied to solve this task. The back propagation algorithm with a feed-forward neural network with hidden layers is a powerful non-linear supervised learning algorithm (Rumelhart and McClelland [170]). This algorithm has been widely used for the task of facial identification (e.g., Intrator et al. [101], Lawrence et al. [117]) or detection (e.g., Rowley et al. [169]), learning a mapping between an input representation space and a set of variation parameters such as identities of faces. The radial basis function (RBF) network proposed by Poggio and Girosi [161] is another powerful non-linear functional approximation algorithm. It expands a multivariate function in terms of a network of radial basis functions with parameter values that are learned from training samples. Edelman and Poggio [60] further developed a theory of 3D object representation based on the RBF network with Gaussian RF representation described in section 2.1.1(b). This technique was applied for representing facial images by Edelman et al. [61]. In this study, a Gaussian RBF classifier is built for each known person by learning a mapping function between an identity and multiple 2D views of the person. Another global network was also built to account for ensemble knowledge of the output patterns of an array of the classifiers in order to improve the recognition performance. Gutta and Wechsler [84] proposed a hybrid

36

classifier which consists of an ensemble of RBF and inductive decision tree networks and applied it to classification tasks of identity, gender, and ethnicity. An extension of this technique in the context of pose transformation of faces will be revisited in section 2.2.2. The support vector machine (SVM) proposed by Vapnik [200] is also a well-known method for the task of multivariate classification and regression. Recently, it has been applied for a variety of facial processing tasks such as pose estimation (e.g., Huang et al. [96], Ng and Gong [135], Li et al. [119]) and face detection (e.g., Osuna et al. [144], Terrillon et al. [188]).

2.1.3 Combination of Geometric and Pictorial Features

As reviewed in section 2.1.1, two types of feature, geometric and pictorial, have been used for single-view representation of faces. The geometric features describe the **shape information** of faces, whereas the pictorial features mainly capture the **texture information**. These earlier studies were based on either of the two types of feature, not both. It is a tempting idea to utilize both shape and texture information in order to enhance the representation power. Recently, a number of researchers have investigated a single-view representation which consists of both geometric and pictorial features.

Vetter and Troje [205] were the first to apply an optical flow technique to separate the shape and texture information from 2D facial images. They used a coarse-to-fine gradient-based optical flow algorithm to establish a pixel-wise correspondence field between two facial images. In their approach, the shape information is represented by 2D shape deformation as a dense pixel-wise correspondence field from an input face to a reference face. In their study, an averaged facial image from a number of samples is used as the reference face. The texture information is then represented by a shape-free texture image created by warping the input image to the reference image according the corresponding field. They constructed linear models with PC component vectors separately for the shape and texture representations for frontal facial images of multiple persons and demonstrated the representation accuracy of the linear model.

Craw et al. [49, 44, 46, 48] represented the shape information by a vector of image coordinates of 34 facial landmarks which are manually located. The shape-free texture representation of an input facial image is derived by warping the input to a fixed reference face linearly. They showed that the performance of a PCA-based face recognition system similar to the eigenface system by Turk and Pentland [195] was the best when a face was represented by both shape and shape-free texture PCs, with comparison to cases of only shape or texture PCs. Furthermore, they showed that a system only with texture PCs outperformed a system only with shape PCs. These results suggest that both shape and texture contains information that is crucial to identification process of faces, however texture may contain more identity information than shape.

Lanitis et al. [116, 114, 115] proposed a more complete face recognition system using a similar technique to the one by Craw et al. In their system, 152 facial landmarks are automatically located by multi-resolution Active Shape Model search (Cootes et al. [43, 113]) which elastically deforms the shape model by varying shape model parameters maximizing a proximity of local gray-level profiles. The shape-free representation was derived by warping an input to an average shape by a thin plate spline-based algorithm with 14 anchor points. Last, an input face was represented by **appearance parameters** that are a linear concatenation of model parameters from the shape PC model, texture PC model, and PC models for 1D local texture profiles. With this representation scheme, they demonstrated applications for facial tracking, pose estimation, facial identification, and gender and expression recognition.

These three studies [205, 49, 116] are similar in that they modeled the shape and shape-free texture representations *independently*. Under certain kinds of variations such as object rotation, however, these two types of information are not necessarily independent. There are only a few studies which addressed this dependency between the shape and texture information. For example, Edwards et al. [62, 63] proposed the **combined appearance model** which models the correlations between shape and shape-free texture information by applying PCA to the appearance parameters used by Lanitis et al. They successfully applied this representation technique to improve a model-fitting algorithm [62] and a facial identification and tracking system [63]. However, they did not explicitly discuss the correlation between the shape and texture captured in their representation.

2.1.4   Summary of Methods for Representing Faces

We classified various object/face representation methods into *single-view representations* and *multiple-view representations*. The single-view representation is derived solely from a single 2D image and consists of two types: *geometric features* and *pictorial features*. The geometric features are suitable for the tasks such as pose and expression analysis based on geometric properties of objects, whereas the pictorial features seem to capture information which is crucial for the identification process.

The multiple-view representation captures a spectrum of continuously varying appearances of objects/faces. We classified it into three types of approach: *3D model-based approach*, *2D template-based approach*, and *2D model-based approach*. The 3D model-based approach explicitly reconstructs a model of 3D shape structure from 2D views. For dealing with pose variation, which is a target of our investigation, this 3D model-based approach could be an appropriate choice. However, the task of 3D reconstruction from 2D views is ill-posed and often requires expensive computations. The 2D template-based and the 2D model-based approaches represent the spectrum of appearances of 3D objects implicitly by a set of 2D views. **The 2D model-based approach is preferred to the 2D template-based approach because a model provides a continuous and compact coverage of the different appearances of objects, whereas the template approach is based only on discrete samples of the continuously varying appearances.**

In the context of the 2D model-based approach, we studied four types of method: a) the *template-based linear subspace model*, b) the *PC-based linear subspace model*, c) the *non-linear subspace model*, and d) the *transformation model*. The first three methods are based on a *subspace model* which describes objects/faces by a weighted linear combination of component vectors which span a low-dimensional space embedded in an input representation space. They differ in the method used to construct the basis of the subspace. **The PC-based linear and the non-linear subspace models statistically learn the component vectors from training samples, whereas the template-based model relies on a manual selection of the component vectors.** While the PC-based model provides a simple framework for the analysis and synthesis processes of a linear model, the non-linear subspace model complicates these model processes. **Although the non-linear subspace model could potentially be an appropriate choice in terms of properly describing variations, the PC-based model is preferred due to its simplicity.** On the other hand, the transformation model uses a different strategy from these subspace models. The model learns a direct mapping function between an input representation space and a parameter space of variations. **The advantage of this method is that it makes the variations *explicit*.** The difficulty of this method is that the mapping function often tends to be complex and hard to learn (non-linear).

In the context of utilizing both shape and texture information, a number of studies have showed that combining the shape and texture information represented independently improves the representation power for the task of facial identification. **However, the correlations between the shape and texture information is still not fully investigated yet.**

2.2 Processing Faces with Pose Variations

In this section, we study literature which specifically concerns *processing* of pose variations of human faces. In order to make pose variations explicit, a model needs to undergo an **analysis** process of head pose from an input view and a **synthesis** process of a model view from an input pose. In the literature, this analysis process is often called **pose estimation** and the synthesis process is called **pose trans-**

formation. We are interested in realizing both analysis and synthesis in a single framework. Many researchers have investigated the pose variations of human faces, however they often concentrate on either the analysis or synthesis process, not both. We are also interested in making facial identification robust against pose variations. Previous studies addressing this **pose-invariant face recognition** are also reviewed in this section.

2.2.1   Head Pose Estimation

Pose estimation plays a crucial role in the process of face recognition. The similarity measure between two different views of the same person decreases as the difference in head pose increases. Furthermore, since the basic features of faces are similar across different individuals, the similarity between two views of different persons with the same pose could be higher than a pair of views from the same person but with different poses. This situation easily leads to misidentification. Therefore, the pose of the face needs to be estimated and compensated prior to the recognition process.

The task of pose estimation (or analysis of head pose variation) also plays a crucial role in many computer vision applications such as interactive human-computer interfaces and automatic video indexing. In such applications, the pose can be treated as an information channel which is associated with actions of the person involved and carries certain domain-specific semantics. A number of studies have addressed this task in various domains. The following provides reviews of such studies of pose estimation of human faces classified into four categories.

3D Model-Based Methods

When a 3D shape model of a face is available *a priori*, the head pose in 2D facial images can be estimated by finding a geometric transformation between a set of control points of the 3D model and corresponding points in the images. Since an analytical form of this transformation is known as a perspective or affine projection, the pose can be computed explicitly from this transformation matrix in a straightforward manner. This strategy can be viewed as matching a 3D shape model to a 2D input by aligning a 2D projection of the 3D control points to the input in order to deduce the transformation. An advantage of this method is that the analysis process is solely based on geometric shape information thus illumination variations which would affect texture information does not influence this procedure. However, facial deformation, often caused by facial expression, can influence the precision of the estimate.

It was Ullman [98] who pioneered a technique of this 3D model matching. He showed that three corresponding points or lines are usually sufficient to determine the transformation that aligns a 3-D model to a 2-D image, assuming the object can undergo only rigid transformations. Haralick [86] evaluated iterative matching methods for pose estimation of generic objects which are robust against incorrect correspondences between points. Recently, Heinzmann and Zelinsky [89] demonstrated head pose and gaze direction estimation based on the same three-point model fitting algorithm in their real-time face tracking system. Choi et al. [41] applied an EM-algorithm to the 3D model matching, improving Ullman's algorithm with a least-square fitting. This 3D model matching can also be achieved with edge curvature information. Shimizu et al. [181] proposed a 3D model fitting algorithm based on curvature alignment. In their approach, 3D curvature derived from a generic 3D facial model is iteratively fit to 2D curvature information extracted from an edge image of a 2D facial view.

Another strategy is based on reconstruction of 3D structure information from a set of 2D views. This method derives a pose estimate by generating a 3D model instead of assuming it *a priori*. For example, Xu and Akatsuka [220] proposed a stereo method for computing relative head pose. Using correspondences of basic facial landmarks such as pupils and the mouth in a stereo image pair, the 3D depth of the landmarks is first reconstructed. The normal direction of a triangular plane region defined by the 3D coordinates of three facial landmarks provides the head pose relative to the camera axis. Gordon [78] demonstrated a pose estimation system using a structure-from-motion algorithm (Horn [94]) based on a factorization method proposed by Tomasi and Kanade [190]. This algorithm factorizes a feature position matrix derived from a video sequence into two matrices, one providing a 3D location of the feature points (structure) and the other providing the rotational relationship between the object and the camera at each frame.

A generic 3D model can also be used to synthesize artificial templates of rotated faces (e.g, Tsukamoto et al. [194]) in order to automate the manual collection of templates for the 2D pictorial template-based methods which will be described in the next section. These artificial templates are then used for a simple template matching in order to estimate the head pose.

As discussed in section 2.1.1(a), the disadvantages of these methods are due to the overhead for reconstructing a 3D structure model for each subject. When a single generic model is used for different individuals, shape differences across individuals can influence the precision of the estimate greatly. Moreover, the accuracy of the landmark finding process which is often based on illumination-sensitive pictorial features directly affects the precision of the estimate.

2D Pictorial Template-Based Methods

This approach is based on a template matching algorithm with a set of pictorial feature-based templates, each of which is associated with its head pose. The input face is subjected to a nearest-neighbor search with these templates, resulting in the template most similar to the input. The pose associated with the most similar template is interpreted as an estimate of the input pose. The pose estimate could approximate the input's head pose well when the set of templates covers the complete viewing sphere with an adequate sampling density and variations of individuals and illumination, etc. For example, Bichsel and Pentland [18] used templates based on 2D gray-level image features to estimate head orientation. Instead of the simple nearest-neighbor search, they used a coarse-to-fine template matching with a Gaussian pyramid of multi-pose templates. Kruger et al. [108] and Elagin et al. [64] also demonstrated a technique with templates based on a facial graph whose nodes are labeled by 2D Gabor jets and with a simple nearest-neighbor search. The above examples only provide a rough classification of discrete poses with a limited number of templates. In order to estimate the head poses accurately and continuously, these techniques require a dense sampling of the viewing sphere, resulting in an prohibitively large number of templates as discussed in section 2.1.1(b). Since these templates are often collected manually by the operator, the preparation of the templates becomes labor-intensive. Moreover, since these methods utilize texture information, it is inherently sensitive to texture variations from sources other than pose variations such as illumination and deformation. Recent studies by McKenna and Gong [128, 75, 180, 135] utilized densely sampled templates using a specialized data acquisition system with a magnetic sensor and a calibrated camera. Their system [128] aimed to mitigate the problems of coarse sampling and illumination sensitivity by using template matching based on the magnitude of the Gabor wavelet transform. However, their reported average estimation error for known persons was roughly 7.0 degrees along 2 rotation dimensions, which is still suboptimal. Their extension to pose estimation for unknown persons [75] used iterative error minimization algorithms using the similarity-based method (Edelman and Duvdevani-Bar [58, 59, 56, 57]) with a vector of similarities to multi-personal templates of fixed poses. This extended system gave a better average error of 3.5 degrees. Ng and Gong [135] demonstrated a multi-view face detection and pose estimation system using an ensemble of localized support vector machines, each of which is responsible for detecting faces in a local region of the viewing sphere. Their pose estimation was based on a nearest-neighbor matching of an input sample to a number of learned support vectors. Their average pose estimation error is, however, 8 degrees which is again suboptimal.

2D Geometric Transformation-Based Methods

Because a 3D model is not always available, there has been a need for pose estimation algorithms solely based on geometric information in a set of 2D views.

Brunelli [30] proposed an algorithm which is based on quantifying the asymmetry between the aspect of the two eyes in an intensity image. In his system, 1D (in-depth) head poses are directly derived from a parameter computed as an integral projection of vertical gradients of the two eye regions. 3D facial models with ray-tracing and texture mapping technique were used to synthesize training samples which varies in pose and illuminant direction. This method, however, suffers from the asymmetry heuristics which restrict its use to only vertical rotation. More holistic strategies can be derived from using a geometric transformation of a set of 2D facial feature positions between a pair of 2D views. The three point 3D model fitting algorithm described in section 2.2.1 can be extended to 2D geometric feature-based templates, assuming that there is no depth in the surface of faces. For example, this technique was used by Maurer and von der Malsburg [127] to derive head pose from a single 2D input view by computing an affine transformation between positions of a set of facial landmarks in an input and in a reference template. The pose of the input face was analytically deduced from the computed transformation matrix. The advantage of this technique is that it is able to estimate poses from any pair of 2D views, though it can suffer from errors due to the assumption that there is no depth on a face. Furthermore, this technique is sensitive to the precision of the landmark finding process similar to the 3D model-based methods previously described. Chen et al. [39] also proposed an algorithm based on geometrical properties of the hair and face regions derived from color cues. Rotation angles of faces along three axes are analytically related to the first and second order moments of hair and face regions. Although this algorithm realizes the pose estimation without locating landmarks, instability in the region finding system can result in problems similar to those for the landmark finding process.

General Transformation-Based Methods

The last approach is to view the task of pose estimation as approximating an **explicit function** which directly maps an input representation space to a pose parameter space, described as a transformation model in section 2.1.2. This is a more general approach which allows us to apply general learning systems. It is also characterized by a minimum usage of *a priori* variation-specific knowledge (e.g., the analytical knowledge of 3D rotation in an affine transformation, etc). The most simple way for realizing this type of method is to define this mapping function as a linear system. An advantage of this approach is that such a linear system can be solved analytically by standard algorithms such as singular value decomposition (SVD) [164]. Lanitis et al. [115] estimated the depth-rotation angles along two axes from two PCs derived from the shape representations. A linear mapping function from a PC to a corresponding rotation angle was computed for each rotation axis by linear regression. The nature of this mapping function is, however, often non-linear. Thus it is tempting to approximate the mapping function by a general non-linear supervised learning algorithm as described in section 2.1.2. For the task of facial pose estimation, Lando and Edelman [112] have used a Gaussian RBF network to approximate mapping from texture information in a high frequency band to head poses. This RBF network is trained to classify an input pose into five different poses. (This system will be revisited in the context of pose transformation and face recognition in sections 2.2.2 and 2.2.3, respectively.) Huang et al. [96] applied a support vector machine (SVM) for classification of head poses into three discrete poses by learning a direct mapping from 2D gray-level image representation to head poses. Recently, Wu and Toyama [217] demonstrated a pose estimation system robust against person- and illumination-variations. In their system, the task of pose estimation is formulated as Bayesian inference from probability density functions of Gabor and Gaussian features annotated on an ellipsoid point-distribution model. The maximum *a posteriori* pose is derived by finding a maximum likelihood solution of the inference. Although they claimed insensitivity to the named variations, their average estimation error was 10 degrees in the best case.

These general transformation-based methods provide a simple framework to make the pose variations explicit by directly associating a single-view representation with its 3D head angles. An inherent problem is the approximation accuracy of the mapping function. Non-linear learning algorithms often result in a near to perfect fit to training samples but have poor generalization capabilities. The work by Lanitis et al. utilized a linear transformation model which often has better generalization capabilities, however they only provided preliminary results without quantitative analyses.

2.2.2 Head Pose Transformation

As pointed out in section 2.1.1(b), pictorial features are sensitive to pose variations; the similarity measure between two different views of the same person decreases as the difference of the head poses in the two views increases. This problem makes recognition of faces with different poses a difficult task. A solution to this problem is to align the head pose of an input and a stored model by applying a pose transformation which is learned from example 2D views. A number of studies have attempted to solve this pose transformation problem and can be categorized into two approaches as shown in figure 2.2.

In the first approach, the pose transformation relates facial appearances with one pose to appearances with another pose (e.g., a transformation between a frontal appearance to a profile appearance). Thus this type of pose transformation can be formalized as a transformation between two points in a single vector space. We call this approach **discrete-transformation**. In the second approach,

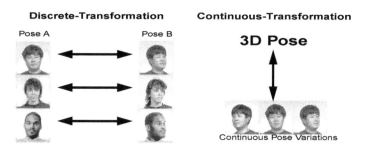

Discrete-Transformation

Pose A   Pose B

Continuous-Transformation

3D Pose

Continuous Pose Variations

Figure 2.2: Two Types of Pose Transformation

the pose transformation directly relates pose variation parameters to facial appearances. This type of pose transformation can be formalized as a mapping between two different vector spaces: from a parameter space of the pose variations to an input representation space of the facial appearances. We call this approach **continuous-transformation**

Discrete-Transformation Methods

Poggio and his colleagues were the first to show that, given one example view at a known pose, it is possible to synthesize views of the face as seen from different poses by exploiting *a priori* knowledge in the form of a class-specific transformation described in section 2.1.2. This class-specific transformation was defined as a discrete-transformation generalized over different individuals (**class-specific discrete-transformation**). In other words, it was defined as a mapping between a pair of template-based linear subspace models, each of which models facial appearances of different people at a specific pose. This class-specific discrete-transformation can be pre-computed with a pair of prototypical template sets at two poses and applied to rotate an arbitrary input face.

Vetter and Poggio [204] proposed an algorithm using a delta function of model parameters as a class-specific discrete-transformation. The use of delta function is postulated by the linear class theory proposed by Poggio [162], in which different views of an object share the same model parameters. In their algorithm, an example face is analyzed by a linear model of the *same* pose, resulting in model parameters which give the most similar model view to the example. In order to synthesize a model view of a target pose, these model parameters are then *directly* translated to model parameters of the target pose, synthesizing the model view by a linear combination. They also treated shape and texture information separately in the same manner, Vetter and Troje [205] (see section 2.1.3 for details). The

45

shape information of an input is extracted as a pixel-wise correspondence field of an input from a reference face of the same pose using an optical flow or a recursive bootstrapping algorithm (Vetter et al. [203]). Using this correspondence field, the input face is warped to the shape of the reference face, resulting in a shape-free texture representation. Both shape and shape-free texture representations of an input face are independently transformed to a target pose by the linear class algorithm described above. In order to generate a final model view, the rotated shape and texture are merged by linear interpolation of the nearest three pixel values (forward-warping).

Beymer and Poggio [16] proposed an algorithm which synthesizes novel views from a single-view example according to a linear combination of 2D shape deformations between pairs of prototypical faces at *different* poses. This algorithm, called **parallel deformation**, utilized a template-based linear subspace model of pixel-wise correspondence fields between the pairs of prototypical faces at different poses. It also synthesized a novel view directly from the input's texture, unlike Vetter and Poggio who extracted texture of a novel view from a linear texture model of a target pose. Similar to Vetter and Poggio's algorithm, shape information of an input is first represented as a pixel-wise correspondence field to an averaged face used as a reference. This input's correspondence field is then expressed as a linear combination of correspondence fields of prototypical templates with the input pose, resulting in model parameters that describe the decomposition. Using these model parameters, a correspondence field from the input's pose to a target pose is synthesized by a linear combination of prototypical pixel-wise correspondence fields between the two poses. The final model view is then generated by a forward-warping of the input face according to the synthesized correspondence field without using prototypical texture information at the target pose.

The two algorithms of Vetter and Beymer are similar in that they both used the linear class theory with a delta function and the shape and texture decomposition by an optical flow computation. One advantage of Vetter's approach is that it is only required to find correspondence fields of faces at the *same* pose, whereas Beymer's approach requires correspondence fields of faces at *different* poses. The optical flow algorithm used in both algorithms can perform poorly as the shape difference between a pair of faces increases. Since shape deformation caused by a pose difference often exceeds deformation caused by an individual difference, it is more difficult to find the correspondence fields of faces at different poses than of faces at the same pose. Moreover, when the shape of an input face cannot accurately be described by prototypical shape templates, the resulting model view by parallel deformation will appear geometrically distorted. The parallel deformation algorithm also requires the existence of pixel correspondences between two different poses, which does not necessarily exist due to self-occlusion. This is not

46

a requirement for Vetter's algorithm. An advantage of parallel deformation over Vetter's approach is its ability to preserve peculiarities of texture such as moles. Since Vetter's algorithm synthesizes the texture of a model view from a linear model of target pose, not from an input, such peculiarities in the input often fail to be recovered. Since both algorithms are based on template-based linear subspace models, they suffer from the same problems of template selection described in section 2.1.1(b).

Maurer and von der Malsburg [126] proposed a different approach for synthesizing novel views from a single-view example according to *a priori* knowledge of the pose transformation. In their algorithm, a face is represented by a graph whose nodes are located at facial landmarks and labeled by 2D Gabor jets in the same manner as Wiskott et al. [215] described in section 2.1.1(b). With an assumption that an image region around each facial landmark is painted on a local flat 3D surface plane, they related two jets, sampled at the same landmark of a face with two different poses, by a linear transformation as a function of normal angles at the landmark for both poses. They used a simple exhaustive search algorithm [125] to learn the normal angles at each landmark for different poses. These normal angles are learned from pairs of prototypical template sets, each of which contains faces of different individuals at a specific pose, and are used as *a priori* knowledge. Since the knowledge of the normal angles are in the basic-level, the linear jet transformation together with this knowledge can be seen as a class-specific discrete-transformation. This algorithm is different from the previous two in that it uses explicit 3D structure information which is learned from a set of 2D views. Because of the assumption of locally planar faces, the learning results can be unstable and inaccurate, which limits the precision of the pose transformation.

Lando and Edelman [112] proposed a pose transformation algorithm based on a class-specific discrete-transformation in an RF representation space (see section 2.1.1(b) for descriptions of this RF representation). Their system first classifies a head pose of an input view by an RBF network, as described in section 2.2.1. Using the classified pose, the input view was transformed to a fixed canonical pose by applying the class-specific discrete-transformation computed as an average of difference vectors between prototype pairs at the input and canonical poses. The approximation of a class-specific discrete-transformation by a simple mean difference vector limited the overall accuracy of their pose transformation.

These four algorithms based on class-specific discrete-transformations realize the task of synthesizing novel views from a single-view example using the transformation as *a priori* knowledge. These algorithms also serve as computational models of generalization capabilities from a single-view in human visual systems (Schyns and Bülthoff [178], Troje and Bülthoff [192, 193], O'Toole et al. [146]). The problem of these algorithms is due to the characteristics of the discrete-transformation. The discrete-transformation covers the viewing sphere only *discretely*. Therefore, a prohibitively large number of different transformations need to be computed in order to continuously cover the complete viewing sphere. Furthermore, in order to learn a single transformation between a reference and target pose, training samples with the specific head poses need to be collected for many subjects. This makes the collection of training samples a practically difficult task requiring assistance of an operator and collaboration of the subjects, especially as the number of transformations increases.

Continuous-Transformation Methods

The continuous-transformation is a mapping between two different vector spaces. For the task of pose transformation, a continuous-transformation from a parameter space of pose variations to an input representation space is learned as a transformation model explained in section 2.1.2 (similar to the general transformation-based methods for pose estimation described in section 2.2.1). This transformation model provides a simple framework to synthesize a single-view representation (**model view**) directly from an *explicit* 3D head angle.

Note that this type of pose transformation can be easily realized by a texture mapping or ray tracing when a 3D structure of a face is given. As described in section 2.1.1(b), a number of view-based methods for reconstructing such 3D models are available such as, for example, a linear class of 3D model recorded by a Cyberware scanner (Blanz and Vetter [24]), an illumination cone estimation by using a generalized bas-relief transformation (Georghiades et al. [73]), and a structure-from-shading technique (Zhao and Chellappa [223]). Although much attention has been given to these methods with explicit 3D models, pose transformation based on a continuous-transformation of 2D views has scarcely been reported.

Beymer et al. [17] demonstrated an example of a pose estimation and transformation system using a transformation model based on an RBF network [161]. For pose estimation, a mapping from a representation space (based on normalized 2D gray-level images) to a parameter space of pose and expression variations are approximated by a Gaussian RBF network with 4 examples (**analysis network**). This analysis network continuously estimates an input pose by interpolation between two examples (the two examples code pose variations and the other two code expression variations). For pose transformation, an inverse mapping from the parameter space to the representation space is approximated by a regularization network [161] with tensor products of piece-wise linear splines (**synthesis network**). These networks are trained to account for facial appearances of a single person from a number of example views. The shape of these example views, as well as test views, are normalized to a reference face by a coarse-to-fine gradient-based optical flow algorithm. They successfully showed a reconstruction of an input face by an **analysis-synthesis chain**, a sequential application of the analysis and synthesis networks, using an output of the analysis network as an input of the synthesis network. Moreover, the model was applied to generate a model view of one person with pose and expression extracted from another person by connecting an analysis network learned for the latter person and a synthesis network learned for the former person. A limitation of this work is that they only considered pose variations along one axis (horizontal rotation). Furthermore, their model requires finding pixel-wise correspondences between different poses, which is often a difficult task as discussed in section 2.2.2.

The general advantage of this approach is that, given a proper distribution of training samples, it provides a continuous transformation between the two parameter spaces, whereas the discrete-transformation approach covers the viewing sphere only discretely. Moreover, this approach is data-driven; the learning algorithm does not require training samples with a specific pose as is the case for the discrete-transformation approach. This implies a solution to the problem of manual sample collection, however it also suggests that the quality of a learned transformation directly relies on the distribution characteristics of the training samples. An open problem in the continuous-transformation approach is how to approximate this mapping function which is often non-linear. As discussed in section 2.2.1, non-linear learning algorithms which can achieve high approximation accuracy have a tendency to overfit training samples. This overfitting decreases the generalization capability of a model. An alternative is to use a linear learning system, however, the linear assumption often limits the approximation accuracy.

2.2.3 Pose-Invariant Face Recognition

Most studies in the face recognition literature address the issue of pose-invariance at least to a certain extent since it is one of the most obvious difficulties for automating the task. As mentioned earlier, the pose transformation for providing model views of specific head poses is originally motivated by this need for making existing identification systems robust against the pose variation. In this section, we provide a review of such studies from the viewpoint of identifying individuals from 2D facial images. Because literature on this topic is vast, this review only concerns a number of characteristic studies. Surveys of face recognition systems in general (e.g., Samal and Iyengar [173], Valentin et al. [199], and Chellappa et al. [38]) are recommended for supplemental examples. It is also worth noting that the term, **pose-invariant**, has been used very loosely in the literature and most of the previous recognition systems are not completely invariant against pose variation. Although other terms such as **pose-insensitive** may be better suited for describing these systems, we choose to use this term, even for these non-invariant systems, in order to maintain consistency with the literature.

Different Approaches

We classify a number of previous methods into three categories: **single-view**, **multiple-view**, and **non-nearest-neighbor** approaches. They are characterized by a general framework for realizing the identification process and also by a specific method used for accommodating the pose variations.

The first two approaches are based on a template-based nearest-neighbor classification. These approaches postulate that each known person is associated with a stored template (or a set of templates) which is directly comparable to a preprocessed input, and that there exists a reasonable metric which gives similarity measures between the inputs and templates. In the framework of the nearest-neighbor classification, an identity associated with the template most similar to an input gives an estimate of the input's identity. In order to make a system of this framework insensitive to the pose variations, head poses of the inputs and templates need to be aligned.

The first two approaches differ from each other in the number of templates used to represent each known person. The single-view approach represents each known person by a single view of the person, while the multiple-view approach represents each known person by multiple views. Because of this difference, the two approaches achieve the pose alignment between the inputs and templates in a different manner. For clarity, see figure 5.1 which illustrates these two approaches.

The last approach utilizes other classification methods such as a multivariate non-linear function learned in an artificial neural network. Such a function can be learned from a number of training samples for various individuals in order to classify the identity of arbitrary inputs. In order to make a system of this approach insensitive to the pose variations, the structure and/or learning algorithm of a system need to be modified such that the outputs of the learned classification function are not influenced by the pose variations.

Single-View Approach

The single-view approach is based on a template-based nearest-neighbor classification, in which each known person is represented by a single-view template. The head pose of these templates are usually assumed to be constant and called a **canonical pose**. In this approach, each test sample undergoes a pose transformation that synthesizes a canonical view of the test sample. This can be viewed as a normalization of various head poses of test samples into a fixed known pose. In order to automate this type of recognition system, it is necessary to estimate head poses of each test sample.

Maurer and von der Malsburg [126] demonstrated a recognition system of this approach with the Gabor jet-based single-view representation. Each test sample with various but known head poses were transformed to a frontal pose as the canonical pose. As described in section 2.2.2, their pose transformation utilized a linear class-specific discrete-transformation of Gabor jets with different head poses as a function of a crude 3D structure of generic faces learned from pairs of training samples. The input's head poses were assumed either given *a priori* or estimated by their 2D geometric transformation-based system [127]. They reported 53% average correct-identification rate using 90 known person pairs of the FERET database with frontal and roughly ±45 degree rotated poses along one depth-rotation axis. This average correct-identification rate improved the rate of a system without the pose transformation by 17%.

Lando and Edelman [112] proposed a pose-invariant face recognition system based on a class-specific discrete-transformation in an RF representation space. As described in sections 2.2.1 and 2.2.2, their RBF network-based system classified an input head pose exploiting high frequency information of the RF representation, and transformed the input view to a fixed canonical pose by an average difference vector between prototype pairs of the input and canonical poses. The identification process was realized by another RBF network utilizing a low frequency RF representation. This network was trained to identify faces with the canonical pose. With 18 known persons with ±34 degree 1D depth-rotation, the average correct-identification rate was 76% when the bilateral symmetry assumption was used to increase the number of training samples. Note that this system can also be categorized as a non-nearest-neighbor system since the identification process is realized by the multivariate function approximated by the RBF network.

A number of studies employed a generic 3D facial structure model to transform input views to the canonical pose. In a pose-invariant face recognition system reported by Imaoka and Sakamoto [100], each known person was represented by 6 raw-image-based localized templates. Given a 3D head pose of an input, these templates were geometrically transformed to templates of a frontal pose using correspondences between the rotated 3D structure and 2D views. They reported 84% average correct-identification rate with a database of 100 known persons with 1D depth-rotation between 0 to 90 degrees. Zhao and Chellappa [223] reported a similar approach using 3D model-based image warping for transforming input views of a known pose into a frontal head pose. Their system which combined the PC-subspace method and LDA resulted in 66.7% average correct-identification rate using 42 pairs of the FERET database which was a subset of data used in Maurer's study [126].

The subspace models described in section 2.1.2 can be used to provide a pose-invariant face description, whose effect is similar to transforming input views of arbitrary head poses to the canonical pose. Pentland et al. [149] proposed a pose-invariant face recognition system based on a **view-specific eigenspace**. Their system consists of a set of subspace models (as system knowledge), each of which describes a specific pose of faces. Using the distance-from-face-space metric, a view-specific eigenspace, which describes the input view of an arbitrary pose most accurately, is found in the nearest-neighbor manner. The input view is then encoded by this pose-aligned view-specific eigenspace, followed by the eigenface-based identification process shown by Turk and Pentland [195].

An advantage of this approach is the relatively small size of the database of known persons. Because each known person is represented by only a single template, a system can be compact which is a favorable characteristics towards developing a scalable and/or real-time recognition system. However, the shortcomings of the class-specific discrete-transformation, needed to align head poses, hurt this approach. The transformation needs to be class-specific because inputs without identity information are subjected to this transformation. The nature of the discrete-transformation poses a tradeoff between the size of database and the accuracy of the transformation. Because of these shortcomings, previous studies in this approach reported either relatively poor accuracy or experimental results in a very limited setting.

Multiple-View Approach

The multiple-view approach is based on a template-based nearest-neighbor classification, in which each known person is represented by multiple templates of the person in different poses. If the head poses of stored templates for each known person cover the viewing sphere sufficiently, each test sample is guaranteed to find a template with a matching head pose. With the fair assumption that a pair of pose-aligned samples gives a higher similarity than a pair of samples with different poses, an identification system which is insensitive to the pose variation can be constructed based solely on nearest-neighbor classification. Therefore, in theory, the pose estimation and transformation of inputs or templates are not necessary for automating a recognition system of this type.

The simplest way to realize a face recognition system of this approach is to manually prepare multiple-view templates for every known individual. Beymer [15] demonstrated this type of system based on a correlation metric of raw-image-based single-view representation. Each input view was geometrically registered to the known person's templates by using locations of eyes and nose which were automatically located by his system. Their experiments with 62 unknown persons with ±30 degree 2D head rotations resulted in 98.7% average correct-identification rate.

As discussed in the introduction, however, manual collection of multiple-view templates is often impractical because the number of all possible views is simply too large. This obvious disadvantage motivated an approach which utilizes a pose transformation synthesizing the multiple-view templates from a single view.

Beymer and Poggio [16] demonstrated a recognition system which utilized a multiple-view database synthesized from a single-view database of a canonical pose by using a technique which is already described in the context of pose transformation in section 2.2.2. A depth-rotated pose was used as a canonical pose in order to reduce the number of target poses by using a bilateral symmetry of facial structure. Class-specific discrete-transformations were constructed for 9 fixed poses, in order to generate 15 different views for every known individual. This study compared the discrete-transformations based on parallel deformation algorithm and the linear class algorithm [204] described in section 2.2.2. With a database of 62 known persons with ± 30 degree 2D head rotations, their experiments showed that a system with the parallel deformation (85.2%) outperformed one with the linear class transformation (73.5%). This is perhaps because the parallel deformation system can preserve individual peculiarities such as facial moles. It is also worth mentioning that either system could not perform as well as the real-view system, indicating that errors of the pose transformation process greatly influence the identification performance.

Such multiple-view synthesis from a single-view can also be realized by a number of different methods. Tsukamoto et al. [194] reported a face detection and pose estimation system which utilized templates of various poses synthesized from a single view of arbitrary persons. This multiple-view synthesis was carried out by rendering a generic 3D facial structure model whose texture was mapped from known single-views. Their study did not, however, address the identification task. Georghiades et al. [73] demonstrated a pose- and illumination-invariant recognition system based on a 3D surface reconstruction from a set of training samples. Arbitrary images of a convex Lambertian object was modeled by an **illumination cone** which was a superposition of image models due to different point-light sources. This illumination cone was completely characterized by the product of the albedo with the inward pointing unit normal at 3D surface points corresponding to each pixel-point. 3D surface structure was reconstructed by iteratively improving the generalized bas-relief transformation ambiguity. Once the surface was reconstructed, views with arbitrary pose and illumination could be synthesized by ray tracing.

The above studies were based on the nearest-neighbor classification framework, in which each known person is associated with many templates that are directly comparable to an input by a simple similarity metric. An obvious disadvantage of these methods is that their known-person database becomes very large as the number of known persons increases. There are a number of studies which resolved this issue by representing each known person by a compact representation model trained by different views of each individual. These systems can still be viewed as a multiple-view approach by considering the multiple-view templates as training samples for each individual model.

Murase and Nayar [133] proposed a pose- and illumination-invariant generic object recognition system based on a **parametric eigenspace**. Their system consisted of two different eigenspaces, **universal eigenspace** and **object eigenspace**, which corresponded to the basic and subordinate levels of object classes. Each different object was represented by a manifold (or a locus of different views of an object) in the universal eigenspace, which was interpolated by cubic splines. Their system identified a test object by finding the object-specific manifold which minimized the distance to a projection of the test sample in the eigenspace. This minimization task was realized by a binary search algorithm or an RBF network. After finding the identity of test objects, the object was further analyzed for pose estimation by an object eigenspace, which was trained for the specific object. Their experiments with 4 known objects with complete 360 degree 1D depth-rotation resulted in 100% correct-identification rate when tested with views whose poses lie between the training views.

Graham and Allinson [80, 79] demonstrated a face recognition system based on a linear combination of prototypical manifolds. They trained an RBF network which reconstructed a full manifold representation in a universal eigenspace from a single view of an arbitrary pose. The universal eigenspace was learned by images of 20 people whose head poses varied between 0 and 90 degrees along one depth-rotation axis in 10-degree intervals. A **virtual manifold** of an unknown person was then interpolated by 9 manifolds derived from 9 different views of the person. Their system resulted in a 93.1% average correct-identification rate with a database of 20 known persons.

Wieghardt and von der Malsburg [210] recently proposed a learning method for constructing a parametric eigenspace representing an object without using explicit knowledge of 3D head angles. They utilized a similarity-based clustering algorithm to construct view-specific local eigenspaces. These local eigenspaces were then pieced together in a global coordinate space by using multi dimensional scaling (MDS). Their experiments showed a successful construction of a global space for a specific object which maintained the topology of pose variations. Their study did not report the identification performance of their system. Tenenbaum et al. [186] also proposed a related learning method utilizing a combination of PCA and MDS (Isomap algorithm), which addresses the same problem. This study demonstrated a successful application of their algorithm to facial images, hand images, and hand-written numbers.

In summary, a study by Beymer showed that the simple multiple-view system with templates of recorded samples performs very well against pose variations. In terms of accuracy and identification performance, the multiple-view system is preferred to the single-view system. However, the obvious shortcoming of this approach is that the size of the known-person database becomes enormous. A number of studies attempted to resolve this problem by constructing a multi-view database from a single-view database by a class-specific discrete-transformation. These methods, however, have not been too successful in terms of their identification performance because of the limitation of their pose transformation accuracy.

A subspace-manifold-based system by Murase and Nayar gave an alternative, in which each known person was represented by a compact and continuous model in a form of a continuous-transformation. In this method, the models can be relatively accurate because each model captures a subordinate level transformation which is expected to behave better than the class-specific transformation for the generic face class. The continuous nature of the model also helps to improve its accuracy. The two systems based on the subspace-manifold, however, utilized non-linear interpolation methods for constructing the continuous-transformation. Therefore, their identification process required an expensive search in parameter space, which was a shortcoming of their methods.

Studies by Wieghardt and Tenenbaum raised an interesting point questioning a role of the ground-truth pose information. Many systems which explicitly address pose variations consisted of pose-specific models learned or constructed with ground-truth 3D pose information for each training sample. Their studies, in contrast, showed the possibility of constructing a parametric eigenspace without such ground-truth information. Another study by Tenenbaum [185] also addressed the same point using a different approach which attempts to solve a two-factor problem: separating two different types of information such as identity and pose directly from facial images by using a factorization method similar to the one by Tomasi and Kanade [190]. These considerations for the cases in which ground-truth parameter information is not available is theoretically significant and very attractive in certain application scenarios.

Non-Nearest-Neighbor Approach

The previous single- and multi-view approaches are based on the nearest-neighbor classification framework for realizing identification. This section presents a few samples of studies based on multivariate functions approximated by artificial neural networks

Duvedevani-Bar et al. [57] proposed a pose- and expression-invariant face recognition system based on their similarity-based object representation method [58, 56], using an ensemble of prototype RBF networks and the Gabor jet-based single-view representation. Their system consisted of 10 prototype networks, each of which was trained to output a constant for different views of a specific person and lower values for different people's faces. A vector of these networks' outputs described the proximity of a face to the 10 prototypical faces. For identification, an input view with an arbitrary pose was first subjected to the 10 prototype networks, resulting in an output vector. Next, the 10 coefficients of the output vector were subjected to a weighted summation whose weights were pre-computed for each known person. A person associated with the weights which resulted in the highest sum gave an identity estimate of the input. These individual-specific weights were computed as an inverse of an output vector from each person's frontal view with a neutral expression by the same 10 prototype networks. Their experiments with 18 known persons of 14 discrete poses within ±34 degree 1D depth-rotation resulted in 69% average correct-identification rate.

Huang et al. [95] demonstrated a pose-invariant face recognition system based on an ensemble of view-specific backpropagation 3-layer networks. Their system was constructed with 2 levels. The first level consisted of 4 view-specific modules, each of which was a combination of a view-specific eigenspace and a 3-layer backpropagation network which models transformation from the eigen manifolds to identities. Another combinatorial neural network was used on top of these view-specific modules in order to achieve the final identification. Their experiments with a database of 5 known persons with ±30 degree 1D depth-rotation resulted in 98.7% average correct-identification rate.

Bartlett et al. [10] reported two neural network-based face recognition systems. The first system was based on ICA of a training image ensemble described in section 2.1.2. Their experiments with 40 known persons with 5 discrete poses of ±30 degree 1D rotation showed that the ICA system performed slightly better (87%) than the PCA system using the same data (84%). The second system explicitly utilized the temporal continuity of visual stimuli, in which patterns presented in the proximal time were more likely to be associated with each other. The continuity was modeled by an attractor network which consisted of a competitive Hebbian learning network with a temporal low-pass filter. Their experiments with 20 known persons resulted in 73% correct-identification rate while the ICA system resulted in 89% using the same database.

Gong et al. [75] also reported a face recognition system utilizing temporal continuity information for real-time facial analysis from continuous video input. In their system, each input sample was represented by a vector of its similarities to a set of pose-varying prototype templates generalized over different people. Both pose estimation (as described in section 2.2.1) and face identification were formulated as a maximization of likelihood functions which included a temporal continuity term. Their experiments with prototype templates of 11 discrete poses (20 degree interval between ±90 degrees of 1D depth-rotation) for 11 different persons resulted in 97% average correct-identification rate when tested with 6 known persons.

Face recognition systems in this approach are restricted by the difficulty of scaling their neural network-based systems to the large number of known persons and various 3D head poses (**curse of dimensionality**). As the number of unknown persons increases, the learning of such non-linear networks becomes extremely difficult. A common compromise for this type of system is to consider only a subset of the 3D rotation dimensions or to crudely discretize the viewing sphere into a few number of prototype views. Therefore, these systems often result in poor accuracy in terms of processing the pose information, or poor practicality. A simple function approximation approach such as the one used by Huang et al. also poses difficulties for incrementally introducing new persons into the system. Each time a new person is added, the system needs to be re-learned from scratch. In contrast, in the case of template-based nearest-neighbor approach, this can be done by simply adding a new single-view template into a known-person database. A study by Duvedevani-Bar et al. showed that this problem could be solved by describing a novel view by a combination of prototypes, however their identification performance is still suboptimal due to its discrete handling of pose variations.

2.2.4 Summary of Methods for Processing Faces with Pose Variations

A number of recently proposed systems for pose estimation are classified into four types: 1) *3D model-based methods*, 2) *2D pictorial template-based methods*, 3) *2D geometric transformation-based methods*, and 4) *general transformation-based methods*.

The 3D model-based method is perhaps the most rational choice for this task, since pose estimation is formally a problem of 3D geometry. There is the least ambiguity in the estimation process in comparison to other types of method. This method is, however, limited by an overhead for 3D model construction as discussed in section 2.1.4. The state-of-the-art systems in this method use either special hardware or expensive algorithms for reconstructing 3D structure from 2D views. The special hardware is not widely available and the 3D reconstruction algorithms often require tedious manual steps, while automatic algorithms are unstable and suboptimal in accuracy. Moreover, this method is intrinsically limited to this special case of pose and does not constitute a general method for handling other types of image variation. **Therefore, it is still highly desirable to realize the task of pose estimation based on 2D sample views.** The 2D pictorial template-based method classifies an input pose by a template matching algorithm with templates based on pictorial features. These methods are limited by using pictorial features, which are sensitive to illumination variations, and furthermore the 2D template-based approach prohibits continuous estimation of all possible head poses (classification rather than continuous estimation). On the other hand, the 2D geometric transformation-based method which is based on a restricted three point model fitting algorithm improves the two disadvantages of the 2D pictorial template-based methods by using geometric features. Disadvantages of these methods are, however, that strict assumptions are required to apply the fitting algorithm in 2D and that the accuracy of the estimate is greatly influenced by the precision of the landmark finding process (see section 2.1.1(a) for details). The general transformation-based method views the task of pose estimation as approximating an explicit mapping function which directly associates an input representation space to a pose parameter space. The transformation is general because it does not assume variation-specific analytical knowledge. Both geometric and pictorial feature-based single-view representations have been utilized in this method. Using the transformation model in section 2.1.2, these methods provide a simple framework to make the pose variations explicit directly from a single-view representation. **An open problem of the transformation model also applies to these methods; there is no clear answer for learning the non-linear mapping function accurately without compromising the generalization capability.**

Comparing performances of the reviewed systems is difficult since most studies only provide qualitative performance analyses with either angular errors only along one or two rotation dimensions within a small range of pose variations or rates of classification errors for coarsely sampled discrete head poses. Among a few studies which reported results of quantitative error analysis, **the best average pose estimation error was roughly 3 degrees to our best knowledge.** The stereo-based system by Xu and Akatsuka [220] reported an average angular error of 3.2 degrees for full 3D rotations within ±10 degrees along each axis. The 3D shape model fitting system using an EM algorithm by Choi et al. reported approximately 3 degrees average error for full 3D rotations within ±40 degrees along each axis. The similarity-based method with Gabor magnitude images by Gong et al. reported 3.5 degrees for 2D depth-rotations within ±90 and ±40 degrees for yaw and tilt axes. For many application scenarios, a pose estimation error of 3 degrees, as reported at best, is still not adequate. The parametric eigenface system by Murase and Nayar [133] reported very high pose estimation accuracy with average angular errors of 1.0 and 1.5 degrees for known and unknown faces, respectively. However, this result cannot be directly compared to the ones by the above systems because their study consider only one rotation dimension and generic objects instead of faces.

Algorithms for pose transformation are categorized into two types: methods for 1) *discrete-transformation* and *continuous-transformation*. We reviewed four state-of-the-art systems based on a class-specific discrete-transformation. These systems realize the task of synthesizing novel views from a single-view example by exploiting a transformation mechanism constructed on the basis of *a priori* knowledge. The first two systems by Vetter and Beymer are based on the linear class theory with separate shape and texture representations. Therefore, there are problems in selecting templates for the template-based linear subspace model. Moreover, the method requires computation of pixel-wise correspondence fields, which is an ill-posed problem. Maurer's system is based on an analytical linear jet transformation with 3D normal angles of facial landmarks learned from 2D template sets. Because of its locally planar face assumption, the resulting jet transformation is limited in accuracy. Lando's system exploits a class-specific discrete-transformation in an RF representation space, implemented as an average of difference vectors between prototypical RF feature vectors at two poses. This approximation by an average also limits accuracy of the system.

An inherent limitation of these systems lies in the fact that they only realize discrete-transformations. A discrete-transformation covers the viewing sphere only discretely and requires training samples with specific head poses, which makes the sample collection procedure a difficult task requiring collaboration of the subjects.

Realization of full continuous-transformation solves these problems, because the resulting pose transformation can cover the viewing sphere continuously. **An open problem is how to approximate the mapping function accurately without compromising the generalization capability.** We are aware of only one system, proposed by Beymer, which exploited this approach with RBF networks.

A number of face recognition systems robust against the pose variation are classified into three approaches: 1) *single-view approach,* 2) *multiple-view approach,* and 3) *non-nearest-neighbor approach.*

In the single-view approach, the size of the known-person database is relatively small, which is a favorable characteristic towards scalability and the real-time speed of a system. However, the class-specific discrete-transformation, needed to align head poses, limits the accuracy of this approach. In the multiple-view approach, on the other hand, the very large size of a known-person database becomes a problem, while **the identification performance of the multiple-view approach tends to be better than the single-view approach.** Solutions with class-specific discrete-transformations to derive pose-varying views from a given single view do not seem to give good identification rate. PC-manifold-based (parametric eigenspace) systems based on individual-specific continuous-transformations give a solution to this problem by modeling each known individual by a compact and continuous model. These systems still require an expensive search for pose estimation and facial identification because of its use of non-linear interpolation. The non-nearest-neighbor approach often suffers from the curse of dimensionality problem which limits system scalability. Systems of this type commonly consider only a subset of the 3D rotation dimensions or crudely discretize the viewing sphere into a small number of prototype views, resulting in poor accuracy, or in difficulty in constructing a system for a realistic scenario.

Table 2.1 summarizes the identification performance of face recognition systems reviewed in this chapter. The first three columns of this table give system descriptions. They denote 1) system type, 2) authors of the study, and 3) year of

Sys	Authors	Year	Rate	DOF	#Pos	Range	#Per
SV	Maurer-Malsburg [126]	1995	53%	1D	2	±45°	90
SV	Lando-Edelman [112]	1995	76%	1D	5	±34°	18
SV	Imaoka-Sakamoto [100]	1999	84%	1D	8	0-90°	100
SV	Zhao-Chellappa [223]	2000	67%	1D	2	±45°	42
SV	Pentland et al. [149]	1994	87%	1D	9	±90°	21
MV	Beymer [15]	1993	99%	2D	15	±30°	62
MV	Beymer-Poggio [16]	1995	85%	2D	15	±30°	62
MV	Vetter-Poggio [16]	1995	74%	2D	15	±30°	62
MV	Georghiades et al. [73]	2000	97%	2D	117	±24°	10
MV	Murase-Nayar [133]	1995	100%	1D	72	360°	20
MV	Graham-Allinson [80]	1998	93%	1D	10	0-90°	20
NN	Duvedevani-Bar [57]	1998	69%	1D	5	±34°	18
NN	Huang et al. [95]	2000	99%	1D	4	±30°	5
NN	Bartlett(ICA) [10]	1997	87%	1D	5	±30°	40
NN	Bartlett(AtNet) [10]	1997	73%	1D	5	±30°	20
NN	Gong et al. [75]	1998	97%	1D	11	±90°	11

Table 2.1: Comparison of Pose-Invariant Face Recognition System's Performance

publication, respectively. The codes for system type, SV, MV, and NN, denote the single-view, multiple-view, and non-nearest-neighbor approaches, respectively. The last five columns of this table summarize experimental results. They denote 4) the best correct-identification rate, 5) the number of rotation dimensions considered, 6) the number of the discrete head poses used, 7) the range of pose variation in the samples, and 8) the number of known persons in the database.

Comparing performances of these systems is difficult since the studies use different databases and experimental settings. However, it is obvious that **most of the studies considered only a subset of the 3D rotation dimensions and/or a rather narrow range of pose variations.** Numerical experiments of 1D pose variation cannot provide meaningful insights about pose generalization in a full 3D head angle space. In terms of the pose variation range, the reviewed systems were limited to either a relatively wide pose range only along one rotation dimension or a narrow range along one or two rotation dimensions. The former, using very dense sets of pose variation samples, tend to result in a high correct-identification rate, however their generalization capability is still questionable because of the above argument. The latter impose too strict limitation on the variations since pose variations of a freely moving human head often surpass these ranges. **These observations of the previous studies urge us to investigate our recognition system for**

a much wider pose range in full 3D rotation dimensions. This need for increasing the range and dimensionality of the variation parameter space also agrees with our goal of realizing a widely applicable method, for which its parameter space becomes intrinsically high-dimensional.

2.3 Discussion: Why Our Approach?

2.3.1 Open Problems

The review of literature in this chapter revealed that the state-of-the-art systems for the analysis and synthesis of human faces with pose variations have the following open problems;

1. The discrete-transformation.

   (a) Covers the viewing sphere only discretely which leads to poor overall accuracy.

   (b) Sampling points connected by a transformation are chosen manually rather than learning from samples.

   (c) Requires operator assistance and subject collaboration for acquiring training samples with a specific head poses.

2. Suboptimal accuracy and limited pose variation.

   (a) Only a few report systematic performance analysis of pose estimation systems.

   (b) The best performance of pose estimation in the literature is not high enough.

   (c) Accuracy of pose estimation is inevitably influenced by accuracy of finding pixel-wise correspondences or facial landmarks in 2D views.

The main problem of many systems in the literature stems from the discreteness of the coverage of 3D head angle space (1, 1a). Such systems are *rigid*: they require an enormous number of templates or discrete-transformations in order to accurately cover the complete viewing sphere. In reality, their accuracy is often compromised by only using a small number of templates or transformations. Moreover, these rigid systems are bounded to be a variation-specific solution, confronted by the curse of dimensionality problem, when considering other types of variation. This discreteness also makes it difficult for the systems to be *data-driven* (1b, 1c). The discrete sampling points in pose parameter space are often determined *a priori*, which implies that samples with specific head poses need to be collected. This imposes operator assistance and subject collaboration, preventing the systems from being *on-line* and increasing the labor for sample collection. In practice, many learning systems suffer tremendously from this type of difficulty. For pose transformation, several studies have utilized the continuous-transformation which mitigates the above problems, however none of them addressed full three DOF of 3D rotations.

For pose estimation, many of the reviewed studies utilized *geometrical features* for characterizing facial information from 2D views. This is perhaps a natural choice since the problem of pose estimation can be formulated strictly as a problem of 3D geometry. The main disadvantage that is innate in this type of feature is sensitivity to errors of feature localization (2c); finding the accurate position of features in 2D images is not a trivial task. In practice, the state-of-the-art automatic systems for this task (e.g., Wiskott et al. [215]) are often less accurate than pixel width due to image digitization and influences from all sorts of image variations. [2] Because of this unavoidable inaccuracy in feature localization, algorithms which derive pose information from geometrical features need to be robust against input errors. Most of studies reviewed in this chapter did not address this problem. Another pitfall of these systems is that a usage of analytical knowledge of rotation variation makes it difficult for them to be data-driven. Therefore, they also tend to be a variation-specific solution only applicable for head pose variations. Furthermore, most systems in the literature are incomplete; they are often limited in the number of DOF or the range of the angle space (2). The performance of the systems has not been analyzed rigorously nor with high accuracy (2a, 2b).

There will be further discussion of the issues of pose-invariant face recognition in chapter 5, in which our proposed method is compared with several methods derived from the previous studies reviewed in this chapter.

2.3.2   Our Approach

In the introduction, we discussed how a compact, generalizable, data-driven and flexible representation model parameterized by 3D head angles can solve the problems of processing pose variations in 2D facial images. We furthermore proposed a method of implementing the model by **LPCMAP model** (Linear Principal Component MAPing functions), a combination of two linear systems; 1) a *PC-based linear subspace model* and 2) *linear mapping functions* between the face representation and 3D head angle spaces. The PC-based linear subspace model (hereafter

---

[2]Note that the Wiskott's system in theory achieves sub-pixel accuracy, although the above argument still holds when it is applied for practical problems.

PC-LSM) was described as a *2D model-based approach* for *multiple-view representation* in section 2.1.2. This representation model provides us with a compact and continuous (flexible) LSM that is learned from sample statistics (and is thus data-driven). However, it does not provide explicit physical parameterization. On the other hand, the linear mapping function (hereafter LMF) is equivalent to the *transformation model* in a simple linear form described in section 2.1.2. It provides a platform for the explicit parameterization missing in the PC-LSM, by learning a mapping function between the two vector spaces. As a format of *single-view representation*, the LPCMAP model utilizes separate representations for shape and texture information. Shape and texture representations are related by a linear transformation model capturing the correlation between them, while only the shape representation based on geometrical features is related to head angles for processing pose variations.

How does this proposed system help to solve the open problems described above? As discussed in the introduction, the nature of the data-driven flexible model innately solves the discreteness problem by continuously covering 3D head angle space. This leads to improved accuracy and generalizability of the system while reducing its size. Moreover, it has the advantage of reducing labor during sample collection, enabling the system's extension towards an on-line learning system.

The design of the LPCMAP model as a combination of two linear models derives advantage from the models' nature. While the PC-LSM provides the core of a model which satisfies the criterion of being compact, generalizable, data-driven and flexible, the LMF achieves the task of pose estimation and pose transformation directly in terms of the absolute values of 3D head angles. The combination then provides us with a continuous-transformation instead of a discrete-transformation whose disadvantages were discussed previously.

The use of the transformation model, however, poses an open problem, namely how to approximate the mapping function accurately without compromising generalization capability. A mapping between head angles and facial appearances is non-linear in general. However, we assume as our working hypothesis that this mapping can be linearly approximated. See figures 1.1 and 1.2 for illustrations of this linear idea. We prefer linear approximations to non-linear ones because of their robustness against errors in inputs and their computational simplicity. Moreover, linear approximations have the potential for generalization while avoiding overfitting statistical peculiarities of training samples that are not innate characteristics of the objects to be learned.

Decomposition of shape and texture information from 2D images is motivated by the fact that the two types of information have different advantages. Shape information based on geometrical features is suitable for pose processing. Ullman and Basri [197] showed that the shape information based on image coordinates

63

of facial landmarks is sufficient to recover the 3D pose of faces. On the other hand, texture information based on pictorial features is suitable for identity processing. Studies by Brunelli and Poggio [33] and by Craw et al. [49] showed that face recognition systems based on texture representation outperform ones based on shape representation. The LPCMAP model as a representation model should benefit from this shape and texture decomposition not only for the accuracy of pose processing but also for that of recognition tasks.

Lastly, the data-driven and flexible nature of the proposed model facilitates its extension to other types of variation. As discussed in the introduction, our long-term goal is to realize a simple unified framework which extracts all possible image variation sources. Although our focus in this study is limited to pose variation, it would not be a success if our solution cannot be extended to other variation sources. The nature of our model assures that it does not depend on the specifics of our particular problem (e.g., view-invariant features) thus does not pre-suppose theoretical analysis of the problem (e.g., in terms of geometry, optics, facial muscle physiology, etc). By this emphasis, our model improves the previous studies reviewed in this chapter whose applicability to other types of variation is limited.

2.3.3 Advantages of Single-View Representation by 2D Gabor Jets

As described in the next chapter, we use **2D Gabor jets** as representation of localized texture information. This representation scheme has been used for the state-of-the-art face recognition system whose performance has been proven by the FERET tests (Phillips et al. [157, 153, 152, 156, 154, 155]). There are also a number of psychological studies which support the system as a biological model of human face processing (Kalocsai et al. [104, 105], Biederman and Kalocsai [20], Hancock et al. [85], Bruce et al. [27]). Our model with the 2D Gabor jet-based texture representation is therefore expected to improve recognition performance of the previous pose processing systems that are based on features with raw pixel-values. Another advantage of the Gabor jet-based representation is that it allows for a spatially sparse graph representation. Although each jet is localized at a single pixel, it captures contrast variations within a region surrounding the center pixel. Therefore, only a few jets sampled at sparse locations are sufficient to represent the whole face. This frees our system from the difficulty of finding pixel-wise correspondences used in other pose processing systems.

2.3.4   Related Work

There are a few previous studies that are closely related to our approach. A study of 3D object recognition by Murase and Nayar [133] addressed the advantage of the continuous coverage of the viewing sphere by parameterized, compact, data-driven, and flexible models. They proposed the parametric eigenspace which models pose-dependent manifolds (trajectory of pose varying samples) in PC-spanned subspaces by a cubic spline technique. Our LPCMAP model can also be viewed as a type of the parametric eigenspace but with linear systems while they use a non-linear (cubic-spline) system to derive the explicit mapping which connects representations to 3D pose angles. The differences of their system from our approach include; 1) their system targeted generic 3D objects while we focus on faces specifically, 2) only 1D depth-rotation was considered in their experiments while our model accounts for the full 3D head rotations, 3) an issue of generalization to unknown poses was not seriously investigated, 4) their system was entirely based on image-based global texture representation while both shape and texture information are utilized for different tasks in our approach, and 5) manifolds in PC subspaces were modeled by a non-linear system while our approach uses a linear map for the same purpose. As discussed in the introduction, we favor linear models for parameterizing the manifolds, emphasizing the generalization capability of our systems. Moreover, their non-linear interpolation of the PC-manifolds makes the process of pose estimation more complicated requiring an expensive exhaustive search in a potentially very high-dimensional parameter space. Regardless of these differences, their study successfully showed very accurate pose estimation and object identification. Therefore, their results can serve as a bench mark of our numerical experiments which will be described in later chapters.

Beymer et al. [17] proposed a system based on a continuous-transformation learned by RBF networks which is capable of pose estimation and transformation. This is another implementation of a data-driven flexible model parameterized by pose variations. Their approach is different from ours in that; 1) only 1D depth-rotation was considered in their experiments while our model accounts for the full 3D head rotations, 2) the issue of generalization to unknown poses was not seriously investigated, 3) their system suffered from the difficulty of finding pixel-wise correspondences for shape normalization, 4) head poses were estimated based on an image-based texture representation while pose estimation in our approach is based on shape information, 5) their study did not address the task of person identification using the model as a representation model, and 6) our model utilizes localized Gabor jet features for representing texture. We expect our specific model design, with geometrical features and a linear 2D model-based approach, helps to improve Beymer's algorithm in performance of pose estimation. For pose transformation, their focus was rather on computer graphics and animation applications which are out of the scope of our current investigation.

Another related study by Lanitis et al. [115] showed that their PC-LSM-based system could perform pose estimation using a simple linear regression of shape model parameters. Although their system consists of a combination of two linear systems that are very similar to our model, their approach differs in that; 1) their study did not attempt to construct a representation explicitly parameterized by physical variations. 2) their study did not address explicitly the problem of pose transformation parameterized by 3D head angles, 3) only 2D depth-rotations were considered in their experiments while our model provides the full 3D head rotations, 4) an issue of generalization to unknown poses was not investigated at all, and 5) a specific PC for each rotation dimension was manually picked while our model is purely data-driven in that we do not give any bias to specific PCs, Although their PC-LSM-based system provides a well-structured architecture for various tasks using facial information, the aspect of head pose variation was not fully investigated in their study. Our approach is expected to improve the accuracy of processing head pose variation.

Chapter 3

Description of the LPCMAP Model

In this chapter, we describe the LPCMAP model (Okada et al. [140]) introduced in the previous chapters as an implementation of a compact, generalizable, data-driven and flexible representation model parameterized by 3D head angles.

3.1 Definition of Our Problem

Let a pair of vectors $(\vec{v}^m, \vec{\theta}^m)$ denote a training sample of our model, where $\vec{v}^m$ is the m-th vectorized facial image and $\vec{\theta}^m = (\theta_1^m, \theta_2^m, \theta_3^m)$ is the vector of 3D head angles of the face and we suppose that we have M training samples consisting of a set of the M pairs,

$$\{(\vec{v}^1, \vec{\theta}^1), ..., (\vec{v}^m, \vec{\theta}^m), ..., (\vec{v}^M, \vec{\theta}^M)\}. \tag{3.1}$$

Our focus is to find a mapping function between $\vec{v}$ and $\vec{\theta}$ from the M training samples,

$$\begin{aligned} \mathcal{A} &: \vec{v} \mapsto \vec{\theta} \; (Analysis) \\ \mathcal{S} &: \vec{\theta} \mapsto \vec{v} \; (Synthesis). \end{aligned} \tag{3.2}$$

An **analysis map** $\mathcal{A}$ gives an estimate of 3D head angles $\hat{\vec{\theta}} = \mathcal{A}(\vec{v})$ while a **synthesis map** $\mathcal{S}$ synthesizes a vectorized facial images $\hat{\vec{v}} = \mathcal{S}(\vec{\theta})$.

Given the above training samples, we can formulate two error functions, ERR and $\overline{ERR}$, of the mapping functions $\mathcal{A}$ and $\mathcal{S}$,

$$ERR = \sum_{m=1}^{M} |\vec{\theta}^m - \hat{\vec{\theta}}| + \sum_{m=1}^{M} |\vec{v}^m - \hat{\vec{v}}|, \text{ and} \tag{3.3}$$

$$\overline{ERR} = \sum_{i=1}^{\infty} |\vec{\theta}^i - \hat{\vec{\theta}}| + \sum_{i=1}^{\infty} |\vec{v}^i - \hat{\vec{v}}|, \tag{3.4}$$

where the $(\vec{v}^i, \vec{\theta}^i)$ are samples, $(\vec{v}^i, \vec{\theta}^i) \notin \{(\vec{v}^1, \vec{\theta}^1), .., (\vec{v}^m, \vec{\theta}^m), .., (\vec{v}^M, \vec{\theta}^M)\}, \forall i$. ERR denotes an average error of estimates for training samples given as ground-truth, while $\overline{ERR}$ denotes an average error of all the samples in the same object class that are not included in the training sample set.

ERR represents the **accuracy** of the mapping functions; how well the learned functions approximate an individual transformation of each training sample. On the other hand, $\overline{ERR}$ represents the **generalization capability** of the mapping functions; how well the learned functions approximate a general transformation of the object class between facial images and their corresponding 3D head angles. These error functions provide the tools to guide our design of the mapping functions.

Obviously, our wish is to learn mapping functions which minimize both errors. In reality, however, it is impossible to compute $\overline{ERR}$ because it is impossible to collect an *infinite* number of samples. Therefore, we are forced to approximate $\overline{ERR}$ by $\overline{ERR}'$ which is an average error of a *finite* number of I test samples,

$$\overline{ERR}' = \sum_{i=1}^{I} |\vec{\theta}^i - \hat{\vec{\theta}}^i| + \sum_{i=1}^{I} |\vec{v}^i - \hat{\vec{v}}^i|. \tag{3.5}$$

Therefore, our problem is reduced to the determination of a structural design and learning algorithm of $\mathcal{A}$ and $\mathcal{S}$ which minimizes both ERR and $\overline{ERR}'$ together,

Find $\mathcal{A}$ and $\mathcal{S}$ which minimize ERR and $\overline{ERR}'$ together. $\quad$ (3.6)

Additionally, it is important to note here that the choice of training and test samples directly influences the validity of this criterion as in any problem which involves a learning process. Therefore these choices need careful consideration to avoid oversampling from a small data domain.

3.2   Overview of the Model

In this section, we present an informal illustration of the LPCMAP model. As proposed in the introduction, the LPCMAP model, consisting of a combination of two linear models (*PC-based linear subspace model* and *linear transformation model*), serves as a representation model that is compact, generalizable, data-driven, flexible, and parameterized by 3D head angles. The model realizes the bidirectional linear mappings $\mathcal{A}$ and $\mathcal{S}$ learned from training samples $(\vec{v}^m, \vec{\theta}^m)$, providing a solution to the problem 3.6.

As a first step, we determine a type of *single-view representation*. As discussed in section 2.3, we decompose a facial image into shape and texture information. Figure 3.1 illustrates this decomposition process.

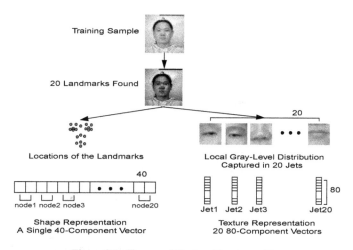

Figure 3.1: Shape and Texture Decomposition

First, a set of facial landmarks are located in a facial image. The figure shows a case of 20 landmarks. The localization of the landmarks can be achieved either by an automatic system, such as a facial feature tracking system developed by Maurer and von der Malsburg [127], or by manual labor with the aid of a user-interface system. At each landmark, information of local image contrast variation is extracted from the image and stored in a **jet**. A jet is a representation of the texture in the local image region around a landmark. It contains responses of multi-level multi-directional 2D **Gabor filters** and is computed by extracting image structure with a filter bank at a landmark location. A topological graph, whose nodes are located at the set of landmarks and labeled by a set of corresponding jets, has proven to be one of the best single-view representations of 2D facial images for the task of facial identification (Wiskott et al. [214] and Okada et al. [141], see section 2.1.1 for more details.).

Next, information of the facial shape and texture is decomposed. Shape information is captured in the form of configurations of the set of facial landmarks. In order to achieve translation invariance, 2D image coordinates of the landmarks are transformed into an object-centered 2D coordinate system whose origin is set at the center of gravity of all the landmarks. We call the array of object-centered 2D coordinates the **shape representation** of a facial image. On the other hand, texture information is captured in the set of Gabor jets. We call the set of Gabor jets the **texture representation** of a facial image. Note that the texture informa-

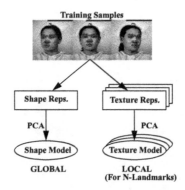

Figure 3.2: Shape and Texture Models

tion is organized in a set of **local** representations; each landmark has a separate vector representation. In contrast, the shape information is organized in a **global** representation; a face is represented by a single vector.

As a second step, the PC-based linear subspace models for shape and texture representations are learned from training samples. Figure 3.2 illustrates this step. Given a set of facial images, the previous step results in a set of shape and texture representations. For the shape representations, a rectangular box in the figure denotes the set of the representations. Because of its locality, the set of texture representations are organized at each landmark separately, resulting in a set of local texture representations (jets) at each landmark. For the texture representation, therefore, a rectangular box in the figure denotes a local texture set for a single landmark.

These sets of representations are subjected to principal component analysis (hereafter PCA), resulting in a set of principal components (hereafter PCs) for each representation set. They are orthonormal and ordered by their corresponding variances. We call PCs for shape representations **shape PCs** and PCs for texture representations **texture PCs**. A subset of the PCs can be treated as the basis of a vector space whose dimensionality is reduced from the original representation space. This subset of PCs constitutes a PC-based linear subspace model and is known to have optimal reconstruction accuracy in the least-square sense when the subset is spanned by PCs whose variances (eigenvalues) are larger than those of any discarded PCs. We call a linear subspace model with shape PCs the **shape model**, and the set of linear subspace models, one for each landmark, the **texture model**.

The linearity of the PCs simplifies the process of parameterizing an input sam-

70

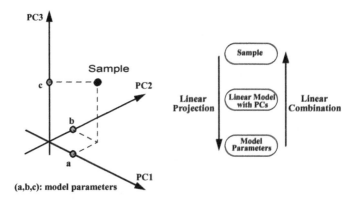

Figure 3.3: Linear Subspace Model

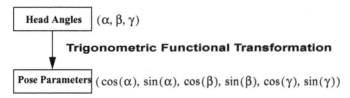

Figure 3.4: Trigonometric Functional Transformation

ple by a subspace model, as illustrated in figure 3.3. An input is parameterized by projecting it onto the PCs of the model. We call a vector of the projection coefficients **model parameters** and this parameterization process **linear projection**. More specifically, model parameters of the shape representation are called **shape parameters** and those of the texture representations are called **texture parameters**. Reconstruction of a sample from model parameters is possible by a **linear combination** of the PCs weighted by the parameters. The orthonormality of the PCs assures that the same PCs can be used for both linear projection and combination.

We represent the 3D head pose of a face by 3D rotation angles $\vec{\theta}$ (roll or shaking within a view plane, pitch or nodding, and yaw or shaking in depth) from a frontal pose. We refer to the 3D angular deviations by **3D head angles**. For training samples, knowledge of the 3D head angles is required for each facial image as ground truth. They can be measured by a physical device such as a magnetic tracker. In order to mitigate non-linearity in mapping between shape

71

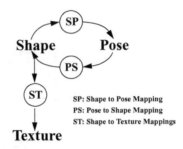

Figure 3.5: Linear Transformation Models

representation and 3D head angles, we have expanded the 3D vector space of head angles to a feature space spanned by trigonometric functions of the angles and products of the functions. In a simple 1st order case shown in figure 3.4, the feature space becomes a 6 dimensional space. We call a coefficient vector in this feature space, derived from a sample's 3D head angles, **pose parameters**. This expansion of dimensionality in the representation space is related to a recently proposed non-linear learning technique, kernel PCA (Schölkopf et al. [177] and Mika et al. [129]). Note that this introduction of non-linearity is qualitatively different from a type of non-linear learning method in which a functional form itself is non-linear. We have earlier discussed shortcomings of such methods, hindering generalizability and extendability of a model and making its learning process more complicated and time-consuming. Our method, which keeps a linear functional form, is therefore expected to avoid these pitfalls, however this claim needs to be carefully evaluated by thorough numerical experiments.

As a third step, shape, texture, and pose parameters are linearly related with each other in order to realize an explicit parameterization of our model with physical variations by using a *transformation model*. Figure 3.5 illustrates this step. Pose parameters are only related to shape parameters because pose variation correlates better to its influence on shape than to texture (see section 4.2.2 for experimental results supporting this argument). Bidirectional mappings need to be learned in order to support both the analysis and synthesis processes. Texture parameters are then linearly related to shape parameters. As a consequence, texture representation can be directly synthesized from shape representation. Note that the shape-to-texture map is localized at each landmark as shown in figure 3.6. This localization of mapping is necessary in order to accommodate different depth profiles of faces at different landmarks. These mappings are computed by a singular value decomposition (hereafter SVD) algorithm with a set of corresponding parameter pairs derived from training samples.

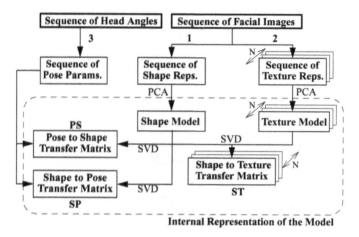

Figure 3.6: Model Learning Processes

Figure 3.6 summarizes the learning process of the LPCMAP model. The two boxes with thick lines denote the set of training samples. Processes of shape and texture decomposition and trigonometric functional transformation are referenced in the figure by 1, 2, and 3, respectively. Note that texture models are localized at N facial landmarks. After learning, data entities inside the dashed box are stored as **model knowledge** while training samples can be discarded.

Figure 3.7 illustrates the analysis and synthesis processes. The task of pose estimation is realized by the analysis process of a model. Shape representation is first derived from an input facial image by finding a set of landmarks. It is then projected to a learned shape model, resulting in shape parameters. Pose parameters are next transformed from the shape parameters by a shape-to-pose linear map. Finally, 3D head angles of the input can be derived from the pose parameters by applying arcsine and arccosine functions. [1] Note that the manifold or trajectory of shape parameters always goes through the origin of shape PC subspace. Therefore, *sine* of head angles should align better with a shape parameter distribution than *cosine* of angles. For this reason, 3D head angles can also be derived solely from arcsine of the pose parameters.

On the other hand, the task of pose transformation is realized by the synthesis process of a model. Input 3D head angles are first expanded to pose parameters. Shape and texture parameters are then linearly transformed from the pose parame-

---

[1] or by applying arctangent functions for simplicity.

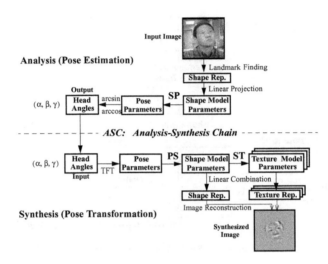

Figure 3.7: Model Matching Processes

ters sequentially by pose-to-shape and shape-to-texture linear maps, respectively. Shape and texture representations are then synthesized by a linear combination process of learned shape and texture models. A facial image can be reconstructed from the synthesized shape and texture representations by a reconstruction algorithm of Gabor jet-based facial representation developed by Pötzsch et al [163]. Sequentially applying the analysis and synthesis processes to an input image results in an estimate of the input image based solely on model knowledge. We call this process **analysis-synthesis chain** or **model matching**. As will be described in chapter 5, this process plays a crucial role in utilizing the LPCMAP model as a representation unit of a database of known persons for identification tasks.

3.3   Formal Description of the Model

3.3.1   Shape and Texture Decomposition

The set of the facial images, $\vec{v}^1, .., \vec{v}^m, .., \vec{v}^M$, are first subjected to a landmark finder, resulting in a localization of N landmarks in each image. Using this information, a set of shape and texture representations are extracted from the image set. The shape representation stands for object-centered 2D coordinates of the N landmarks while the texture representation stands for a set of N Gabor jets sampled at the N landmarks.

Let $2N$-component vector $\vec{x}^m$ denote the shape representation of the $\vec{v}^m$,

$$\vec{x}^m = (x_1^m - u_x^m, y_1^m - u_y^m, .., x_n^m - u_x^m, y_n^m - u_y^m, .., x_N^m - u_x^m, y_N^m - u_y^m)^t,$$
$$u_x^m = \frac{1}{N} \sum_{n=1}^{N} x_n^m,$$
$$u_y^m = \frac{1}{N} \sum_{n=1}^{N} y_n^m,$$

$$(3.7)$$

where x_n^m and y_n^m are x and y image coordinates of the n-th landmark in the $\vec{v}^m$.

Let also L-component vector $\vec{j}^{m,n}$ denote the texture representation of the $\vec{v}^m$,

$$\vec{j}^{m,n} = (j_1^{m,n}, .., j_l^{m,n}, .., j_L^{m,n})^t, \tag{3.8}$$

where $j_l^{m,n}$ is the l-th jet coefficient derived from a response of the l-th Gabor filter with $\vec{v}^m$ at the n-th landmark.

As a result of the above operations, each image is decomposed into shape and texture representations,

$$\vec{v}^m \mapsto (\vec{x}^m, \vec{j}^{m,1}, .., \vec{j}^{m,n}, .., \vec{j}^{m,N}). \tag{3.9}$$

Let $\mathcal{D}_x$ and $\mathcal{D}_j$ denote operations of shape and texture decomposition, respectively,

$$\mathcal{D}_x(\vec{v}^m) = \vec{x}^m,$$
$$\mathcal{D}_j(\vec{v}^m) = \vec{j}^{m,1}, .., \vec{j}^{m,n}, .., \vec{j}^{m,N}. \tag{3.10}$$

3.3.2 Linear Subspace Models for Shape and Texture Representations

A set of the shape representations, $\vec{x}^1, .., \vec{x}^m, .., \vec{x}^M$, are subjected to principal component analysis (hereafter PCA), resulting in P principal components (hereafter PCs) of the shape representations.

Let $2N$-component vector $\vec{y}^p$ denote the p-th shape PC and a scalar λ_y^p denote variance of $\{\vec{x}^m\}$ along the direction of $\vec{y}^p$. Then $\vec{y}^p$ satisfies,

$$XX^t\vec{y}^p = \lambda_y^p\vec{y}^p, \tag{3.11}$$

where X is a centered column matrix of $\vec{x}^m$,

$$X = (\vec{x}^1 - \vec{u}_x, .., \vec{x}^m - \vec{u}_x, .., \vec{x}^M - \vec{u}_x),$$
$$\vec{u}_x = \frac{1}{M} \sum_{m=1}^{M} \vec{x}^m. \tag{3.12}$$

PCA solves equation (3.11) as eigen decomposition of a covariance matrix of X, resulting in an ordered array of pairs of eigenvalue and eigenvectors,

$$(\lambda_y^1, \vec{y}^1), .., (\lambda_y^p, \vec{y}^p), .., (\lambda_y^P, \vec{y}^P),$$
$$\lambda_y^1 >, .., > \lambda_y^p >, .., > \lambda_y^P,$$
$$\vec{y}^1 \perp, .., \perp \vec{y}^p \perp, .., \perp \vec{y}^P,$$
$$|\vec{y}^1| =, .., |\vec{y}^p| =, .., |\vec{y}^P| = 1. \tag{3.13}$$

For each landmark n, a set of the texture representations, $\vec{j}^{1,n}, .., \vec{j}^{m,n}, .., \vec{j}^{M,n}$, are also subjected to PCA, resulting in S PCs of the texture representations for each landmark.

Let L-component vector $\vec{b}^{s,n}$ denote the s-th texture PC at a landmark n and a scalar $\lambda_b^{s,n}$ denote variance of $\{\vec{j}^{m,n}\}$ along the direction of $\vec{b}^{s,n}$. Then $\vec{b}^{s,n}$ satisfies,

$$(J^1)(J^1)^t \vec{b}^{s,1} = \lambda_b^{s,1} \vec{b}^{s,1},$$

$$\cdot$$

$$(J^n)(J^n)^t \vec{b}^{s,n} = \lambda_b^{s,n} \vec{b}^{s,n}, \tag{3.14}$$

$$\cdot$$

$$(J^N)(J^N)^t \vec{b}^{s,N} = \lambda_b^{s,N} \vec{b}^{s,N},$$

where J^n is a centered column matrix of $\vec{j}^{m,n}$,

$$J^n = (\vec{j}^{1,n} - \vec{u}_j^n, .., \vec{j}^{m,n} - \vec{u}_j^n, .., \vec{j}^{M,n} - \vec{u}_j^n),$$
$$\vec{u}_j^n = \frac{1}{M} \sum_{m=1}^M \vec{j}^{m,n}. \tag{3.15}$$

Solving the set of equations (3.14) by PCA results in a set of ordered eigenvalue and eigenvector arrays,

$$(\lambda_b^{1,1}, \vec{b}^{1,1}), .., (\lambda_b^{s,1}, \vec{b}^{s,1}), .., (\lambda_b^{S,1}, \vec{b}^{S,1}),$$

$$\cdot$$

$$(\lambda_b^{1,n}, \vec{b}^{1,n}), .., (\lambda_b^{s,n}, \vec{b}^{s,n}), .., (\lambda_b^{S,n}, \vec{b}^{S,n}), \tag{3.16}$$

$$\cdot$$

$$(\lambda_b^{1,N}, \vec{b}^{1,N}), .., (\lambda_b^{s,N}, \vec{b}^{s,N}), .., (\lambda_b^{S,N}, \vec{b}^{S,N}),$$

where $\lambda_b^{s,n}$ and $\vec{b}^{s,n}$ hold the same properties as in (3.13).

Next, we construct linear models of shape and texture representations in order to optimally parameterize them in a vector space with reduced dimensions. A vector space spanned by a subset of these PCs in decreasing order of corresponding variances assures the optimal L^2 error in the reconstruction of a training sample. We call these subsets of PCs a *linear subspace model.*

A linear subspace model Y for shape representation (hereafter shape model) is constructed with the first P_0 shape PCs as a row matrix of $\vec{y}^p$,

$$Y = (\vec{y}^1, .., \vec{y}^p, .., \vec{y}^{P_0})^t. \tag{3.17}$$

Let P_0-component vector $\vec{q}^m$ denote a parameterization of a shape representation $\vec{x}^m$ by Y (by linear projection),

$$\vec{q}^m = Y(\vec{x}^m - \vec{u}_x), \tag{3.18}$$

where,

$$\begin{aligned} \vec{q}^m &= (q_1^m, .., q_p^m, .., q_{P_0}^m), \\ q_p^m &= \vec{y}^p \cdot (\vec{x}^m - \vec{u}_x). \end{aligned} \tag{3.19}$$

We call this $\vec{q}^m$ shape parameter of $\vec{x}^m$. The original shape representation can be approximated from the shape parameter (by linear combination),

$$\vec{x}^m \approx \vec{u}_x + Y^t \vec{q}^m. \tag{3.20}$$

Note that (3.20) becomes an equation when $P_0 = P = 2N - 1$.

For each landmark n, a linear subspace model B^n for local texture representation (hereafter texture model) is constructed with the first S_0 texture PCs as a row matrix of $\vec{b}^{s,n}$,

$$B^1 = (\vec{b}^{1,1}, .., \vec{b}^{s,1}, .., \vec{b}^{S_0,1})^t,$$

$$\cdot$$

$$B^n = (\vec{b}^{1,n}, .., \vec{b}^{s,n}, .., \vec{b}^{S_0,n})^t, \tag{3.21}$$

$$\cdot$$

$$B^N = (\vec{b}^{1,N}, .., \vec{b}^{s,N}, .., \vec{b}^{S_0,N})^t.$$

Let S_0-component vector $\vec{r}^{m,n}$ denote a parameterization of a texture representation $\vec{j}^{m,n}$ by B^n,

$$\vec{r}^{m,1} = B^1(\vec{j}^{m,1} - \vec{u}_j^1),$$

$$\cdot$$

$$\vec{r}^{m,n} = B^n(\vec{j}^{m,n} - \vec{u}_j^n), \tag{3.22}$$

$$\cdot$$

$$\vec{r}^{m,N} = B^N(\vec{j}^{m,N} - \vec{u}_j^N),$$

where,

$$\vec{r}^{m,n} = (r_1^{m,n}, .., r_s^{m,n}, .., r_{S_0}^{m,n}),$$
$$r_s^{m,n} = \vec{b}^{s,n} \cdot (\vec{j}^{m,n} - \vec{u}_j^n). \tag{3.23}$$

We call this $\vec{r}^{m,n}$ a texture parameter of $\vec{j}^{m,n}$. The original texture representation can be approximated from the texture parameter,

$$(\vec{j}^{m,1}, .., \vec{j}^{m,n}, .., \vec{j}^{m,N}) \approx (\vec{u}_j^1 + (B^1)^t \vec{r}^{m,1}, .., \vec{u}_j^n + (B^n)^t \vec{r}^{m,n}, .., \vec{u}_j^N + (B^N)^t \vec{r}^{m,N}). \tag{3.24}$$

Note that (3.24) becomes a set of equations when $S_0 = S = L - 1$.

3.3.3   Linear Mappings between Different Parameter Spaces

Lastly, we construct bidirectional maps between $\vec{v}^m$ and $\vec{\theta}^m$ by linearly relating different parameters. We call a map from image to 3D head angles ($\vec{v}^m \mapsto \vec{\theta}^m$) analysis mapping and an inverse map ($\vec{\theta}^m \mapsto \vec{v}^m$) synthesis mapping.

3D head angles $\vec{\theta}^m$ are first non-linearly transformed to a T-component vector $\vec{\varphi}^m, T \geq 3$ by a trigonometric functional transformation $\mathcal{K}$,

$$\vec{\varphi}^m = \mathcal{K}(\vec{\theta}^m), \tag{3.25}$$

where the function $\mathcal{K}$ first centers the distribution of the M 3D angle vectors $\vec{\theta}^1, .., \vec{\theta}^M$ and expands the angular deviations from the average to a vector of trigonometric functions of these angles (and their products),

$$\mathcal{K}(\vec{\theta}^m) =$$
$$(\cos(\theta_1^m - u_{\theta 1}), \sin(\theta_1^m - u_{\theta 1}),$$
$$\cos(\theta_2^m - u_{\theta 2}), \sin(\theta_2^m - u_{\theta 2}),$$
$$\cos(\theta_3^m - u_{\theta 3}), \sin(\theta_3^m - u_{\theta 3})), \tag{3.26}$$

where,

$$\vec{u}_\theta = (u_{\theta 1}, u_{\theta 2}, u_{\theta 3}) = \frac{1}{M} \sum_{m=1}^{M} \vec{\theta}^m. \tag{3.27}$$

We call the $\vec{\varphi}^m$ pose parameter. There exists an inverse transformation $\mathcal{K}^{-1}$ such that,

$$\vec{\theta}^m = \mathcal{K}^{-1}(\vec{\varphi}^m) = \vec{u}_\theta + (\arctan(\frac{\varphi_2^m}{\varphi_1^m}), \arctan(\frac{\varphi_4^m}{\varphi_3^m}), \arctan(\frac{\varphi_6^m}{\varphi_5^m})). \tag{3.28}$$

As discussed in section 3.2, another form for deriving 3D angle vectors from pose parameters is to use only sine components of pose parameters,

$$\vec{\theta}^m = \mathcal{K}^{-1}(\vec{\varphi}^m) = \vec{u}_\theta + (\arcsin(\varphi_2^m), \arcsin(\varphi_4^m), \arcsin(\varphi_6^m)). \tag{3.29}$$

This transformation looses information by discarding cosine components of pose parameters, however this function performs better than the equation (3.28) when there exist measurement errors which influence the cosine components of pose parameters more strongly than their sine components.

For the analysis mapping, the shape parameter $\bar{q}^m$ is linearly related to the pose parameter $\bar{\varphi}^m$,

$$\bar{\varphi}^m = F\bar{q}^m, \tag{3.30}$$

where F is a $T \times P_0$ transfer matrix. A combination of equations (3.10), (3.18), (3.30), and (3.29) in this order, therefore, constitutes the analysis mapping. Let a symbol $\mathcal{A}$ denote this mapping.

For the synthesis mapping, the pose parameter $\bar{\varphi}^m$ is first linearly related to the shape parameter $\bar{q}^m$,

$$\bar{q}^m = G\bar{\varphi}^m, \tag{3.31}$$

where G is a $P_0 \times T$ transfer matrix. The texture parameter $\bar{r}^{m,n}$ at each landmark is then linearly related with the shape parameter $\bar{q}^m$ instead of the pose parameter $\bar{\varphi}^m$,

$$\bar{r}^{m,1} = H^1\bar{q}^m,$$

$$\cdot$$
$$\cdot$$

$$\bar{r}^{m,n} = H^n\bar{q}^m, \tag{3.32}$$

$$\cdot$$
$$\cdot$$

$$\bar{r}^{m,N} = H^N\bar{q}^m,$$

where H^n is a $S_0 \times P_0$ transfer matrix at landmark n. As a result, a combination of equations (3.25), (3.31), and (3.20) in this order constitutes the synthesis mapping for shape representation and a combination of equations (3.25), (3.31), (3.32), and (3.24) in this order constitutes the synthesis mapping for texture representation. Let symbols SS and TS denote synthesis mappings for shape and texture representations, respectively.

F, G, and $H^1, .., H^N$ are learned from the training samples in (3.1). Let $P_0 \times M$ matrix Q denote a column matrix of M shape parameters,

$$Q = Y \cdot X. \tag{3.33}$$

Let $S_0 \times M$ matrix R^n denote a column matrix of M texture parameters at each landmark n,

$$R^1 = B^1 \cdot J^1,$$

$$\cdot$$
$$\cdot$$

$$\tag{3.34}$$

$$R^N = B^N \cdot J^N.$$

79

Let $T \times M$ matrix Φ denote a column matrix of M pose parameters,

$$\Phi = \mathcal{K}(\Theta), \text{ where } \Theta = (\vec{\theta}^1, .., \vec{\theta}^m, .., \vec{\theta}^M). \qquad (3.35)$$

Substituting transposes of (3.33), (3.34), and (3.35) to transposes of (3.30), (3.31), and (3.32) results in the following overcomplete sets of linear equations,

$$Q^t \cdot F^t = \Phi^t,$$
$$\Phi^t \cdot G^t = Q^t,$$
$$Q^t \cdot (H^1)^t = (R^1)^t,$$

$$\cdot$$

$$Q^t \cdot (H^N)^t = (R^N)^t, \qquad (3.36)$$

respectively. The transfer matrices $F, G, H^1, .., H^N$ are computed from (3.36). Singular Value Decomposition algorithm (hereafter SVD) is used for computing inverse matrices,

$$F^t = (Q^t)^{-1} \cdot \Phi^t = V_{Q^t} \cdot [diag(\frac{1}{w_k})]_{Q^t} \cdot U^t_{Q^t} \cdot \Phi^t,$$
$$G^t = (\Phi^t)^{-1} \cdot Q^t = V_{\Phi^t} \cdot [diag(\frac{1}{w_k})]_{\Phi^t} \cdot U^t_{\Phi^t} \cdot Q^t,$$
$$(H^1)^t = (Q^t)^{-1} \cdot (R^1)^t = V_{Q^t} \cdot [diag(\frac{1}{w_k})]_{Q^t} \cdot U^t_{Q^t} \cdot (R^1)^t,$$

$$\cdot$$

$$(H^N)^t = (Q^t)^{-1} \cdot (R^N)^t = V_{Q^t} \cdot [diag(\frac{1}{w_k})]_{Q^t} \cdot U^t_{Q^t} \cdot (R^N)^t, \qquad (3.37)$$

where V_{Q^t} and V_{Φ^t} are orthogonal matrices of $P_0 \times P_0$ and $T \times T$, U_{Q^t} and U_{Φ^t} are column-orthogonal matrices of $M \times P_0$ and $M \times T$, and w_k is the k-th singular value.

Finally, we define a LPCMAP model LM as a set of data entities and mapping functions,

$$LM = \{\vec{u}_x, \vec{u}_j^1, .., \vec{u}_j^N, \vec{u}_\theta,$$
$$Y, B^1, .., B^N,$$
$$F, G, H^1, .., H^N,$$
$$\mathcal{A} : \vec{v}^m \mapsto \vec{\theta}^m,$$
$$\mathcal{SS} : \vec{\theta}^m \mapsto \vec{x}^m,$$
$$\mathcal{TS} : \vec{\theta}^m \mapsto (\vec{j}^{m,1}, .., \vec{j}^{m,N})\}, \qquad (3.38)$$

where $\vec{u}_x$ and $\vec{u}_j^1, .., \vec{u}_j^N$ are average shape and texture representations, $\vec{u}_\theta$ is an average 3D head angle vector, Y and $B^1, .., B^N$ are shape and texture models, F is a shape-to-pose parameter map, G is a pose-to-shape parameter map, $H^1, .., H^N$ are shape-to-texture parameter maps, $\mathcal{A}$ is a function of analysis mapping, and $\mathcal{SS}$ and $\mathcal{TS}$ are functions of synthesis mappings for shape and texture representations, respectively.

3.3.4 Applying the LPCMAP Model

In this section, we demonstrate a number of applications of the LPCMAP model.

Suppose we are given a facial image $\vec{v}$ which was not present in the training sample set,

$$\vec{v} \notin \{\vec{v}^1, .., \vec{v}^M\}. \tag{3.39}$$

The problem of finding 3D head angles of $\vec{v}$ is called *pose estimation*. This problem can be solved by using an analysis mapping $\mathcal{A}$ of LM. Let $\hat{\vec{\theta}}$ denote the estimated 3D head angles of $\vec{v}$ by LM,

$$\hat{\vec{\theta}} = \mathcal{A}_{LM}(\vec{v}) = \mathcal{K}^{-1}(F_{LM} \cdot Y_{LM} \cdot (\mathcal{D}_x(\vec{v}) - \vec{u}_x^{LM})). \tag{3.40}$$

Suppose, next, we are given a 3D head angle vector $\vec{\theta}$ which was not present in the training sample set,

$$\vec{\theta} \notin \{\vec{\theta}^1, .., \vec{\theta}^M\}. \tag{3.41}$$

The problem of synthesizing a corresponding facial image is called *pose transformation* or *model animation*. This problem can be solved by using synthesis mappings $\mathcal{SS}$ and $\mathcal{TS}$ of LM. Let $\hat{\vec{x}}$ denote the synthesized shape representation from $\vec{\theta}$ by LM,

$$\hat{\vec{x}} = \mathcal{SS}_{LM}(\vec{\theta}) = \vec{u}_x^{LM} + Y_{LM}^t \cdot G_{LM} \cdot \mathcal{K}(\vec{\theta}). \tag{3.42}$$

And let $(\hat{\vec{j}}^1, .., \hat{\vec{j}}^N)$ denote the synthesized texture representation from $\vec{\theta}$ by LM,

$$(\hat{\vec{j}}^1, .., \hat{\vec{j}}^N) = \mathcal{TS}_{LM}(\vec{\theta})$$
$$= (\vec{u}_j^{1,LM} + B_{LM}^1 \cdot H_{LM}^1 \cdot G_{LM} \cdot \mathcal{K}(\vec{\theta}), .., \vec{u}_j^{N,LM} + B_{LM}^N \cdot H_{LM}^N \cdot G_{LM} \cdot \mathcal{K}(\vec{\theta})). \tag{3.43}$$

There exists an operation which reconstructs a facial image $\vec{v}$ from shape and texture representations $\vec{x}, \vec{j}^1, .., \vec{j}^N$. Let a symbol $\mathcal{R}$ denote this operation $(\vec{x}, \vec{j}^1, .., \vec{j}^N) \mapsto \vec{v}$,

$$\vec{v} = \mathcal{R}(\vec{x}, \vec{j}^1, .., \vec{j}^N). \tag{3.44}$$

Now let $\hat{\vec{v}}$ denote the synthesized facial image from $\vec{\theta}$ by LM. Substituting (3.42) and (3.43) to (3.44) results in,

$$\hat{\vec{v}} = \mathcal{R}(\mathcal{SS}_{LM}(\vec{\theta}), \mathcal{TS}_{LM}(\vec{\theta})). \tag{3.45}$$

Another application of the LPCMAP model is to represent faces with arbitrary head poses. Suppose a LPCMAP model is learned by a set of training samples. When the set consists of facial images of a single person with many head poses, the model acquires the knowledge of how a facial image of the person transforms under various poses. A facial image of the same person with an arbitrary head pose can then be described purely by the internal model knowledge by fitting the model to the input image,

$$\hat{\vec{v}} = \mathcal{R}(\mathcal{SS}_{LM}(\mathcal{A}_{LM}(\vec{v})), \mathcal{TS}_{LM}(\mathcal{A}_{LM}(\vec{v}))), \qquad (3.46)$$

where $\hat{\vec{v}}$ is an input's description by the internal knowledge of LM. We call the operation of fitting the model to an input *model matching*, and the synthesized facial image $\hat{\vec{v}}$ *model view*.

3.4 Why the LPCMAP Model?

In section 2.3, we have argued how different aspects of our general approach will solve open problems found in the current literature. In this section, we extend our theoretical arguments, introduced in section 1.5, to validate particular design decisions of the LPCMAP model which emphasize linearity.

The difficulty of designing the mapping functions $\mathcal{A}$ and $\mathcal{S}$ stems from a problem known as the **bias/variance dilemma** described in Geman et al. [72]. The bias/variance dilemma depicts a trade-off between **overfitting** and **oversmoothing** in a learning system. In their argument, the number of internal degrees of freedom (hereafter internal DOF) plays a key role. Given a mapping that has an innate complexity with a certain number of DOF (hereafter innate DOF), a system whose internal DOF is larger than the innate DOF adapts itself to the peculiarities of the given training samples, such as noise, and cannot generalize to unknown samples of the same class (overfitting). On the other hand, a system with fewer internal DOF than the innate DOF cannot accurately capture the innate characteristics of the mapping due to too few DOF (oversmoothing) although it may have better generalization capability.

In our problem, it is known *a priori* that there are 3 innate DOF. However, these 3 DOF interact non-linearly with each other in the mapping functions. We choose to linearly approximate the non-linear mapping functions because 1) it helps to avoid overfitting and 2) it helps to avoid the necessity for iterative optimization. Carelessly introducing explicit non-linear terms into a learning system often leads to overfitting. To avoid overfitting is a priority since one of the key criteria for our model is generalization capability. When the functions are linearly formulated, they can be analytically computed by matrix operations. This helps to avoid the necessity for iterative optimization which is often deteriorated when its solution is trapped in local minima.

Due to the bias/variance dilemma, however, our emphasis on avoiding overfitting may create a situation of oversmoothing. More specifically, the inability of the linear approximation to fully represent the non-linearity may produce a large error outside of a very limited range of 3D head angles which a single model is only capable of capturing. This range limitation depends on the degree of non-linearity; the stronger the non-linearity, the narrower the range. This poses a problem since it directly violates the flexibility criterion which we want to meet with our model.

We have proposed to decompose the learning process of the mapping functions into two parts in order to mitigate this shortcoming of the linear model. One part is dedicated to extracting a set of statistical modes or components, which correspond to the innate DOF, from a set of training facial images. The other is dedicated to learning a linear map between the modes and 3D head angles. This decomposition provides our model with the capability to control which components should be included or not. Although our analysis and synthesis mappings between the 3D head angles $\vec{\theta}$ and the facial images $\vec{v}$ are intrinsically non-linear, those between the angles and the shape model parameters $\vec{q}$ of components corresponding to the innate DOF modes are expected to become more linear when a set of components to be included in a shape model are found correctly. This means that the model should capture a complete spectrum but nothing more of a given non-linear variation. Therefore, our model needs to be constructed by extracting only shape components corresponding to the innate DOF and discarding the rest of the components.

From a number of methods for extracting statistical modes or component vectors from data ensemble (reviewed in chapter 2), we have chosen principal component analysis (PCA) for this task. We favored PCA because of its linear nature, the general advantages of which have been discussed above. A disadvantage of PCA is its inaccuracy: PCA will result in more than three significant component vectors for our 3 innate DOF problem because the linear nature of PCs does not allow for capturing curve-linear or correlated statistical modes. Moreover, their orthogonality further restricts flexibility of linear models spanned by them. This inaccuracy increases non-linearity in the mapping we linearly approximate. We mitigate this problem by applying an explicitly non-linear transformation $\mathcal{K}$ to the 3D angle vector $\vec{\theta}$, such that mapping functions between model parameters of the inaccurate PCs and the transformed pose parameters $\vec{\wp}$ become approximately linear. Therefore, our model should remain accurate while maintaining its generalization capability. Because this non-linearity is derived from formal analytical knowledge of pose variations and is not included within a functional form of the mappings, it should not exhibit the disadvantages of the general non-linear model discussed above.

3.5   Issues for Further Discussion

In this section, we address a number of issues that need to be clarified by numerical experiments. We will present results and discussion of several experiments in the next two chapters.

Our model's design, described in the previous sections, is based on a number of implicit assumptions which still need to be proven. They are listed below:

1. Should the analysis mapping only use shape information?

2. Should a shape-to-texture map be used instead of pose-to-texture for synthesis?

3. What type of non-linear function should be used for $\mathcal{K}$?

Other concerns involve the characteristics of our model during its learning process. The following questions should be answered in order to claim feasibility for the proposed model:

1. Can the model generalize (by interpolation)?

2. If not, in what range of the head poses can the model be accurate?

3. What is the minimum number of samples needed to achieve good accuracy in the model?

4. How do different distributions of training samples influence the accuracy of the model?

5. Can the model generalize over different individuals?

6. Can the model extrapolate?

Related to the above learning issues, a trade-off problem between the accuracy and size of a model needs to be further discussed. In order to apply a LPCMAP model for representation purposes, the size of the model needs to be small while it maintains acceptable accuracy. If the size of the model is allowed to become large, we may simply store the set of all the training samples, which defeats the purpose of the proposed model. The optimal number of size parameters P_0 and S_0 for a linear subspace model needs to be found for resolving this trade-off.

Lastly, it is again worth stressing the importance of the generalization capability of the model. If the model does not possess this capability, we are forced to collect an enormous number of all possible pose conditions as training samples. This makes the model infeasible, even if the model can represent the given training samples very accurately. Therefore, the generalization performance of our model needs to be examined rigorously.

Chapter 4

Analysis and Synthesis of Human Faces with Pose Variations by the LPCMAP Model

In this chapter, we evaluate the performance of the analysis (pose estimation) and synthesis (pose transformation) processes of the LPCMAP model by a series of numerical experiments. The purpose of this chapter is to empirically assess the feasibility of the proposed model described in chapter 3. These experiments are conducted with a C++ implementation of our model as a part of FLAVOR, a class library for computer vision applications developed by a group of researchers headed by von der Malsburg.

4.1 Numerical Experiments with Artificial Data

In this section, we present results of experiments using shape representations that are created artificially. The purpose of these experiments is to give experimental proof of the correctness of our model. Additionally, we seek to find an optimal non-linear function $\mathcal{K}$ described in section 3.3.3 for improving the accuracy of the mappings between shape representation and 3D head angles.

4.1.1 Data Set

We generated a set of artificial shape representations by orthographically project-ing a set of 3D control points located on the surface of a unit sphere to a 2D plane, while we rotate the sphere around its center. We used 25 control points on a 5 by 5 square grid pasted on the sphere. The 2D coordinates of the projected points are scaled and translated in order to fit into a 128 by 128 image coordinate space.

Since the rotation is explicitly controlled by a program, 3D rotation angles for each shape representation are available without measurements. We prepared two types of training samples which differ in the sphere's rotation. For the first type, pure samples (PUR), the sphere is rotated along only one axis at a time. Along each axis, the sphere was rotated from -30 to 30 degrees and the orthographic projection was carried out at 2 degrees intervals, resulting in 31 samples for each axis. Therefore, the PUR set consists of 93 samples, each one-third of which contains sphere rotations along strictly one axis. For the second type, noisy samples (NOI), the sphere is rotated in the same way as the PUR but with a small (between ± 5) degrees of rotations along the other two axes. The NOI set consists of 186 samples, including samples from the PUR set. This set corresponds to more realistic training samples since one cannot strictly control head rotations of subjects. In order to assess the generalization capability, a test set (TST) was also prepared. The TST set consists of 62 samples which are derived from rotating the sphere along three axes simultaneously so that the 3D rotation angle of these samples is different from any of the training samples.

4.1.2   Non-Linear Filter $\mathcal{K}$ for 3D Head Angles

As described in section 3.3.3, we apply a non-linear transformation $\mathcal{K}$ to the 3D head angles, projecting the angles to the pose parameter space spanned by trigonometric functions of the angles and their products (**trigonometric functional transformation**). After this transformation, a mapping between these pose and the shape parameters is expected to become less non-linear. Thus, the accuracy of pose estimation and shape synthesis of our model should become better. However, due to its possible shortcomings discussed in section 3.2, we need to carefully examine the feasibility of this non-linear process. We test three types of function as candidates for $\mathcal{K}$:

A a delta function, $(\alpha, \beta, \gamma) \mapsto (\alpha, \beta, \gamma)$,

B 3 angles to 6 trigonometric functions,
  $(\alpha, \beta, \gamma) \mapsto (cos(\alpha), sin(\alpha), cos(\beta), sin(\beta), cos(\gamma), sin(\gamma))$, and

C 3 angles to 6 trigonometric functions and 12 products,
  $(\alpha, \beta, \gamma) \mapsto (cos(\alpha), sin(\alpha), cos(\beta), sin(\beta), cos(\gamma), sin(\gamma),$
  $sin(\alpha)sin(\beta), sin(\alpha)cos(\beta), cos(\alpha)sin(\beta), cos(\alpha)cos(\beta),$
  $sin(\alpha)sin(\gamma), sin(\alpha)cos(\gamma), cos(\alpha)sin(\gamma), cos(\alpha)cos(\gamma),$
  $sin(\beta)sin(\gamma), sin(\beta)cos(\gamma), cos(\beta)sin(\gamma), cos(\beta)cos(\gamma))$

For analysis, 3D head angles are derived from pose parameters by using the equation 3.29, which disregards cosine components of pose parameters. This is

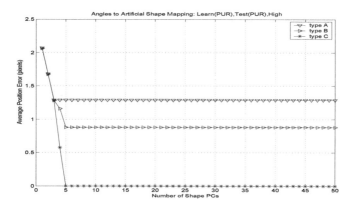

Figure 4.1: Accuracy of Pose-to-Shape Mapping with Toy Data, (PUR,PUR,High)

because arccosine function often amplifies small errors in these components, resulting in unreliable pose estimates. Our pilot study indicated that this equation performs the best among others including the equation (3.28).

4.1.3 Experimental Results

First, we compared the three types of non-linear transformation $\mathcal{K}$ in terms of the accuracy of shape synthesis from 3D rotation angles (pose-to-shape mapping). Figure 4.1 displays the average landmark position errors of the synthesized shapes in pixels as a function of P_0, the number of shape PCs included in the shape model. In this experiment, a model was trained with the PUR set and tested with the same PUR set. We also used float (High) precision for each vector component of the shape representation. Shape models with the type C transformation resulted in a *perfect* synthesis when the size of the model was more than 5 PCs. The accuracy of models with the type A and B transformations was lower than that of the type C.

Figure 4.2 shows the results of an experiment evaluating the influence of using more realistic (noisy) data. In this case, the models were trained with the NOI set and tested with the same NOI set. We also used integer (Low) precision for each component of the shape representation. This is a natural setting when the shape representation is extracted from a facial image, since we only have pixel-level precision for the location of landmarks. The results indicate that the perfect synthesis can no longer be achieved with this setting. However, models with type B and C transformations still reach acceptable accuracy (1 pixel error).

87

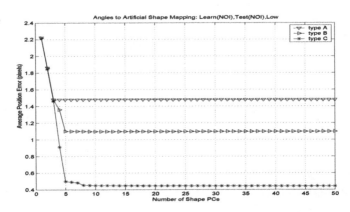

Figure 4.2: Accuracy of Pose-to-Shape Mapping with Toy Data, (NOI,NOI,Low)

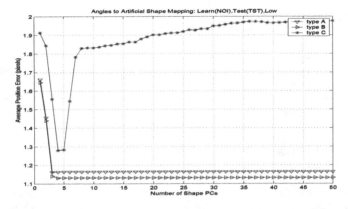

Figure 4.3: Accuracy of Pose-to-Shape Mapping with Toy Data, (NOI,TST,Low)

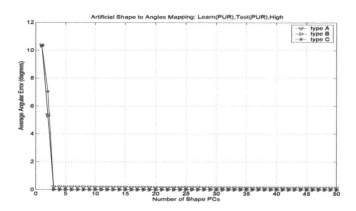

Figure 4.4: Accuracy of Shape-to-Pose Mapping with Toy Data, (PUR,PUR,High)

Figure 4.3 shows the results of an experiment assessing the generalization capability of the models. In this case, the models were trained with the NOI set and tested with the TST set. Integer precision was used also for this experiment. Unlike the previous two cases, models with the type C transformation resulted in much less accuracy, while the accuracy of models with the type A and B was maintained. A possible reason for the inaccurate results of the type C is that the model overfit the noise presented in the training samples. The results from these three experiments suggest that models with the type B transformation provide the best balance between accuracy and generalization capability.

Next, we conducted the same three experiments for the task of pose estimation (shape-to-pose mapping). Figure 4.4 displays the average angular errors (in degrees) of 3D rotation angles estimated by our model's analysis process with different types of $\mathcal{K}$. The set of training samples, test samples, and precision of sample vector components are the same as in the case for figure 4.1. Models with both the type B and C transformations resulted in *perfect* pose estimation when the size of the models was more than 3 PCs. This result matches with the fact that there are 3 DOFs in the pose variation.

Figure 4.5 displays the pose estimation accuracy for the same setting as in figure 4.2. The average angular errors were about 1 degree with sufficiently sized models and there were no significant differences in the value of errors across different types of the $\mathcal{K}$.

Figure 4.6 shows the pose estimation accuracy in the most realistic setting as in figure 4.3. Similar to the results of the experiment for the shape synthesis, the accuracy of models with the type C transformation was reduced, while models

89

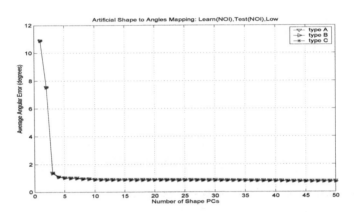

Figure 4.5: Accuracy of Shape-to-Pose Mapping with Toy Data, (NOI,NOI,Low)

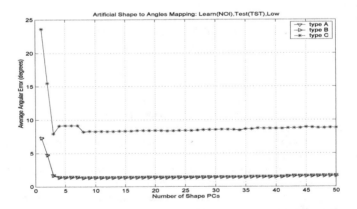

Figure 4.6: Accuracy of Shape-to-Pose Mapping with Toy Data, (NOI,TST,Low)

Figure 4.7: Examples of Training Samples

with type A and B resulted in acceptable accuracy.

In summary, the results of our experiments with artificial data indicate that 1) mappings between the shape representations and 3D head angles can be correctly learned by our model in an optimal setting and 2) the type B transformation provides the best balance between the accuracy and generalization capability of our model in a more realistic setting.

4.2 Numerical Experiments with Real Faces

In this section, we test the performance of the analysis and synthesis processes of our model with samples derived from 2D images of real faces. According to the results in the previous section, we used the type B transformation as the trigonometric functional transformation $\mathcal{K}$ throughout this section.

4.2.1 Data Set

In this section, we describe our methods used to derive training and test samples from a video sequence of continuously rotating faces. Figure 4.7 shows examples of facial images in the video sequence used for training samples.

For each person, we collected 1600 images of 128 by 128 pixels from a continuous video stream capturing rotating faces. Three quarters (1200) of the total samples are used as training samples while the rest of the samples (400) are used as test samples. For training samples, each third of the 1200 samples contains

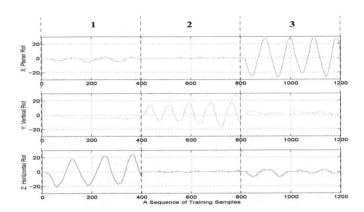

Figure 4.8: Variation of 3D Head Angles in the Training Samples

faces rotated mainly along one axis while rotations along the other two axes are minimal. We verbally instructed subjects to perform these specific head rotations. The acquisition took place after several practice sessions. For test samples, each subject was asked to rotate the head freely. We collected these samples for 4 people. During the acquisition of these samples, the lighting conditions and background remained unchanged.

We also measured the 3D head angles of each sample in degrees with the help of a magnetic sensor synchronized to a frame grabber used for the image acquisition. Horizontal (shaking), vertical (nodding), and planar (plane-shaking) rotations of the head (denoted in the figure as **1,2,3**, respectively) are measured as a continuous 3D angular deviation from the frontal pose of the head. Figure 4.8 displays the 3D head angles of the training samples shown in figure 4.7. Each plot illustrates the angles along x (planar), y (horizontal), or z (vertical) axis for the total sequence of 1200 training samples. The maximum range of the head angles was approximately ±25 degrees on average.

Next, these samples are subjected to a landmark finding system in order to generate both the shape and texture representation for each sample. Figure 4.9 illustrates the definition of the facial landmarks. Locations of 20 landmarks are defined mainly around the inner region of faces (i.e., eyes, nose, and mouth). They are indexed by numbers between 0 to 19 as shown in this figure. We used this definition throughout this dissertation.

We used a facial feature tracking system developed by Maurer [127] in order to locate the landmarks in images of a rotated face. This tracking system utilizes the phase information of Gabor jets in order to track a local feature within a continu-

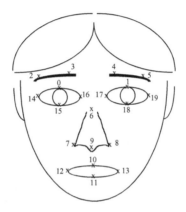

Figure 4.9: Definition of Facial Landmarks

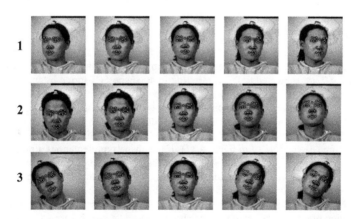

Figure 4.10: Examples of Training Samples after Landmark Finding Process

ous image sequence. In this system, we first find the landmarks in a frontal face using elastic graph matching [215], then each landmark is independently tracked over the sequence. Although the precision of the facial feature tracking system is sub-pixel between two frames, the system can accumulate errors over time. Thus we corrected a few ill-located landmarks manually in order to achieve the highest accuracy of the landmark locations for our analysis. Figure 4.10 shows the examples of the training samples with the correctly located facial landmarks.

After these landmarks are found for each sample, we generate a shape representation as a 40-component vector of object-centered image coordinates of these landmarks, and a texture representation as a set of jets, one for each landmark. To compute a jet, we used a set of Gabor filters varying in 5 frequency levels and 8 orientations. Thus, a jet can be seen as an 80-component vector. [1]

4.2.2 Statistical Analyses of the Data

In this section, we evaluate statistical properties of the data described in the previous section. In the LPCMAP model, the shape and texture information is modeled by the PC-based linear subspace models. Analyses of both shape and texture PCs derived from our training samples illustrate the functionality of the two subspace models, and help to determine P_0 and S_0, the number of PCs to be included in both models. We also study linear correlations between shape, texture, and pose parameters in this section, whose results prove our design of the LPCMAP model.

Shape Representation

In this section, we evaluate the PCs extracted from a set of shape representations (shape PCs). 1200 shape representations extracted from the samples shown in figure 4.7 are subjected to PCA, resulting in 40 shape PCs sorted by the size of variance. Figure 4.11 illustrates variations coded in the first 5 shape PCs. To display the variations, we computed the average of all the shape representations displayed in the middle column and move or distort it along the direction of each PC. Intervals of the movement along each PC are normalized by the standard deviation (denoted as sd in figure 4.11) of the shape representations along each PC. The first PC clearly coded variation of the planar rotation angle($r = 0.99$). Variation of the head size, horizontal rotation, and vertical rotation were coded in the second, third ($r = 0.88$), and fourth ($r = 0.65$) PCs, respectively.

We now investigate how many shape PCs are needed to accurately describe the variation present in the set of training shape representations. Figure 4.12 displays

---

[1] Note that a response of a Gabor filter is a complex value. Thus the number of vector components of a jet becomes $80 = 5(\text{level}) \times 8(\text{orientation}) \times 2$.

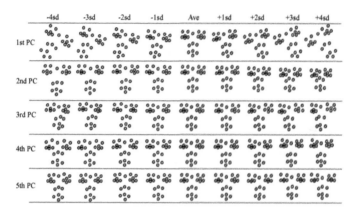

Figure 4.11: Variations Coded in the First 5 Shape PCs

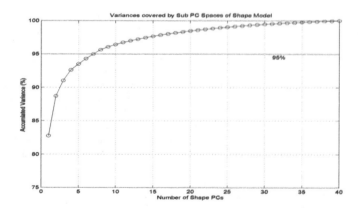

Figure 4.12: Accumulated Variances in Shape Models of Different Sizes

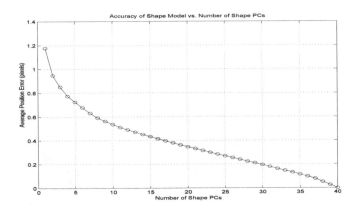

Figure 4.13: Accuracy of Shape Models of Different Sizes in Average Position Errors

the accumulated variances covered by the shape models of different size. The vertical axis denotes the accumulated variance, while the horizontal axis denotes the number of shape PCs included in the shape model, which always includes the subset of PCs with the largest accumulated variance. For example, a shape model with 10 PCs means that it includes the shape PCs with the first to tenth largest variance. The figure shows that a small number of PCs can account for most of the shape variations in the training samples; only 8 PCs are enough to cover 95% of the total data variance.

Next we evaluate the accuracy of the shape models of different size by means of reconstruction errors. Each test sample is first parameterized by the shape model by linear projection, yielding shape parameter vectors whose length depends on the size of the model. By linear combination of the model components, we then reconstruct each test sample from the shape parameters. Similarity of the test and reconstructed samples depends on the size of the model and expresses the model's accuracy. Figure 4.13 shows average landmark position errors of the reconstructed training samples for different model size. The errors are averaged over 4 persons, 1200 samples, and 20 nodes. An average error of the shape model with the first 8 PCs (which are enough to cover 95% of the total variances shown in figure 4.12) was 0.6 pixels.

The feature tracking system we used has sub-pixel accuracy in theory, although it generates errors because of the use of a Taylor expansion and loss of information when objects move fast. Once an error is generated, the system accumulates it over time. We therefore consider a shape model to be accurate if the

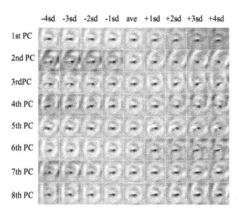

Figure 4.14: Variations Coded in the First 8 Texture PCs at Node 0 (Left Eye)

average error is within 1 pixel (**sub-pixel accuracy**). The above results indicate that a shape model has long become accurate in the above sense when it includes the first 8 PCs.

Texture Representation

In this section, we evaluate the PCs extracted from the set of texture representations at each landmark (texture PCs). The format of the evaluation is same as that of the shape PCs in the previous section.

PCA is performed for the set of 1200 texture representations at each landmark, resulting in 80 texture PCs at each landmark. Figure 4.14 illustrates variations coded in the first 8 texture PCs at node 0 (top of the left eye) by the same manner used in figure 4.11. For visualization, we reconstructed gray-level images from the texture representations by an algorithm developed by Pötzsch et al [163]. At node 0, the first PC encodes variation of the illumination. This is natural because the head rotation greatly changes the distribution of image irradiance. The rest of the PCs code the different appearances of the left eye rotating in various ways. Note that, unlike shape PCs, the texture PCs do not code the head rotation exclusively along any specific axis. This is caused by either degeneration of PCs or non-linear interaction of pose variations in the texture representation. In the former case, PCA will results in an arbitrary mixture (rotated components) in the space of degenerate components which have the same eigenvalue. In the latter case, orthogonal PCs cannot separate the variations into a few PCs. The same result was observed for the texture PCs at the other 19 landmarks.

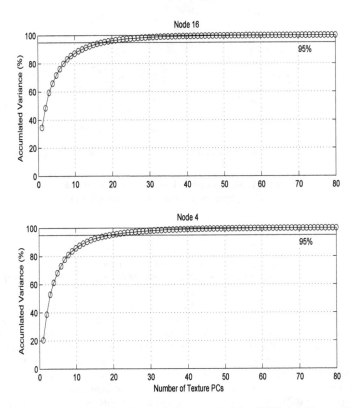

Figure 4.15: Accumulated Variances in Texture Models of Different Sizes at Node 16 and 4

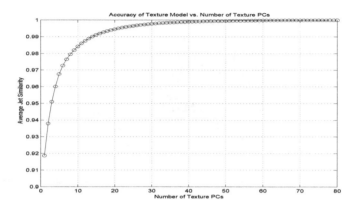

Figure 4.16: Accuracy of Texture Model of Different Sizes in Average Jet Similarities

Figure 4.15 displays accumulated variance covered by texture models of different size at nodes 4 and 16 (see figure 4.9 for their positions). The legend of these figures is the same as figure 4.12. The case for node 16 was the best. It shows that the first 19 texture PCs were enough to cover 95% of the total variance present in the texture representations. The worst case was at node 4. The first 21 PCs were needed to cover 95% of the total variance. The fact that a large number of PCs are needed to cover the variance of 3 DOF indicates that the pose variations in the texture representation interact non-linearly with each other in greater extent than in shape representation.

Lastly, we evaluate the accuracy of the texture models for different size by means of the error of reconstruction from a subspace model. The format of the evaluation is the same as the shape models in figure 4.13. Figure 4.16 shows average jet similarities of the reconstructed training samples as a function of model size. The jet similarity is computed as a normalized dot-product of the two jets compared. The similarities are averaged over 4 persons, 1200 samples, and 20 nodes. For simplicity of the evaluation, we do not vary S_0, the number of shape PCs, for different landmarks. The average similarity of the texture model with the first 21 PCs (which are enough to cover 95% of the total variance) was 0.995.

Although the first three texture PCs cannot capture the innate 3 DOF of the pose variations, the above results show that a compact texture model with only 21 texture PCs (25% of the total number of texture PCs) can accurately account for the pose variation of faces.

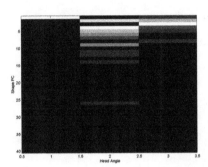

Figure 4.17: Correlation Matrix between 3D Head Angles and Shape Parameters

Correlation between Different Parameter Spaces

In this section, we investigate the nature of mappings between pose, shape, and texture parameters. We examine Pearson or linear correlation coefficients [55] between them because we linearly approximate these mappings as described in chapter 3. The results of these experiments provide us with answers to two questions raised in section 3.5 regarding the design of the LPCMAP model,

1. Should the analysis mapping only use shape information?

2. Should shape-to-texture map be used instead of pose-to-texture for synthesis?

4.2.2(a)   Correlation between the Pose and Shape or Texture Parameters
In this section, we study linear correlations of the 3D head angles to the shape and texture parameters. Both for analysis and synthesis, the LPCMAP model relates the pose parameters only to the shape parameters. The results of these experiments strongly support this design decision by showing that the head angles correlate much better to the shape than to the texture parameters.

Figure 4.17 illustrates a matrix of correlation coefficients between the 3D head angles and shape parameters derived from the training samples in figure 4.7. Each cell of this image corresponds to the magnitude of a correlation coefficient between one of the 3 head angles and one of the 40 parameter components of the shape representations. Thus, this figure shows the linear relationship between the 3D head angles and the shape parameters. In the image, the magnitudes of the coefficients are expressed as 8-bit gray-level values between black (0) and white (255) where black represents correlation 0 and white represents correlation 0.5 and

100

Best Case: Node 11 (Lower Lip)   Worst Case: Node 0 (Left Eye)

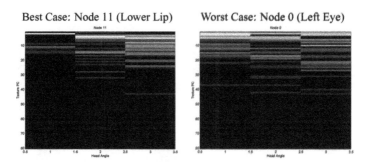

Figure 4.18: Correlation Matrices between 3D Head Angles and Texture Parameters

above. In the figure, the planar, vertical, and horizontal head angles are denoted as 1, 2, and 3, respectively. The maximum correlation coefficient was $r = 0.993$ between the planar head angles and first shape PC. The horizontal and vertical angles displayed their highest correlations to the third shape PC ($r = 0.878$) and the fourth shape PC ($r = 0.648$), respectively. A mean of these three highest correlation coefficients for each head angles was $r_{\mathrm{mean}} = 0.840$. We use this mean correlation value for comparing mappings between different parameter spaces. Note also that only the first few PCs correlated to the angles. This coincides with results of the previous section shown in figures 4.12 and 4.13.

Next, we study the nature of the mapping between the 3D head angles and the texture parameters. Since the texture model is localized, we analyze 20 separate correlation matrices, one for each landmark. Figure 4.18 displays two correlation matrices between the head angles and the texture parameters, at node 11 (bottom of lower lip) and node 0 (top of the left eye). They are the best and worst cases in terms of the value of r_{mean}, the mean of the three highest correlation coefficients. The maximum mean correlation value was $r_{\mathrm{mean}}^{11} = 0.775$ at node 11 and the minimum was $r_{\mathrm{mean}}^{0} = 0.544$ at node 0. The average of the mean correlation values $r_{\mathrm{mean}}^{0}, ..., r_{\mathrm{mean}}^{19}$ over 20 landmarks was $r_{\mathrm{mean}} = 0.598$.

The results of these experiments indicate that 1) the shape PCs linearly separate 3 statistical modes of the 3D pose variations well and 2) the 3D head angles are much more tightly correlated to the shape parameters ($r_{\mathrm{mean}} = 0.840$) than the texture parameters ($r_{\mathrm{mean}} = 0.598$). This supports our design of the LPCMAP model, in which the pose parameters are linearly related solely to the shape parameters.

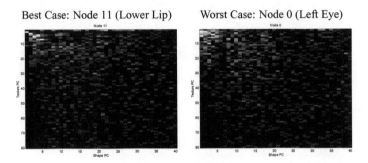

Best Case: Node 11 (Lower Lip)   Worst Case: Node 0 (Left Eye)

Figure 4.19: Correlation Matrices between Shape and Texture Parameters

4.2.2(b)   Correlation between the Shape and Texture Parameters   Lastly, we study linear correlations between the shape and texture parameters. The LPCMAP model synthesizes texture from the shape parameters instead of the pose parameters. This design assumes that the texture parameters correlate better to shape than the pose parameters. This experiment empirically assesses this assumption.

Figure 4.19 shows two correlation matrices between the shape and texture parameters at the node 11 and node 0 as the best and worst case, respectively. Similar to the analyses of the pose-to-texture mapping in figure 4.18, we analyze 20 separate correlation matrices, one for each landmark. The maximum of the mean of the three highest correlation coefficients was $r^{11}_{\text{mean}} = 0.795$ at the node 11 and the minimum was $r^{0}_{\text{mean}} = 0.503$ at the node 0. The average of the 20 mean correlation values $r^{0}_{\text{mean}}, ..., r^{19}_{\text{mean}}$ was $r_{\text{mean}} = 0.620$.

Although the difference is small, the average mean correlation between shape and texture is larger than the one between head angles and texture. This is also the case for the other three individuals. These results support our model design, in which the texture parameters are related to the shape parameters instead of the pose parameters. Note also that most of the white-colored cells representing strong correlations are located in a small region around the top-left corner of the images. This suggests the compactness of our model, in that only a small number of PCs in the shape and texture models suffice to describe the correlation structure.

4.2.3   Pose Estimation

In this section, we empirically evaluate the accuracy and generalization capability of the pose estimation process of the LPCMAP model. For evaluating the accuracy

# of Shape PCs	Planar (x)	Vertical (y)	Horizontal (z)	Average
1	1.17	4.87	4.17	3.41
8	**0.98**	**2.29**	**1.72**	**1.66**
20	0.92	2.14	1.45	1.50
30	0.90	2.08	1.44	1.47
40	0.90	2.06	1.42	1.46

Table 4.1: Accuracy of the Pose Estimation in Ave. Angular Errors (degs.)

# of Shape PCs	Planar (x)	Vertical (y)	Horizontal (z)	Average
1	1.17	2.72	4.26	2.72
8	**0.93**	**2.26**	**2.36**	**1.85**
20	0.94	2.33	1.71	1.66
30	0.96	2.30	1.70	1.65
40	0.95	2.31	1.58	1.61

Table 4.2: Generalization of the Pose Estimation in Ave. Angular Errors (degs.)

of the process, we first learn a shape-to-pose analysis mapping $\mathcal{A}$ from 1200 training samples, and then test the mapping on the same training samples (**accuracy test**). For evaluating the generalization capability, the mapping is tested with the test samples of the person described in section 4.2.1 (**generalization test**) after the same learning process. This experiment is conducted for 4 different persons. The numerical results are averaged over these 4 persons.

Table 4.1 shows the results of our experiments for the accuracy test. We compute average angular errors (AAE_i) for each rotation axis i and for 5 different sizes of the shape model. The average angular error is an average error of estimated 3D head angles in degrees, $AAE_i := 1/4M \sum^4 \sum_{m=1}^M \|\theta_i^m - \hat{\theta_i^m}\|$. For comparison, we also compute an average value (AAE) of these errors over the 3 rotation dimensions, $AAE := 1/3 \sum_{i=1}^3 AAE_i$.

Table 4.2 shows results of our experiments for the generalization test. The errors are computed in the same manner as in table 4.1. With a shape model with the first 8 PCs, the average angular error was 1.7 degrees for the accuracy test and 1.9 degrees for the generalization test. For the accuracy test, standard deviation of the errors and the worst error were 0.9 and 4.8 degrees, respectively. For the generalization test, the standard deviation and the worst error were 1.1 and 5.0 degrees, respectively. We highlight the errors with the 8 PCs and use them for our evaluations according to our experimental results presented in section 4.2.2.

These results support the accuracy and generalization capability of the

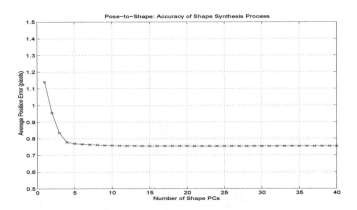

Figure 4.20: Accuracy of Shape Synthesis in Ave. Position Errors (pixels)

LPCMAP model for the pose estimation task. The average angular errors for both the accuracy and generalization tests were small; they were much smaller than the best facial pose estimation accuracy reported in the literature, not better than 3 degrees using a 3D model-based method. These errors were almost the same as those for artificial data shown in figures 4.5 and 4.6. Note that the artificial data is free from errors of rotation angle measurements and of landmark locations, while these errors cannot be avoided for the real face data and can decrease the accuracy of our model. Therefore, they suggest the robustness of our model against these measurement noises. Lastly, the errors for the generalization test were not significantly larger than that for the accuracy test. This displays our model's generalization capability to different poses.

4.2.4 Pose Transformation

In this section, we evaluate the accuracy and generalization capability of the pose transformation process (shape and texture syntheses) of the LPCMAP model. We performed the accuracy and generalization tests, described in section 4.2.3, for the shape synthesis (pose-to-shape) mapping $\mathcal{SS}$ and for the texture synthesis (pose-to-shape-to-texture) mapping $\mathcal{TS}$ of our model. Equivalent to the experiments in section 4.2.3, they are conducted for 4 persons and the results are averaged over these four.

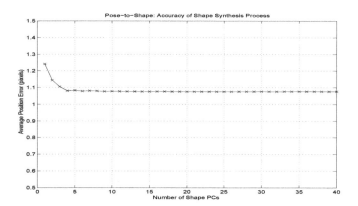

Figure 4.21: Generalization of Shape Synthesis in Ave. Position Errors (pixels)

Shape Synthesis

Figure 4.20 displays the accuracy of the shape synthesis process. We compute average position errors (APE) for different sizes of the shape model. The average position error is an average of root-mean-square errors of synthesized landmarks $\vec{x}$ in pixels. This position error is averaged over M samples and 4 persons, $APE :=$ $1/80M \sum^4 \sum_{m=1}^{M} \sum_{n=1}^{20} \|\vec{x}_n^m - \hat{\vec{x}}_n^m\|$. With only the first 8 PCs, the error was below 0.8 pixels. Standard deviation of the errors and the worst error were 0.2 and 1.4 pixels, respectively. This meets the accuracy criterion of the shape model discussed in section 4.2.2.

Figure 4.21 shows the generalization capability of the shape synthesis process. The average position errors are computed with the test samples of each person in the same manner as the accuracy test in figure 4.20. With the first 8 PCs, the error was about 1.1 pixels. Standard deviation of the errors and the worst error were 0.3 and 2.0 pixels, respectively. It is slightly above the accuracy criterion although the difference is negligible. Moreover, the difference of the errors between the accuracy and generalization tests was very small. These results indicate again the capability of our model to generalize over head poses which are not presented in the training samples.

Texture Synthesis

Figure 4.22 displays the accuracy of the texture synthesis process. Each training sample and the corresponding synthesized texture representation are compared us-

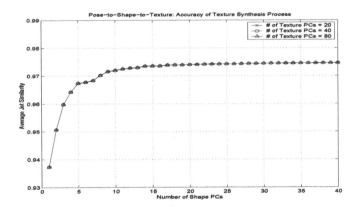

Figure 4.22: Accuracy of Texture Synthesis in Ave. Jet Similarities

ing average jet similarity (AJS) of a pair of texture representations as a similarity metric. The jet similarity (cosine between the two normalized jets) is averaged over 20 nodes, M samples, and 4 persons,

$$AJS := 1/80M \sum_{m=1}^{4} \sum_{n=1}^{M} \sum_{n=1}^{20} (amp(\vec{j}_n^m) \cdot amp(\hat{\vec{j}}_n)) / (\|amp(\vec{j}_n^m)\| \, \|amp(\hat{\vec{j}}_n)\|),$$

where amp transforms a jet $\vec{j}_n^m$ in a Cartesian (real-imaginary) coordinate system to one in a polar (magnitude-phase) coordinate system and extracts only the magnitudes of the polar jet. We conducted this similarity evaluation for varying size of both shape and texture models. Combinations of shape models of 40 different sizes and texture models of 3 different sizes were tested and are shown in figure 4.22. Although the size of the shape model affected the average jet similarities, the size of the texture model did not have a significant influence. The jet coefficients of the synthesized texture representations were indeed influenced by the size of texture models, however, the effect was too small to alter the similarity values. Considering only 8 shape and 21 texture PCs (which had been shown in section 4.2.2 to cover most of variations in the training samples), the average similarity value was about 0.97. Standard deviation of the similarities and the worst similarity value were 0.02 and 0.91, respectively.

Figure 4.23 shows results of the generalization test using the same settings as for the accuracy test, figure 4.22. The jet similarities were also insensitive to the size of the texture model as was the case for the accuracy test. With 8 shape and 21 texture PCs, the average similarity value was about 0.96. The standard deviation

106

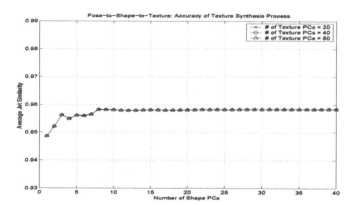

Figure 4.23: Generalization of Texture Synthesis in Ave. Jet Similarities

and the worst similarity value were 0.03 and 0.90, respectively.

The difference of the average similarities between the accuracy and generalization tests with our compact LPCMAP model (8 shape and 21 texture PCs) was small (0.01). This indicates our model's generalization capability to unknown poses similar to the results of the previous experiments for the pose estimation and shape synthesis. The difference of the similarities between these tests and our previous statistical analyses in section 4.2.2 was, however, not negligible. In the analysis for the texture model shown in figure 4.16, we showed that a texture model with 21 PCs can achieve accuracy of 0.99 with the aforementioned similarity metric. Because these similarity values ranging between 0 and 1 are not directly associated with physical units, it is difficult to interpret their implication directly from the values. Although the similarity difference is relatively small in its magnitude, we still need to carefully assess how this loss of similarity influences the proper capabilities of our model, its ability to capture 3D pose variations, innate facial characteristics and to generalize over unknown poses. We suspect that this loss of similarity is due to approximation errors when linearly approximating the non-linear mappings between the shape and texture parameters.

In order to provide a reference for interpreting the jet similarity values, we studied distribution characteristics of the similarity values using the FERET database (e.g., Phillips et al., [157]). This database includes pairs of frontal facial images with slight variation in facial expression (i.e., fa and fb galleries [157]). Figure 4.24 shows two histograms of jet similarity values. A histogram in dark color illustrates a distribution of similarities between facial image pairs of the

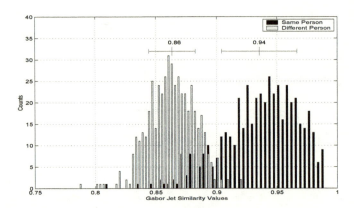

Figure 4.24: Similarity Histogram of the FERET Database

same person, while the other illustrates similarities between facial images of *different person* which are most similar to one another among other persons. The similarity values were computed for 454 image pairs and the same format of the Gabor jet and the similarity metric used throughout this dissertation were also used in this study. A facial representation by a labeled graph with 48 facial landmarks including those on facial contour and hair region (e.g., Okada et al., [141]) was used instead of the 20 facial landmarks for our model. Despite discrepancy of the type of image variation and facial landmarks, this analysis provides an idea of a similarity value range which must be reached for a correct identification. The average and standard deviation of the similarity values were 0.94 and 0.03 for the same person case and 0.86 and 0.02 for the different person case, respectively. The result suggests that the correct identification is assured with a similarity value of 0.94 which is safely above an overlapping region of the two histograms. Note that the average jet similarity values resulted from the texture synthesis process of our LPCMAP model were well above 0.94, supporting its fair accuracy in terms of the identity information.

Reconstructed Images of Synthesized Samples

Next, we visually evaluate the synthesized shape and texture representations by reconstructing gray-level image samples from them. We used an algorithm developed by Pötzsch et al [163] for reconstructing an image sample from a topological graph whose nodes are labeled by Gabor jets. The purpose of these experiments is to visually illustrate the generalization capability of our model to unknown poses.

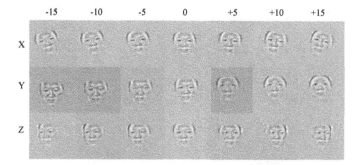

| | -15 | -10 | -5 | 0 | +5 | +10 | +15 |

Figure 4.25: Reconstructed Training Samples

For this purpose, we display synthesized representations that are rotated to poses which are not presented in the training samples. Moreover, in this section, our model's proper faculty to capture the pose variations and the innate facial characteristics is tested. If the similarity loss described in the previous section reduced these abilities of the model, the reconstructed image samples should not look proper.

Figure 4.25 displays reconstructed training samples. The original training samples shown in figure 4.7 are first encoded into the shape and texture representations. The figure shows image samples which are directly reconstructed from these representations by the Pötzsch algorithm. The image quality of these reconstructed samples cannot be perfect because some information of the original image is lost during the encoding process due to the coarse sampling of the jets only at the 20 landmarks. These image samples, however, serve as reference for the images reconstructed from synthesized samples.

Next, we synthesized samples using the pose transformation process SS and TS of the learned LPCMAP model in the same way as described for the similarity analysis in figures 4.22 and 4.23. Figure 4.26 displays image reconstruction of samples synthesized from the 3D head angles of each training sample in figure 4.7 with a LPCMAP model with 8 shape and 21 texture PCs. Therefore, each image in this figure corresponds to the one used in figure 4.25. Although a comparison of these two figures is subjective, the 3D pose variations and the innate facial characteristics presented in the training samples seem to be captured correctly. The shape of faces with large rotations, however, are slightly more distorted compared to the corresponding facial samples in figure 4.25.

Next, we synthesized samples whose head poses were not presented in the training samples in order to assess our model's generalization capability to un-

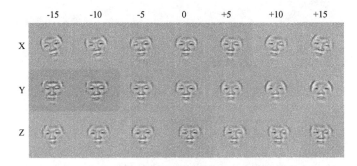

Figure 4.26: Synthesized Samples of Known Poses with 8 Shape and 21 Texture PCs

Figure 4.27: Synthesized Samples of Unknown Poses with 8 Shape and 21 Texture PCs

Figure 4.28: Synthesized Samples of Unknown Poses with 40 Shape and 80 Texture PCs

known poses. In this case, the pose transformation process of our model is used for generating an animation of a face rotating arbitrarily. The same face used in the previous figures was rotated along all three rotation axes simultaneously between ±15 degrees in two different ways (A and B). Figure 4.27 displays reconstructed images of these samples of unknown poses synthesized by a LPCMAP model with 8 shape and 21 texture PCs. It is again up to a subjective evaluation of the reader. However the given pose variations and the innate facial characteristics seem to be captured correctly. This supports our model's generalization capability to unknown poses, discussed with the experimental results of our pose estimation tests shown in tables 4.1 and 4.2. Both the shape and texture of strongly rotated faces in this figure, however, seem to be more distorted compared to the reconstructed images in figure 4.26. This suggests that the generalization capability of our model might be restricted by a range of 3D head angles; the model does not seem to be able to extrapolate the pose variations.

Lastly, we synthesized samples with the same head poses as in figure 4.27 but by a LPCMAP model with complete sets of the PCs (40 shape and 80 texture PC) in order to assess our model's sensitivity to the information loss due to data compression. Figure 4.28 displays reconstructed images of these synthesized samples. A comparison of the two figures 4.28 and 4.27 indicates that there is no significant information loss between them except a slight loss of some peculiar details in figure 4.28. This is a pleasing result since it suggests that the compactness of our model does not influence our model's generalization capability and the ability to capture pose variations and innate facial characteristics correctly.

4.3 Limitation for a Range of Head Poses in Samples

As we discussed in section 4.2.4, a synthesized facial sample loses some information from the original in terms of the average jet similarity value. This was also

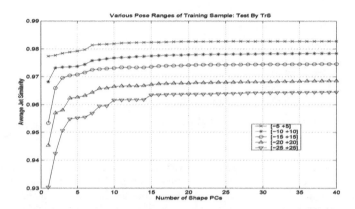

Figure 4.29: Accuracy of Synthesis Process with Various Pose Ranges in Ave. Jet Similarities

visually illustrated in figure 4.27; the reconstructed images of the synthesized samples were more distorted as head rotation angles increased. Although the visual examples and the comparison to the similarity statistics using the FERET database in the previous sections validate that the information loss is not significantly reducing the model's ability to capture pose variations and innate facial characteristics, it is preferable to maintain a higher similarity profile, thereby minimizing the disturbance.

We have discussed that the loss of information is perhaps due to approximation errors of the mapping between different parameter spaces (pose, shape, and texture) because we linearly approximate these non-linear mappings. It is obvious that the non-linear distortion between different parameter spaces becomes stronger as the range of head rotation in the training samples increases. Therefore, we can expect to improve the linear mapping approximation by limiting the range of 3D head poses in the training and test samples. In order to clarify this point, we conducted a number of experiments with various sets of training and test samples, each containing samples with a different range of 3D head angles.

Figure 4.29 shows results of our experiments for the accuracy tests where learned models are tested by the same training samples. Similar to our experiments for the texture synthesis in the previous section, we synthesized samples from the 3D head angles of each training sample by the pose-to-shape-to-texture mappings of a learned LPCMAP model. In these experiments, however, we estimated the head angles of each training sample by our model's analysis process (analysis-synthesis chain) instead of using the angles in the training samples. The

112

size of the texture model is fixed to the first 21 texture PCs while the average jet similarities are computed for 40 different sizes of the shape model. We used five different sets of pose ranges in training and test samples,

1. samples whose head angles are within a range of ± 5 degrees for all three axes,

2. samples within ± 10 degrees range,

3. samples within ± 15 degrees range,

4. samples within ± 20 degrees range,

5. samples within ± 25 degrees range.

The training sets include 450, 526, 621, 686, and 781 samples, respectively. The results of these experiments showed that the average jet similarities between the test and synthesized samples monotonically improves as the range of pose variations is narrowed. Similarity profiles for each pose range set become flatter as the range becomes more limited. The average similarity value between the test and synthesized model with 8 shape and 21 texture PCs was improved to 0.975 with the ± 10 degrees range and to 0.982 with the ± 5 degrees range.

Figure 4.30 shows the results of our experiments for the generalization test, where learned models are tested for test samples with unknown head poses. The settings of the training samples remained the same as in the previous experiments for the accuracy test shown in figure 4.29. The pose range of the test samples were also restricted in the same manner as the training samples. The test sets consist of 162, 204, 271, 293, and 300 samples, respectively. Between the ± 5 and ± 10 degrees ranges, there was a significant decrease in the similarity profiles. A similar decrease of similarity values was observed between the ± 10 and ± 15 degrees ranges. This is perhaps due to the fact that the number of samples was much smaller for the narrower pose range sets than for the wider range sets in the training samples. This result, however, indicates that the generalization capability of our model to unknown poses is limited by the range of pose variation. Beyond 20 degrees, the similarity values decrease rapidly. Therefore, the accuracy of our model is maintained only within a limited pose range.

4.4 Discussion

In this chapter, we presented the results of numerical experiments assessing the feasibility of the LPCMAP model. We have concentrated on analyzing the performance of our model learned with multiple views of a single person. In chapter 8,

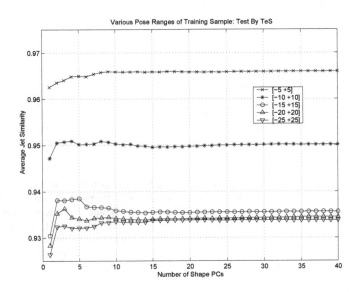

Figure 4.30: Generalization of Synthesis Process with Various Pose Ranges in Ave. Jet Similarities

we will discuss an application of our model towards representing the general class of faces by learning a LPCMAP model with views from multiple persons.

The experimental results in this chapter indicate that our model achieves a good balance between accuracy and generalization capability. Our experiments with artificial data in section 4.1 first proved the correctness of our model by showing perfect accuracy in an optimal setting. The series of numerical experiments using the accuracy and generalization tests in section 4.2 revealed that the LPCMAP model, whose size was derived from the statistics of the data, was able to generalize to unknown poses while maintaining good accuracy. Moreover, good balance was achieved with a compact model, compressing the data size of model knowledge. For example, with the 8 shape and 21 texture PCs, the model compresses an amount of information captured in 1200 training samples to roughly 22 samples, resulting in a compression by a factor of 60. Lastly, a study of the synthesized samples in section 4.2.4 indicated our model's capability to capture pose variations and innate facial characteristics present in the training samples.

Similarity analysis of the synthesized faces in section 4.2.4 showed that the similarity values of the synthesized faces were somewhat lower than expected from the accuracy shown in our statistical study. Although the loss does not seem to significantly disturb the model's ability to capture the pose variations and the innate facial characteristics, it indicates some information loss during the mapping processes. Since our model is designed to compactly represent the pose variations of a face, not to maintain all the pixel-level information for an optimal reconstruction property, it is natural to have lower similarity values among the synthesized faces. A model can be a general and compact representation of a large number of pose-varying views only by eliminating redundant information and irrelevant variational factors. These redundancies and variational factors might contain peculiarities presented in single images which can work as cues that accidentally increase similarity values. In this view, the model should suppress similarity values of specific single views by its nature. The data compression aspect of our model can also be considered a byproduct of this redundancy and peculiarity reduction for enabling the generalization to unknown poses. A question we need to answer here, however, is if this loss of information influences the capability of the model to capture the 3D pose variations and the innate characteristics of a learned face. The study of reconstructed images of synthesized samples in section 4.2.4 supports our model's ability to capture these types of information. In the next chapter, we also explore our model's retainment of the innate facial characteristics by applying the model to a facial identification task.

Figures 4.26 and 4.27 in section 4.2.4 displayed that the synthesized face with large head rotations seemed to be more distorted compared to the original samples. The innate facial characteristics used for the identification task are often sensitive to a slight deformation of configurational information in shapes (Bruce

115

and Humphreys [28]). Therefore, this distortion might have an affect on the innate facial characteristics captured in a learned model. The similarity metric used in our jet similarity analysis in figures 4.22 and 4.23 will also be used for our recognition system which utilizes the innate characteristics. This metric is mostly insensitive to the shape deformation, [2] therefore it might be able to suppress the negative effect of the shape distortion. The next chapter should provide experimental answers to this argument.

This chapter also experimentally revealed an important shortcoming of our model. The proper faculty of the LPCMAP model is limited in the range of pose variations presented in samples. Any limitation in poses of training samples means that the model requires operator assistance and subject's collaboration for sample collection, so that our model would no longer be data-driven and flexible. Therefore, this is clearly an intolerable restriction to our system. Our solution to this problem will be explored in chapter 6.

---

[2]The similarity metric based on the node-wise jet similarities does not account for the location of landmarks. However the shape deformation in configuration can be partially captured in responses of low frequency filters whose receptive fields are relatively large.

Chapter 5

Pose-Invariant Face Recognition by the LPCMAP Model

In this chapter, we present a novel pose-invariant face recognition method using the LPCMAP model for representing each person in a database of known persons (Okada et al. [143]). We first illustrate three different methods of pose-invariant face recognition based on a nearest-neighbor classifier, in order to depict differences of our method from the other two. In section 5.2, we describe our method and illustrate it with qualitative evaluations using the real face data described in section 4.2.1. In section 5.3, the feasibility of our method is assessed by numerical experiments with a data set created by a Cyberware scanner.

5.1 Three Different Methods for Pose-Invariant Face Recognition

In the literature, a number of systems have been proposed for recognizing faces robustly against pose variations (**pose-invariant face recognition**). We have reviewed a number of examples of such systems in section 2.2.3. The review presented the two types of approach based on a nearest-neighbor recognizer, the single-view and multiple-view approaches. In the nearest-neighbor framework, an input's identity is estimated by finding the entry most similar to the input from a known-person database or **gallery** using a specific similarity metric. In other words, the input's identity is derived from the identity associated with a gallery entry which is most similar to the input. In order to robustly recognize faces with pose variations, head poses of arbitrary inputs and gallery entries need to be aligned for each comparison. In this section, we first illustrate two recognition methods based on these two approaches. Next, we compare these methods to our approach. Figure 5.1 schematizes these two methods.

SVM: Single-View Method   **MVM: Multiple-View Method**

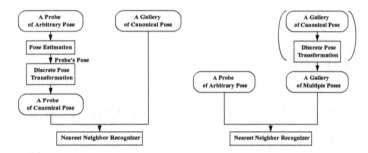

Figure 5.1: Two Basic Methods of Pose-Invariant Face Recognition Systems

The **single-view method (SVM)** utilizes a gallery which represents each known individual by a single view of the person. In this method, all entries of a gallery are supposed to have the same *canonical pose* (e.g., a frontal pose). In order to compensate for pose variations, the input view is transformed to *canonical pose*, thereby aligning the head pose of the input and the gallery entries. After this alignment, the input can be subjected to a nearest-neighbor recognizer for an identification. Recognition systems by Maurer and von der Malsburg [126] and Lando and Edelman [112] are based on this method with a class-specific discrete-transformation. See section 2.2.3 for details.

The **multiple-view method (MVM)** utilizes a gallery which represents each known individual by multiple views. In this case, each entry of the gallery consists of views of different pose for a specific person. The identification process of this method is realized by two-level nearest-neighbor classification. For each gallery entry, an input is compared against all the views of the entry. The gallery view most similar to the input then serves as a **representative view** of the entry and the highest similarity value represents *proximity* of the input to the person. An input's identity is estimated by another nearest-neighbor classification over all the gallery entries finding an entry whose proximity to the input is the highest. Assuming that each entry always contains a view whose pose matches with an arbitrary input, head poses of the representative views are likely to be aligned to the input's head pose. These multiple views of each person are either manually recorded or synthesized from a single-view of a fixed head pose by using a class-specific discrete-transformation. Recognition systems by Beymer and Poggio [15, 16] demonstrated both types of multiple-view gallery construction. See section 2.2.3 for details.

In this dissertation, we propose a novel method for pose-invariant face recog-

118

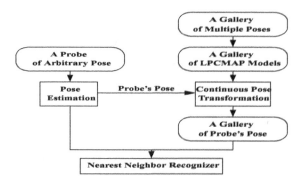

Figure 5.2: Our Method of Pose-Invariant Face Recognition System

nition using the LPCMAP model as the data format of a gallery entry. Figure 5.2 schematizes this recognition method. Using the analysis-synthesis chain of learned models, we align the head pose of each known person to the input pose, by synthesizing the appropriate model views. This method combines the SVM and MVM by that 1) it uses estimated pose information of inputs, similar to the SVM, and 2) it represents each known person by compact knowledge derived from multiple views of the person similar to the MVM. Using the information derived from inputs, the search space within the gallery can be greatly reduced in comparison to the MVM. Moreover, this model-based gallery is more compact than the MVM, which represents each known person by a set of multiple views.

As described in sections 1.4, 2.3, and 3.4, the LPCMAP model is based on continuous-transformation. This continuous-transformation allows the model to cover the viewing sphere continuously, while the discrete-transformation covers it only discretely. Our method is not restricted to a canonical pose, as is often the case in the previous methods. In our approach, knowledge of the canonical pose should be learned directly from sample statistics instead of given *a priori*.

The recognition systems based on the PC-manifold representations (parametric eigenspace) proposed by Murase and Nayar [133] and Graham and Allinson [80, 79] resemble our method in that both systems also represented each known person by a compact and continuous PC-subspace model. However, their systems undergo an exhaustive (or binary in Nayar's case) search of the all possible poses. Therefore, our method, using the input pose estimate, is expected to make the matching process more efficient and potentially more accurate.

119

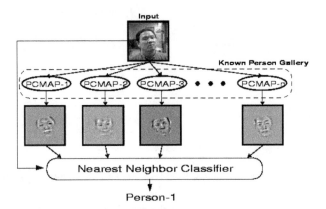

Figure 5.3: Pose-Invariant Recognition System with LPCMAP Models

5.2 Illustration of Our System

In this section, we describe our face recognition system using the method described in the previous section. Figure 5.3 shows an overview. In this system, each gallery entry for a single known person is represented by an LPCMAP model learned for the person. For identification, an arbitrary input is subjected to the analysis-synthesis chain process of the LPCMAP models stored in the gallery. This results in synthesized views of each known person with its pose aligned to the input. After this pose alignment, the input is subjected to a nearest-neighbor classification with these synthesized views. Because of the pose alignment, the identification performance should be robust against pose variations. Furthermore, there is no systematic limitation to particular discrete head poses due to the continuous coverage of the pose parameter space as a result of using the LPCMAP model. As long as the learned linear PCMAPs cover a sufficient range of head poses, an input with arbitrary pose can be processed without any pose restrictions.

Next, we qualitatively assess our face recognition system with samples used in section 4.2. For comparison, we build three recognition systems for our method, MVM, and SVM. They all are based on the same nearest-neighbor classification system but differ in a way the known-persons gallery is constructed.

For our system, each known person is represented by a LPCMAP model which is trained by 1200 training samples of the person as shown in figure 4.7. Only 8 shape PCs and 21 texture PCs were included in the shape and texture models, re-

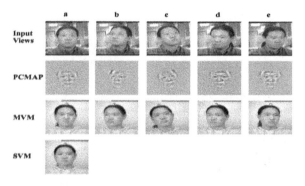

Figure 5.4: Examples of Model Views by the Three Different Systems

spectively, and the type B trigonometric functional transformation is used. With the same 1200 training samples used to train the LPCMAP model, we also construct known-persons galleries for the MVM and SVM systems. For the MVM system, each known person is represented by a number of views with different poses by storing all the 1200 training samples of the person. For the SVM system, each known person is represented by a single frontal view taken from the training samples. Pose transformation described in the previous section was not used for both MVM and SVM systems for simplicity.

Each gallery entry in these systems provides the most similar view to a given input facial image for computing the input-to-entry similarity values. We call this most similar view **model view** of the entry. A model view of our system is synthesized from the input's head pose by the analysis-synthesis chain process of a LPCMAP entry. For the MVM system, a model view is the most similar view to the input among the set of views in the entry. For the SVM system, a model view is the single view of the entry since there is no other choice.

Figure 5.4 compares the model views of 5 different input views by the three systems. This figure only shows model views derived from a gallery entry whose identity is the same as the inputs. We collected 5 facial images with arbitrary head poses in different environments from the one used for the training samples shown in figure 4.7. These input views are shown in the first row of the figure 5.4. The second, third, and fourth row of this figure shows the model views by our system, MVM, and SVM, respectively. A comparison of the model views by LPCMAP and MVM illustrates the advantage of using the LPCMAP models as gallery entries. Note that head poses in the training samples were restricted to rotations along only one axis at a time, while head poses of the inputs were not restricted.

121

Model Type	a	b	c	d	e
LPCMAP	0.915	0.871	0.862	0.891	0.878
MVM	0.930	0.872	0.876	0.913	0.897
SVM	0.926	0.852	0.816	0.878	0.862

Table 5.1: Similarities Between the Input and Model Views in Figure 5.4

Although the gallery entry for both systems contained the same amount of information, having been built from the same training samples, our system's model views are clearly more aligned to the input's poses than those by the MVM. This again suggests our model's generalization capability to unknown poses shown in figure 4.27.

Table 5.1 provides the jet similarity values between the 5 input views and the corresponding model views shown in figure 5.4. The similarity values by the SVM provides the base-line in which the pose variation is not compensated. The similarity values by our LPCMAP system exceeded the base-line similarities except for the image **a**, suggesting the effectiveness of our system's handling of the pose variations. In other words, the head pose alignment between input and model views helped to improve the similarity values from the base-line. The similarity values by our system are, however, slightly lower than those by the MVM. Since our system's model views are more aligned to the inputs than the MVM's model views, one could expect that they have a higher similarity values than the MVM's model views. As discussed in section 4.4, this similarity decrease by the LPCMAP model is due to its reduction of the redundancies and irrelevant variational factors presented in the training samples. This reduction is a key factor which enables the generalization to unknown poses, however it might also give a negative influence to our model's ability to capture the innate facial characteristics.

Next, we conducted an identification test with a gallery of 3 individuals in order to develop insights for our system's performance. 1200 samples for each individual described in section 4.2 are used to train 3 LPCMAP entries which represent the 3 known persons. 400 test samples for each person are used for the identification test. These test samples are recorded in the same environment as the training samples but their head poses are different from any training samples. The 3 LPCMAP entries in the gallery give 3 model views for each test sample. The entry with the most similar model view to the test sample in terms of the jet similarity values provides the estimate of the sample's identity.

Figure 5.5 illustrates 3 examples of such an identification process. Each row of this figure shows a single identification process for different test samples. Three test samples are shown in the left most column of this figure and the rest of columns display the synthesized model views for each test sample by the 3

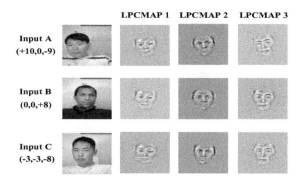

Figure 5.5: Model Views of our System with 3 Person Gallery

Input View	LPCMAP 1	LPCMAP 2	LPCMAP 3
A	**0.920**	0.816	0.871
B	0.849	**0.960**	0.797
C	0.855	0.736	**0.943**

Table 5.2: Similarities Between the Input and Model Views in Figure 5.5

LPCMAP entries. This figure shows that the 3 synthesized views in each row have the same head pose while the 3 views in each column maintains the same personal appearance.

Table 5.2 lists the jet similarity values between the 3 tests and model views shown in figure 5.5. Similarity values between the 3 tests and their corresponding entries are highlighted in the diagonal of this table. The table shows 3 correct identification cases. Using the total test set of 1200 samples, we compared the identification performance of our system and the MVM system described earlier. As a result, our system had no failure, whereas the MVM system failed in 3 cases. The average value of the similarity between the test and model views was again smaller for our system (0.96) than for the MVM system (0.98). We also computed the average of similarity differences between model views of the best and the 2nd best match as a statistical measure of *discrimination-power* of a recognition system. The higher the value of this measure, the more discrimination-power the recognition system possesses. This value was the same for both systems (0.09). This seems to suggest that the similarity decrease in comparison to the MVM system does not negatively influence the identification performance of our system.

Figure 5.6 illustrates one of the failure cases of the MVM system. In this case,

123

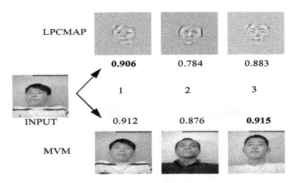

Figure 5.6: An Example of Successful Identification with our System where MVM fails

our system correctly identified the test as the person 1 while the MVM system falsely identified it as the person 3. Two other failure cases by the MVM were also caused by the disagreement of head poses, but our LPCMAP system correctly identified them. This qualitatively shows the advantage of our system by aligning head poses of model views to an arbitrary input pose by the analysis-synthesis chain process of the LPCMAP model for all the gallery entries.

5.3 Numerical Experiments with 3D Cyberware Scanner Data

In this section, we present results of numerical experiments with 3D facial data created by a Cyberware scanner in order to quantitatively assess the feasibility of our method for pose-invariant face recognition. A series of qualitative illustrations in the previous section implied the feasibility of our method, however the multi-person statistics with only 3 gallery entries can not provide a convincing proof. Quantitative experiments with more gallery entries for more individuals in this section aim to show more convincing arguments for supporting our recognition system.

5.3.1 Data Set

In this experiment, we use 2D samples generated from 3D facial models recorded by a Cyberware 3030 scanner. Twenty models (10:female,10:male, shown in figure 5.7) are randomly picked from a 3D facial model database of Japanese faces

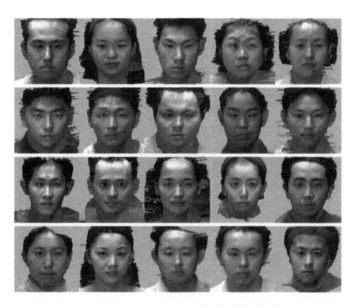

Figure 5.7: 20 Known Persons in 3D ATR-Database

developed at the Human Information Research Laboratories of ATR in Kyoto, Japan (ATR-Database).

A common problem for conducting numerical experiments to evaluate a given recognition system is the difficulty of collecting training and test samples. In our case, rigorous numerical evaluation of our system requires a sufficiently large number of gallery entries and samples with a wide variety of pose variations for each entry. The samples used in sections 4.2 and 5.2 do not serve as a good testbed because there are two few individuals and their pose distributions are specific and arbitrary, although these particular distributions provided a convenient experimental setting to show our model's generalization capability to unknown poses. Although our LPCMAP model is designed to accommodate uncontrolled continuous pose variations, we require a controlled data set for evaluating our system's performance numerically. The collection of real face samples in the manner described in section 4.2.1 is cumbersome because it is hard to control different subjects for the same pose variations and it is vulnerable to measurement errors of landmark locations and 3D head angles. In order to mitigate these problems, we use 3D facial models recorded by a Cyberware scanner. The scanner captures

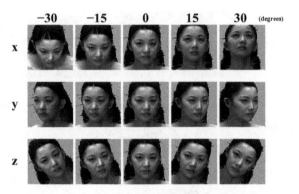

Figure 5.8: Examples of Training Samples from the ATR-DB

a 3D structural models together with their texture images by rotating a slit-laser range finder around a still subject. An advantage of this method is that it is free from the measurement errors since landmark locations and 3D head angles are derived from explicit rotations of the 3D models. This method also provides a convenient way to create arbitrary pose variations without further recording of the same subject.

For each model, test and training samples are generated by rendering 2D snapshot views while explicitly rotating the 3D facial model [102]. We used distributions of pose variations similar to those described in section 4.1.1. For the training samples, each model is rotated along only one axis at a time as shown in figure 5.8. We generated 248 training samples for each rotation axis and 744 training samples for each person. For the test samples, each model is rotated along the three axes simultaneously, as shown in figure 5.9. We generated 186 test samples for each person. We generated these training and test samples for 20 individuals. Locations of the 20 facial landmarks in various poses are determined by explicitly rotating 3D reference coordinates that are found manually for a frontal view of each 3D model. The 3D head angles of each sample are directly given from the explicit rotation angles. One may be concerned about the artificiality of the data due to the 2D rendering process. However, these two figures show that facial appearances in these 2D views are very realistic since the appearances are based on the actual images of the person.

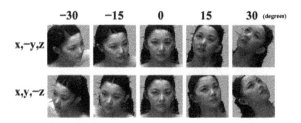

Figure 5.9: Examples of Test Samples from the ATR-DB

5.3.2 Experimental Results

Figure 5.10 shows the result of our numerical experiments for evaluating the identification performance of our system. Using the same training samples, the SVM, MVM, and our proposed systems are built in the manner described in the previous section. 5 different test sets are derived from the test samples for the 20 persons by limiting the range of pose variations to ±5, ±10, ±15, ±20, and ±30 degrees, respectively. The bars in the figure show the percentages of correct identifications by the 3 systems for each test set. The correct-identification rates of our system were constantly better than or equivalent to the SVM system. Our system's performance was equally good in comparison to the MVM within the pose range of ±20 degrees, although the performance of both systems reached the ceiling. The MVM system outperformed our system beyond the ±20 pose range.

5.4 Discussion

In this chapter, we have proposed a novel pose-invariant face recognition system using LPCMAP models as entry format for a known-persons gallery. Our recognition system postulates that pose-invariance can be achieved by providing the memory/knowledge systems, a known-persons gallery in this case with a learning capability, instead of trying to find pose-invariant properties in input representations within a perceptual process. The continuous coverage of the pose parameter space by our LPCMAP model should improve the identification performance of the SVM and MVM systems which can cover the space only at discrete points given *a priori*.

The numerical experiments presented in section 5.3 assess the feasibility of this recognition system. The results showed that identification performance of our system against pose variations improved that of the SVM system, which represented a known person by a single frontal view. The qualitative analysis of our

127

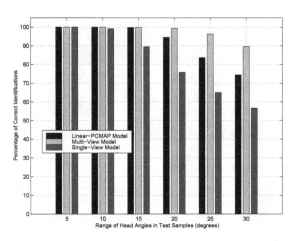

Figure 5.10: Percentages of Correct Identifications with the SVM, MVM, and our Systems

system in section 5.2 also supported the feasibility of this system.

The experimental results, however, clarified a limitation of our recognition system. The MVM system outperformed our system beyond the pose range of ±20 degrees, although the performance of our system was equivalent to the MVM system within this pose range. The results in chapter 4 supported an effectiveness of our model for correctly capturing the pose variations and for generalizing to unknown poses. However, they also showed that the effectiveness was limited to the range of pose variations. Our hope was that this pose limitation does not negatively influence our model's capability to capture the innate facial characteristics, therefore it does not interfere with the correct identifications. Unfortunately, our results showed that the identification performance of our recognition system was also good only within a limited range of pose variations. The choice of the linear approximations in the LPCMAP model provides the advantage of generalization for unknown poses, but unfortunately it leads to this limitation. Moreover, samples derived from 3D Cyberware data contain artifacts that distinguish them and may improve recognition performance unrealistically. Therefore, the absolute values of correct-identification rates need to be interpreted with caution.

One of the encouraging implications from the experimental results is that the identification performance of our system was as good as the MVM system within the pose range of ±15 degrees, in which the LPCMAP model was shown to be

128

accurate in chapter 4. This suggests that our proposed recognition method can be effective if we can mitigate the pose range limitation of the LPCMAP model. Furthermore, the performance of the MVM system was very high; the correct-identification rate was close to 90% even with the test samples of the widest ±30 degrees pose range. This is perhaps due to our choice of the Gabor jet-based single-view representation, which has been successfully shown to be effective for the identification task [141] and to be robust against a small range of pose variations [111]. This high performance is sufficient for many application scenarios, however the system is not practical because the size of its gallery will become too large to handle especially when we deal with additional image variations such as illumination changes. By reducing the pose range limitation of our model, the performance of our recognition system may be able to improve up to this sufficient level, while the size of the known-persons gallery is maintained much smaller because of the model's data compression nature which also improves recognition time by limiting the search space. These arguments clearly set a new goal of our investigation for the rest of this dissertation: extending the LPCMAP model to overcome the pose range limitation. The next chapter will address our solution to this problem using a piecewise linear model approach.

Chapter 6

Extension of the LPCMAP Model to a Piecewise Linear Model Approach

In the previous chapters, we showed that there is a range limitation of 3D head angles which restricts the LPCMAP model's accuracy and generalization capability to unknown poses. In this chapter, we propose a method which overcomes this restriction by piecing together a set of localized LPCMAP models. The idea is to cover the wide range of the 3D angle space by a number of local linear models since a single model cannot cover the whole. There has been a similar idea in the literature of various fields. Borrowing the terminology from these previous studies, we call our approach **piecewise linear model** (hereafter PWLM) approach.

Figure 6.1 shows a sketch of such an approach in a hypothetical 2D parameter space. Each circle in this sketch represents a parameter range that a single model wishes to cover. The broken-lined large circle covers an adequate range of the parameter, however, the model cannot be accurate around the peripheral of the circle. Our approach tries to cover the same parameter range by a number of smaller solid-lined circles. Since each model only covers a limited range with good accuracy, the collection of these models results in better overall fitting accuracy.

Also remember that the pose range limitation of the LPCMAP model was caused by non-linearity of pose variation in our facial representations. Figure 6.2 illustrates how the PWLM approach overcomes the non-linearity problem while keeping virtue of a linear system. The right figure 6.2(b) schematizes a N-dimensional data-cloud embedded in a two-dimensional linear subspace as also shown in figure 1.1. A curved axis of the data-cloud indicates that the sample distribution is non-linear. Because of this non-linearity, the linear basis cannot describe the non-linear variation accurately; $\vec{e_1}$ does not align with the curved axis. The left figure 6.2(a) shows a PWLM approach which covers the same data-

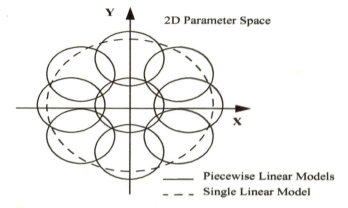

Figure 6.1: A 2D Sketch of the Piecewise Linear Model Approach

cloud by a number of localized linear subspaces (R_1^2, R_2^2, and R_3^2). The non-linear variation axis is collectively covered by linear components from the different subspaces, providing a better alignment than the case in figure 6.2(b).

6.1 Related Studies

In this section, we briefly review the literature related to our piecewise linear model approach. As discussed in chapter 1, one of our main goals is to use samples to learn mappings which directly associate image-based facial representations and physical parameters. This problem can be formalized as a problem of multivariate function approximation. In fact, many problems in various fields such as pattern classification and multivariate regression can be generalized to this problem (Bishop [22]). The difficulty of this problem depends on the nature of the mappings to be learned. When we can expect the mappings to be linear, simple analytical solutions to this problem with well studied behaviors become available. However, these mappings of interest are non-linear in most realistic cases, including the problem of interest here. In such cases, these linear methods fail to approximate the mappings accurately. In past decades, many studies have proposed to solve this function approximation problem by using learning methods which fit a non-linear function to sample statistics. For this purpose, artificial neural networks such as the back-propagation network by Rumelhart and McClelland [170] became popular and have been investigated rigorously. However, they have the following common pitfalls; 1) their performance often depends on the choice of a

131

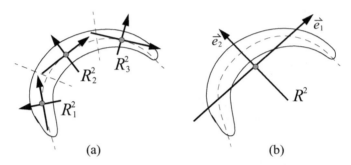

Figure 6.2: Non-linearity and Piecewise Linear Model Approach

specific non-linearity that needs to be given *a priori*, 2) their computational processes tend to be complicated and time-consuming, and 3) they often result in
overfitting, leading to poor generalization (see discussion about the bias-variance
dilemma described by Geman et al. [72] in section 1.6).

Another solution to solve this problem is to use a collection of localized linear functions. The idea is to cover a wide range of parameter space by a number
of linear functions, each of which can only be accurate within a limited range
of the whole parameter space due to its linearity. Since a single linear function
cannot cover the whole space, this type of method utilizes a collection of such
localized linear functions in order to cover the entire space. Because it only consists of linear functions, the common problems of non-linear learning methods
can be avoided. Methods of this type have been called piecewise linear approach.
They have been incorporated into a number of common techniques and applied
to solve various practical problems. The techniques which have been extended to
the piecewise linear approach include the multivariate regression (Brailovsky and
Kempner [25], Schaal and Atkeson [176], and Vijayakumar and Schaal [206]),
the growing neural gas network (Fritzke [69]), the self-organizing map (SOM)
network (Walter [209]), the binary-tree classifier (Chai et al. [36]), and the lay-
ered neural network classifier (Herman and Yeung [90], Vriesenga and Sklansky [208], and Tenmoto et al. [187]). The problems to which piecewise linear
methods have been applied include sensor-motor coordination for robot control
(Mael [121], Schaal and Atkeson [176], Vijayakumar and Schaal [206], and Walter [209]), plane curve approximation (Sato [174]), 3D texture morphing (Venka-
traman and Poston [201]), 2D image warping (Uchida and Sakoe [196]), image
restoration (Acton and Bovik [2]), image compression (Modayil et al. [130]), and
MPEG video decoding (Cheng and Hang [40]).

An important issue for this piecewise linear approach is how to interpolate

132

an intermediate data point with stored local linear models. As illustrated in figures 6.1 and 7.1, there are regions of the parameter space which can be covered by multiple local models or by no models depending on specific sample distributions. For the data points in such a parameter region, it is important to interpolate neighboring linear models in order to cover the parameter space smoothly.

6.2 Description of the Piecewise Linear Model Approach

In the following, the extension of the LPCMAP model to the piecewise linear model (PWLM) approach is demonstrated. In our case, a local linear model is a linear mapping function which is valid only within a specific local area of the model's parameter space. We treat the LPCMAP model described in chapter 3 as local linear model without modifications of its design such as introducing explicit parameter windows. The extension utilizes weighted averaging of the *outputs* of the LPCMAP models for piecing together the local linear models.

Suppose K LPCMAP models are learned from K sets of training samples for a single person, each of which includes a limited range of pose variations,

$$\{LM_1, .., LM_k, .., LM_K\}, \tag{6.1}$$

where each LM_k denotes a single LPCMAP as a local linear model. We assume that the average of the 3D pose distributions of the training sample sets for each local model, $\vec{u}_\theta^{LM_k}$, are appropriately distanced from each other. We call $\vec{u}_\theta^{LM_k}$ the **model center** of LM_k in the 3D angle space.

The analysis mapping of a single LPCMAP model in (3.40) can be extended to the PWLM approach by averaging K pose estimates by the set of the K local models with appropriate weights,

$$\hat{\vec{\theta}} = \sum_{k=1}^{K} w_k \hat{\vec{\theta}_k} = \sum_{k=1}^{K} w_k \mathcal{A}_{LM_k}(\vec{v}), \tag{6.2}$$

where w_k is a weight for the k-th local LPCMAP model LM_k and $\hat{\vec{\theta}_k}$ is a pose estimate of an image sample $\vec{v}$ by the LM_k.

Similarly, the synthesis mapping in (3.45) can be extended by averaging K synthesized representations with the same weights,

$$\begin{aligned}
\hat{\vec{v}} &= \mathcal{R}(\sum_{k=1}^{K} w_k \hat{\vec{z}_k}, \sum_{k=1}^{K} w_k \hat{\vec{z}_k^1}, .., \sum_{k=1}^{K} w_k \hat{\vec{z}_k^N}) \\
&= \mathcal{R}(\sum_{k=1}^{K} w_k \mathcal{SS}_{LM_k}(\vec{\theta}), \sum_{k=1}^{K} w_k \mathcal{TS}_{LM_k}(\vec{\theta})),
\end{aligned} \tag{6.3}$$

where $\hat{\vec{x}}_k$ and $\hat{\vec{t}}_k^{-1}, .., \hat{\vec{t}}_k^{-N}$ are synthesized shape and texture representations from 3D head angles $\vec{\theta}$ by the k-th local model LM_k.

The choice of the weight vector $\vec{w} = (w_1, .., w_k..., w_K)$ is essential for the feasibility of this proposed method. These weights are responsible for the localization of the model's outputs. Their functional behavior also decides the extent to which each single local model influences the averaged output $\hat{\vec{\theta}}$ and $\hat{\vec{v}}$ of our system. For localizing the linear models, the weights should be a function of the distance in the 3D angle space between an input pose and each model centers such that the value of weights decays as the distance increases. We also prefer a fast-decaying weight function since the results of our previous numerical experiments suggested that the accuracy of the LPCMAP model decreases rapidly as the distance between the input pose and the model center increases. In this study, we use a normalized exponentially-decaying weight functions of Gaussian shape in 3D angle space,

$$w_k(\vec{\theta}) = \frac{\rho_k(\vec{\theta} - \vec{u}_\theta^{LM_k})}{\sum_{k=1}^{K} \rho_k(\vec{\theta} - \vec{u}_\theta^{LM_k})}, \text{ where } \rho_k(\vec{\theta}) = \frac{1}{\sqrt{2\pi}\sigma_k} \exp(-\frac{\|\vec{\theta}\|^2}{2\sigma_k^2}), \quad (6.4)$$

where σ_k controls the width of the k-th Gaussian. We consider the σ_k as a function of the sample standard deviation of the training 3D head angle vectors for each local model LM_k,

$$\sigma_k = p \times \sqrt{\frac{1}{M_k - 1} \sum_{m=1}^{M_k} \|\vec{\theta}^m - \vec{u}_\theta^{LM_k}\|^2}, \quad (6.5)$$

where p is a positive scalar factor and M_k is the number of training samples used for the local model LM_k. When not specified, we set p to 1.

6.3 Gradient-Descent Algorithm for Pose Estimation

A shortcoming of this weight function is that it is a function of an input's 3D head angles $\vec{\theta}$. This makes the extended analysis mapping in (6.2) infeasible, although the extended synthesis mapping in (6.3) remains valid.

In order to overcome this shortcoming, another approach is introduced next. The idea is to formulate a gradient-descent algorithm which iteratively improves an estimate of the input's head pose $\hat{\vec{\theta}}$. For each step of the iteration, pose estimate $\hat{\vec{\theta}}$ is modified such that a shape synthesis error decreases relative to the previous pose estimate. Since the modification of the pose estimate in each iteration step utilizes information from the previous step, the extended analysis mapping in (6.2) becomes feasible. By setting an initial condition carefully, this algorithm is expected to find a correct pose estimate and to avoid local minima. The following describes this algorithm.

Let a shape vector $\vec{x}$ be an input to the algorithm. Let a shape vector $\vec{x}_i$ and a 3D angle vector $\vec{\theta}_i$ denote the shape and angle estimates by the i-th iteration of the algorithm. The task of this algorithm is then to accurately approximate the correct pose estimate $\hat{\vec{\theta}}$ in (6.2) by the iterative estimate $\vec{\theta}_i$.

An initial condition $\vec{\theta}_0$ and $\vec{x}_0$ are set with a model center and its corresponding shape vector of the local LPCMAP model whose center (average) shape $\vec{u}_x^{LM_k}$ is the closest to the input shape,

$$
\begin{aligned}
\vec{x}_0 &= \vec{u}_x^{LM_{k_{min}}}, \\
\vec{\theta}_0 &= \vec{u}_\theta^{LM_{k_{min}}}, \\
k_{min} &= index(\min_{k=1}^{K} \|\vec{x} - \vec{u}_x^{LM_k}\|^2),
\end{aligned}
\tag{6.6}
$$

where k_{min} is an index of the local model whose center shape is the closest to the input $\vec{x}$ and a function $index()$ retrieves an index k from a shape vector representing a model center.

Iteration rules are defined as follows,

$$
\Delta \vec{x}_i = \vec{x} - \vec{x}_i,
\tag{6.7}
$$

$$
\Delta \vec{\theta}_i = \sum_{k=1}^{K} w_k(\vec{\theta}_i) \mathcal{A}'_{LM_k}(\Delta \vec{x}_i),
\tag{6.8}
$$

$$
\vec{\theta}_{i+1} = \vec{\theta}_i + \eta \Delta \vec{\theta}_i,
\tag{6.9}
$$

$$
\vec{x}_{i+1} = \sum_{k=1}^{K} w_k(\vec{\theta}_{i+1}) \mathcal{SS}_{LM_k}(\vec{\theta}_{i+1}),
\tag{6.10}
$$

where η is a learning rate which is set to a very small value and $\mathcal{A}'$ is a slight modification of the analysis mapping $\mathcal{A}$ in (3.40), which has an interface with shape vector $\vec{x}$ instead of image sample $\vec{v}$,

$$
\hat{\vec{\theta}} = \mathcal{A}'_{LM_k}(\vec{x}) = \mathcal{K}^{-1}(F_{LM_k} Y_{LM_k}(\vec{x} - \vec{u}_x^{LM_k})).
\tag{6.11}
$$

The algorithm iterates equations (6.7) to (6.10) in this order until the mean-square error $\|\Delta \vec{x}_i\|^2$ becomes sufficiently small.

The equation (6.8) utilizes the shape-to-pose analysis mapping $\mathcal{A}'$ as an approximation of gradients of $\hat{\vec{\theta}}$ with respect to $\vec{x}_i$ at the current pose estimate $\vec{\theta}_i$.

Note that, in our case, such gradients $\frac{\Delta \vec{\theta}}{\Delta \vec{x}}$ are only available at the set of K discrete points (model centers) in the 3D angle space. Therefore, our method interpolates the gradients at an arbitrary point of the space from the K local gradient matrices. In this sense, it is not strictly a gradient-descent algorithm, for which each iteration step would have to precisely take the negative gradient direction assuring local minimization of the energy or error. We also do not know the analytical form of the gradient function required for such algorithms. The good local accuracy of the LPCMAP model shown in chapters 4 and 5, however, suggests that the approximation of the local gradients $\frac{\Delta \vec{\theta}}{\Delta \vec{x}}$ by the shape-to-pose mapping $\mathcal{A}'_{LM_k}(\Delta \vec{x}_i)$ should be valid. The error function is also expected to be smooth and monotonic at least locally so that a small interpolation error of gradients will not greatly influence performance of our method. Our choice of the initial condition should also decrease the chance of being trapped at a local minimum during the iterations as long as a sufficient number of local models are allocated in the 3D angle space and the input is close to one of their model centers.

6.4 Handling of the Self-Occlusion of Facial Landmarks

In the construction of our proposed models we have implicitly assumed that all the facial landmarks are visible regardless of the various 3D head poses. This assumption may be valid when the range of pose variations is kept narrow. However, it inevitably fails when the face is largely rotated because some landmarks can become invisible hidden behind other facial parts. This problem has been commonly called **self-occlusion** of landmarks. It is obviously important for our PWLM system to handle this problem because the system extends the LPCMAP model in order to cover a wider range of head poses, in which such a self-occlusion occurs naturally. This section introduces our solution to this problem.

6.4.1 Missing Data Problem

The self-occlusion of landmarks for certain facial views introduces uncertainties in shape vectors, our single-view representations of shape information. Remember that a shape vector consists of a set of 2D landmark locations in a facial image. When certain landmarks are self-occluded, data values for the corresponding vector components become unavailable. This can be termed either by saying that the length of the shape vectors becomes variable or that arbitrary components of the shape vectors are missing.

These uncertainties cause a great deal of trouble for statistical analysis. When the uncertainties are present, simple moments such as data mean and variance cannot be computed correctly in the same manner. Therefore, common statistical analysis methods based on such moments become erroneous. In the field of statistics, this problem is called the **missing data problem** (e.g., Little and Rubin [120]).

Our problem with landmark self-occlusion is indeed an example of this missing data problem. The missing data problem inevitably hurts our model because of the model's intrinsic statistical nature imposed by the data-drivenness criterion. More specifically, the uncertainties due to missing data hamper the principal component analysis (PCA) used to learn the shape subspace model. As described earlier, PCA involves a sample covariance matrix. Because the uncertainties interfere with the estimation of the covariance, the resulting principal components can be biased or can fail to correctly capture the pose variations. On processing facial images, most of the previous studies did not address the missing data problem. Even studies addressing head pose variation ignored the problem either by using a data set with a limited pose range or by treating it as a minor technical problem.

6.4.2 Sample Manipulation-Based Approaches

There are a number of previous studies addressing the missing data problem in the field of statistics. Strategies for solving this problem can be categorized into two approaches. One approach *manipulates* the data set such that it becomes complete and can be subjected to the statistical analyses such as PCA (e.g., Little and Rubin [120] and Belanche Buñoz [12]). The manipulation includes *deleting* unwanted samples and *filling in* missing vector components. The other approach *estimates* the covariance matrix directly from the available data. This approach utilizes probabilistic tools based on the **maximum likelihood estimation** (e.g., Little and Rubin [120], Ghahramani and Jordan [74], Arbuckle [6], Tresp and Hofmann [191], and Wothke [216]). This section introduces a number of techniques from the former approach based on sample manipulation.

The simplest method is *not* to use sample vectors with missing vector components for the model training by deleting training samples with any uncertainty. This strategy is called the **list-wise deletion** in the statistics literature. By throwing away the samples with missing data, this technique assures a fixed dimensionality of the data set so that a common method for computing a sample covariance can be applied. However, it is obviously suboptimal since it discards samples which may include properly measured vector components carrying valid information.

Another approach is to *fill in* each missing vector component by a certain concrete value which is estimated from the available data. This approach also assures the completeness of the data, which enables the PCA. Moreover, it utilizes all the valid measurements in the data set. Techniques using this approach are called

imputation in the statistics literature. There are two imputation methods which differ in their way of estimating the missing data. The **mean imputation** method fills in each missing vector component by the mean value computed from the available data for the component. Note that a value of each missing component becomes zero when a mean imputated data set is centered. The **regression imputation** method fills in each missing component by an estimated value regressed from other available vector components of the same vector. A regression function for each vector dimension with more than one missing data needs to be learned prior to the imputation process.

A problem of these method is due to the estimation error of the unknowns. The mean imputation treats the missing vector components to be silent by forcing them to be at the mean so that they are ignored for the covariance computation similar to another deletion method called **pair-wise deletion**. However, this treatment introduces an artificial bias which is not related to the true value of the missing vector component and causes an underestimation of the data covariance. The regression imputation depends on the accuracy of the regression function. When the function is accurately learned, it is expected to improve the mean imputation method. However, the regression functions may be hard to learn, depending on the missing data patterns. Their errors, due to a poor function fitting, impose unpredictable noise into the unknowns, which may result in poorly estimated covariances.

6.4.3 Extending the PWLM system for the Missing Data Problem

In this section, we describe an extension of the piecewise linear model (PWLM) system described in this chapter to handle the self-occlusion of the facial landmarks.

Definition of Landmark Visibility Information

In order to handle the missing data problem, visibility information of landmarks for each sample needs to be known prior to any type of our system's processing. Therefore, this visibility information is assumed to be a part of training and test samples and to be visually measured. It is readily possible to acquire such visibility information since a landmark finder system based on a tracking can detect landmarks as missing when it processes a sample.

We introduce a new notation which represents the visibility information as part of the training and test samples. Let an N-component binary-valued vector

$o\vec{}^m$ represent the landmark visibility information of a facial image sample $v\vec{}^m$,

$$\vec{o}^m = (o_1^m, .., o_n^m, .., o_N^m), \text{ where } o_n^m = \begin{cases} 1 & \text{if landmark } n \text{ is visible} \\ 0 & \text{if landmark } n \text{ is occluded} \end{cases} \quad (6.12)$$

We call the $o\vec{}^m$ an **occlusion vector** of a sample m.

For the training samples of the PWLM system, each local model LM_k is now trained with a set of triples,

$$\{(\vec{v}^1, \vec{\theta}^1, \vec{o}^1), .., (\vec{v}^m, \vec{\theta}^m, \vec{o}^n), .., (\vec{v}^{M_k}, \vec{\theta}^{M_k}, \vec{o}^{M_k})\}, \quad (6.13)$$

where M_k is the number of training triples for a local model LM_k. We also extend the test samples from pairs to triples in the same manner.

Missing Data Structure of Shape and Texture Vectors

Upon the self-occlusion of some landmarks in a facial image sample $\vec{v}^m$, the corresponding components of the occlusion vector $\vec{o}^n$ are set to zero. When the image sample is subjected to the operators $\mathcal{D}_x$ and $\mathcal{D}_j$ in (3.10) for decomposing the shape and texture vectors, as described in section 3.3.1, the occlusion vector provides information of which shape and texture vector components are uncertain due to self-occlusion but it does not provide any information of what value can be assigned to the components.

Therefore, the components of the shape vector $\vec{x}^m$ that correspond to the missing landmarks are considered as *unknown*. For example, a hypothetical shape vector of three 2D landmarks $(1, 0, 2, 0, 1, 2)$ becomes $(1, 0, 2, 0, ?, ?)$ when the third landmark is missing. Moreover, Gabor jets which serve as the local texture vectors in our model cannot be computed without explicit landmark locations. Therefore, a local texture vector $\vec{j}^{m,n}$ for a missing landmark n becomes unavailable, too. Since the texture vector is localized at each landmark, the existence of missing landmarks poses only missing *samples* not missing *vector components* of a sample.

Shape and Texture Decomposition with Missing Data

Next, we describe how to apply the methods for handling the missing data described in section 6.4.2. The list-wise deletion method does not require any modification of the structure of the PWLM system. A set of training occlusion vectors are first checked if there are samples with any missing shape vector components. The training triples with missing shape vector components found by this process are then discarded prior to the model training.

The two imputation methods can be adapted to our PWLM system by introducing a filtering operator which imputes or fills in the missing shape vector components. For a complete vector case, an image sample $\bar{v}^m$ is first subjected to the shape decomposition operator $\mathcal{D}_x$, resulting in a $2N$-component shape vector $\bar{x}^m$ as shown in the equation (3.10). When there is landmark self-occlusion, we assume that this operator provides a shape vector $\bar{x}^m$ whose missing vector components according to the corresponding occlusion vector $\bar{o}^m$ get assigned arbitrary values. Therefore, this operation results in a set of shape vectors with a fixed dimensionality but with uncertain values in the missing components.

Next, the shape vector $\bar{x}^m$ is subjected to an imputation filter $\xi()$ for filling in the missing vector components,

$$\bar{x}'^m = \xi(\bar{x}^m, \bar{o}^m, \bar{a}^m) = \begin{cases} x'^m_n = x^m_n & \text{if } o^m_{\lfloor \frac{n}{2} \rfloor} = 1 \\ x'^m_n = a^m_n & \text{if } o^m_{\lfloor \frac{n}{2} \rfloor} = 0 \end{cases}, \qquad (6.14)$$

where the $2N$-component vector $\bar{x}'^m$ denotes a resulting imputated shape vector and a^m_n denotes a missing component estimate for a landmark $\lfloor \frac{n}{2} \rfloor$ of a sample m. [1]

For the mean imputation, the missing component estimate a^m_n is given by a mean of all the available vector components from the M_k numbers of the training samples for each local model LM_k,

$$a^m_n = u'_n = \frac{1}{\sum_{m=1}^{M_k} o^m_{\lfloor \frac{n}{2} \rfloor}} \sum_{m=1}^{M_k} x^m_n \cdot o^m_{\lfloor \frac{n}{2} \rfloor}. \qquad (6.15)$$

For the regression imputation, the a^m_n is estimated by a function which regresses a missing vector component x^m_n from the rest of the vector components $\{x^m_{\bar{n}}\}$ in the same sample,

$$a^m_n = \hat{x^m_n} = \zeta_n(\{x^m_{\bar{n}}\}). \qquad (6.16)$$

The following defines a linear regression function for a vector dimension $\acute{n}$ which includes at least one missing vector component,

$$\begin{aligned} x^m_{\acute{n}} = \zeta_{\acute{n}}(\{x^m_{\bar{n}}\}) = \textstyle\sum_{n \in \{\bar{n}\}} w^{\acute{n}}_n \cdot x^m_n, \text{ where} \\ \acute{n} \in \{n | n \in \{1, .., 2N\}, \exists m o^m_{\lfloor \frac{n}{2} \rfloor} = 0\}, \\ \bar{n} \in \{n | n \in \{1, .., 2N\}, n \neq \acute{n}\}. \end{aligned} \qquad (6.17)$$

For all the vector dimensions with missing components $\{\acute{n}\}$, we prepare a set of the regression functions $\{\zeta_{\acute{n}}\}$ by learning the regression coefficients $\{\bar{w}^{\acute{n}}\}$

---

[1]Note that the index n in the equation (6.14) covers the $2N$-components shape vector. Therefore $\lfloor \frac{n}{2} \rfloor$ correctly indicates a landmark in N-component occlusion vector.

from all the pairs $\{(x_{\hat{n}}^m, \{x_{\hat{n}}^m\})\}$ available from the training samples for a local model LM_k. When more than one missing component are presented in any single shape vector, however, this formulation of the regression function in (6.17) becomes problematic because it introduces uncertainties to the right-hand-side of the equation. This problem can be solved by finding a subset of $\{\bar{n}\}$, in which all the samples are complete without any missing vector components,

$$\{n|n \in \{\bar{n}\}, \forall mo_{\lfloor\frac{n}{2}\rfloor}^m = 1\},$$

and use the subset, instead of the $\{\bar{n}\}$, to train the regression functions. After applying the filtering operator (6.14), both training and test shape vectors can be treated as complete $2N$-component vectors without uncertainties. Therefore, the rest of our models' procedures related to the shape vectors remain the same.

A case for texture vector is less harmful than the case for shape. This is because the texture vectors are *local* while the shape vectors are *global*. While it makes the *components* of shape vectors uncertain, the landmark self-occlusion makes the *entire* local texture vectors uncertain so that the length of texture vectors remains a constant. Therefore, a texture model at a landmark can be correctly learned simply by training it with all the available local training texture vectors at the landmark, disregarding the unavailable vectors due to the self-occlusion. The procedure to acquire the texture models by PCA needs only a slight modification to allow the different number of training samples at different landmarks. When a very large range of head rotations is considered, however, some landmarks can be invisible throughout the entire training samples for a local model. Such a case can be handled by allowing the local model not to construct texture models at the entirely missing landmarks. The rest of procedures of our models related to the texture information remain the same.

6.5 Discussion

In this chapter, we propose the piecewise linear model (PWLM) system which extends the LPCMAP model in order to mitigate its pose range limitation. The system interpolates a set of local linear models by a weighted averaging of local models' outputs such as locally estimated poses and synthesized shapes and textures. For computing the weights for each local model, we utilize a normalized Gaussian function in 3D angle space. An iterative gradient-descent algorithm is also introduced for realizing a pose estimation process by our PWLM system without ground-truth pose information.

In chapters 4 and 5, we showed that our usage of linear systems in the LPCMAP model gives the benefit of good generalization, enabling a model to learn a transformation from a small number of samples which smoothly cover the parameter space. However, the same design choice strictly limits the range of head poses in which our linear model can perform accurately. This is an unbearable restriction to our system since it violates our design philosophy: data-drivenness and flexibility, discussed in the introduction. The PWLM system, extending the LPCMAP model, offers a systematic solution to this problem while maintaining the linearity of our system so that the aforementioned benefit of a linear system still remains valid. The feasibility of this extension will be empirically investigated by a series of numerical experiments in the next chapter.

The missing data problem due to the self-occlusion is an innate consequence of 3D head pose variation. The performance of the sample manipulation-based approaches described in this chapter can, however, be unstable, depending on the frequency and pattern of the missing shape vector components in training samples. In general, they perform well when the number of missing components is small and the components are missing at random. In our case it is assumed that the number of missing shape vector components is relatively small. This is because the LPCMAP model used as a local model of the PWLM system is responsible only within a small pose range in which most samples share the similar landmark visibility configuration. Therefore, within a local model, the number of missing components are kept small with respect to the total number of the shape vector components. Our interest also focuses on analyzing a face, not a complete 3D head. Since the back of a head possesses less information than the frontal face, we may naturally confine the 3D pose range so that the face is fairly visible.

Note that our choice of representing the facial shape by using a distribution of sparse landmarks instead of dense pixel correspondences helps to maintain the number of missing shape vector components. This makes sample manipulation-based methods applicable which can handle only a small number of missing components. If a dense correspondence field is used as the single-view representation such as the systems by Vetter and Beymer, the number of missing components will be much larger than one based on a sparse point-distribution for the same pose range. The simple imputation methods may not be able to handle the missing data problem in those systems.

There are other methods for statistically analyzing data with missing components. For example, Little and Rubin demonstrated an EM algorithm based on a maximum likelihood which estimates sample moments from data sets with missing components more accurately than the imputation methods when the number of missing components are larger. Their study provides a theoretical framework which gives us useful insights. However an implementation of the algorithm is often complicated and its estimation process is time-consuming. In our study, we favor the sample manipulation-based method because of its simplicity. When the number of self-occluded landmarks is small, these sample manipulation-based methods will allow PCA to correctly extract the 3D rotation modes in the shape vectors with missing components. The validation of these methods will be sought by numerical experiments described in the next chapter.

Chapter 7

Numerical Evaluation of the Piecewise Linear Model System

In this chapter, we empirically evaluate the performance of the piecewise linear model (PWLM) system described in chapter 6. The PWLM system is extended from the LPCMAP model using the piecewise linear model approach in order to cover a wider range of pose variations than can be covered by the single LPCMAP model described in chapter 3. We conducted a series of numerical experiments with two different types of data set for assessing the feasibility of this system. This chapter describes the results of these experiments.

7.1 Numerical Experiments with Artificial Data

In this section, we present results of numerical experiments of the PWLM system with artificially created simple data. By using simple and controlled data we seek an experimental proof of the correctness of our PWLM approach and investigate the optimal setting of a PWLM system for maximizing its performance.

7.1.1 Data Set

We generated sets of artificial shape representations consisting of 2D projections of 25 landmarks pasted onto a rotating 3D unit sphere, using the same method described in section 4.1.1. Seven different sets of training samples are created for 7 model centers which deviate ± 40 degrees from the origin along one rotation axis. Figure 7.1 displays 3D pose distributions of these 7 training sample sets with the 7 centers, $(0,0,0), (\pm 40,0,0), (0,\pm 40,0)$, and $(0,0,\pm 40)$. Note that, instead of the sphere with dots, facial images whose poses correspond to these 7 model centers are shown in the figure in order to intuitively describe the pose distribution. Each

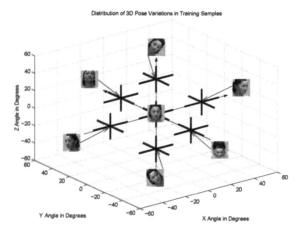

Distribution of 3D Pose Variations in Training Samples

Figure 7.1: Distributions of 3D Pose Variations for PWLM Training Samples

sample set includes 403 samples which are rotated around its model center within ±15 degrees from the center for each axis. The figure only shows samples rotated along one axis at a time, although samples rotated along more than one axis are also included in each set. We construct 7 local LPCMAP models with these 7 training sample sets.

We also generated a set of test samples whose 3D poses are not presented in the above training samples. Figure 7.2 displays the 2D projection of 3D pose distributions of the 804 test samples. In this figure, both training (thick lines) and test (thin lines) samples in the 3D angle space are projected onto the x-y plane. Note that some test samples are outside of the 7 local clusters of the training sets while the other are within one of these clusters. Therefore, these test samples include various topological relations in the space between inputs and local linear models. The pose distribution of the test samples ranges between ±50 degrees from the origin of the 3D angle space for each axis.

For both the training and test samples, 3D rotation angles of each sample are given by the rotation angles of the unit sphere. The self-occlusion of landmarks is artificially simulated by introducing an occluding plane, $z = c$ (c: constant, $\|c\| \leq 1$), which is parallel to the image plane of a view with the initial frontal pose. A landmark whose corresponding 3D point on the unit sphere is below the occluding plane is considered as occluded.

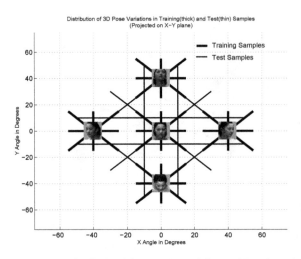

Figure 7.2: 3D Pose Distributions for PWLM Training and Test Samples in 2D

7.1.2 Experimental Results

This section presents results of our numerical experiments with the artificial shape representations described in the previous section. We investigate the correctness of our PWLM system, the optimal σ_k of our weight function, the feasibility of the missing data handling, and the feasibility of the pose estimation process by the gradient-descent algorithm in this section.

Evaluation of the PWLM System

In this section, we evaluate the accuracy and generalization capability of pose estimation and shape synthesis processes of the PWLM system using settings similar to those of the previous experiments, section 4.1. The accuracy and generalization tests used in this section are the same as the ones used in section 4.2; the accuracy test uses the training samples as test samples while the generalization test uses separate test samples described in the previous section. For the accuracy test, in order to show the correctness of our system, we used the type C (2nd-order) trigonometric functional transformation $\mathcal{K}$ which gave perfect accuracy in our previous experiments as shown in figure 4.1 For the generalization test, we used the type B (1st-order) trigonometric functional transformation which was shown to give the best balance between the LPCMAP model's accuracy and generalization

146

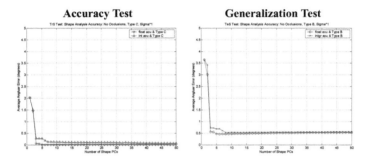

Accuracy Test   **Generalization Test**

Figure 7.3: Accuracy and Generalization Tests of Pose Estimation by the PWLM System with Toy Data

capability to unknown poses. For both tests, we compared two data-precision settings: float and integer accuracy of the shape representations (described HIGH and LOW in section 4.1, respectively). The former gives the most accurate information possible for the correctness evaluation, while the latter enables evaluations in more realistic scenarios. All landmarks are considered to be visible by setting the occluding plane parameter c to -1.

Figure 7.3 shows results of the accuracy and generalization tests for the pose estimation process of the PWLM system. In both plots of this figure, average angular errors in degrees between the test and estimated poses are plotted against 50 different sizes of the shape model. For the accuracy test, the average errors of an PWLM system with a type C transformation $\mathcal{K}$ and float accuracy became zero degrees when more than 5 shape PCs are included in the shape model. This result indicates the correctness of our PWLM system. For the generalization test, the more realistic case with type B $\mathcal{K}$ and integer accuracy resulted in about 0.5 degrees average errors when more than 8 shape PCs are included. This result is very satisfactory supporting a high precision of our system even for this most difficult test case with unknown poses. The accuracy of our PWLM system is significantly improved relative to the similar test for the single LPCMAP model, shown in figure 4.6. This result also shows our system's generalization capability to unknown poses. In the results of both tests, the difference of the errors between the float and integer cases was very small. This indicates the robustness of our system against small measurement errors in landmark locations. The errors reached their minimum with 5 to 8 shape PCs. This agrees with our similar finding from the experiments of the single LPCMAP model in section 4.1.

Figure 7.4 shows results of the accuracy and generalization tests for the shape synthesis process of the PWLM system. Similar to figure 7.3, average landmark

147

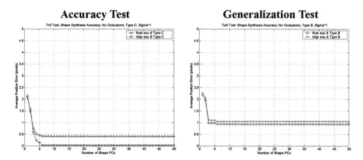

Accuracy Test	Generalization Test

Figure 7.4: Accuracy and Generalization Tests of Shape Synthesis by the PWLM System with Toy Data

position errors in pixels between the test and synthesized shape representations are plotted against the 50 different shape model sizes in this figure. For the accuracy test, the average errors of an PWLM system with a type C $\mathcal{K}$ and float accuracy became very close to zero pixels when more than 6 shape PCs are included. This result also supports the correctness of our PWLM system. For the generalization test, the more realistic case, which is the same for the pose estimation process, resulted in about 1.1 average error in pixels when more than 6 shape PCs are included. As discussed in section 4.1, this is still acceptably accurate because the landmark locations estimated in the facial image only possess the pixel-level precision. Moreover, the average errors in this figure are also improved relative to the similar test for the single LPCMAP model, shown in figure 4.3. This modest improvement is perhaps due to the fact that samples in this test contain a much wider range of pose variation (± 55 degrees) than those used in section 4.1 (± 30 degrees). The results also showed that the difference of the pixel errors between the float and integer cases was very small. This again indicates our system's robustness against a small measurement errors in the landmark locations.

Evaluation of the Weight Function

Next, we evaluate different sizes of the Gaussian of our weight function. As mentioned earlier, the weight function (6.4) makes the localization of the linear models possible. The range of which each local model is responsible for in the 3D angle space is controlled by a Gaussian-width parameter σ_k in this function. The experimental results in chapter 4 showed that the effective range of our single LPCMAP model is about ± 15 degrees. Obviously, our aim here is to find a right value of σ_k which aligns the width of the Gaussian to the effective pose range of our local

148

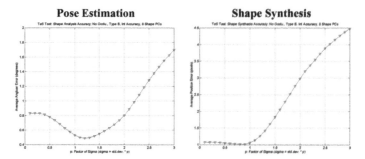

Pose Estimation   **Shape Synthesis**

Figure 7.5: Different Sigma of the Weight Function for Pose Estimation and Shape Synthesis

linear models. In section 6.2, we have proposed the σ_k as a function of the sample standard deviation shown in (6.5). In this formulation, the σ_k is parameterized by a positive scalar factor p. We evaluate our system's errors with different p values in order to find the optimal σ_k. In this section, we conduct only the generalization tests and all landmarks are again considered visible.

Figure 7.5 shows results of the generalization test for pose estimation and shape synthesis processes of our PWLM system with the type B transformation $\mathcal{K}$, integer accuracy, and 8 shape PCs. The average angular and position errors in the figure are plotted against the different values of p. For the pose estimation and the shape synthesis, the minimum error was reached when σ_k was slightly larger than the sample standard deviation ($p = 1.2$) and when σ_k was slightly smaller than the sample standard deviation ($p = 0.9$), respectively.

These results suggest that the optimal balance between the accuracy and generalization capability of our PWLM system is achieved when we set σ_k by the sample standard deviation itself ($p = 1$). The errors with a large p increase rapidly for both cases. This agrees with our findings about the accuracy of the single LPCMAP model discussed in section 4.3. The error curves in both figures are smooth. This suggests that a slight variation of the σ_k value does not greatly influence the system's accuracy.

Evaluation of the Landmark Self-Occlusion Handling

Next, we numerically evaluate the performance of the PWLM system when some landmarks in the training and test samples are occluded. For this evaluation, the trigonometric functional transformation $\mathcal{K}$ was fixed to the type B and only integer accuracy was used. According to the result in the previous section, σ_k was set by

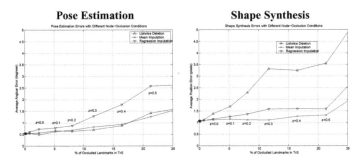

Figure 7.6: Comparison of the Three Methods for Handling the Occlusion

the sample standard deviation of the 3D angle vectors for each local model LM_k by setting p in the equation (6.5) to 1. We conducted only the generalization tests.

First, we compare the three sample manipulation-based methods for handling the occlusion of landmarks, introduced in section 6.4. Figure 7.6 compares the pose generalization errors of the pose estimation and shape synthesis processes of the PWLM system in different conditions of the landmark occlusion. Average angular and position errors are plotted against the percentages of the occluded landmarks in the training samples. As described in section 7.1.1, the frequency of the occlusion is parameterized by a constant parameter c which is a depth of the occluding plane $z = c$. These occluding plane parameters are also shown in the figure for some data points. The up-triangles, crosses, and down-triangles denote the errors by the system with the *list-wise deletion*, *mean imputation*, and *regression imputation* methods, respectively. A shape model with the first 20 PCs are used in each case.

For the pose estimation process, the errors by the list-wise deletion and mean imputation behaved similarly in that they were not greatly influenced by an increase of the occlusion occurrences, while the errors by the regression imputation were largely worsened as the occurrence percentage increased. For the shape synthesis process, the errors by the mean imputation were nearly constant against the various occlusion occurrences. The errors by the regression imputation also behaved well but distinctively worse than those by the mean imputation, while the errors by the list-wise deletion were rapidly aggravated as the occurrence percentage increased. The results show that the mean imputation method performed best for both pose estimation and shape synthesis processes. The error increase of this method was relatively slow against an increase of the occlusion occurrences, which is a favorable characteristic concerning handling of missing data. This graceful decrease of the accuracy was observed when the percentage of occluded

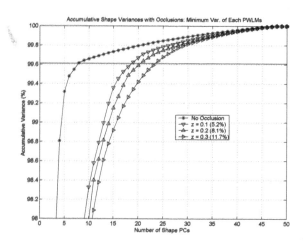

Figure 7.7: Effects of the Occlusion in Accumulated Shape Variances

landmarks was less than roughly 20%. The regression imputation method did not perform well for the pose estimation process. This is perhaps due to a suboptimal fitting of the linear regression functions as discussed in section 6.4.2. On the other hand, the list-wise deletion method performed poorly for the shape synthesis process. Since the method pessimistically discards samples with any missing vector components which are often samples with a large 3D rotation, the PWLM system with this method naturally fails to capture the full pose variation, which perhaps leads to this poor performance.

Next, we investigate the extent to which the missing data influences the performance of the shape subspace model of our system. In chapter 4, we demonstrated that a relatively small number of shape PCs are enough to cover most of the data variance caused by 3D head pose variation, as shown in figure 4.12. A shape subspace model spanned by only 3 PCs cannot cover the complete range of pose variations because the curve-linear shape variation along each of the 3 rotation dimensions is only rendered by a larger number of shape PCs. Nonetheless, the first 8 PCs, including ones that code intuitively interpretable variations such as scaling and stretching, are able to describe the complete range of pose variations without ambiguities. However, missing data due to the occlusion of landmarks cause difficulty in the construction of the shape subspace model by PCA, as described in section 6.4. The artificial biases introduced by the sample manipulation-based method for missing data may provide a negative influence to the linear separation

151

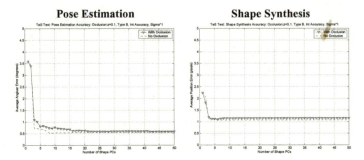

Pose Estimation **Shape Synthesis**

Figure 7.8: Shape Processing Accuracies with and without the Occlusion

process of the 3D pose variation by PCA.

Figure 7.7 shows how the accumulated variance of a shape subspace model is influenced by the presence of the occlusion of landmarks. The figure plots the percentages of the accumulated variances against the 50 different shape model sizes for 4 different conditions of the occlusion, $z = $ -1, 0.1, 0.2, and 0.3. These values of the occluding plane parameter c correspond to 0% (no occlusion), 5.2%, 8.1%, and 11.7% of landmarks missing from the total training samples, respectively. The shape model which results in the least accumulative variance among the 7 local models of the PWLM system is used for this analysis. The missing vector components are filled in by the mean imputation method according to the result of the previous section.

When occlusion was not considered (denoted by a plot with star marks), the first 8 shape PCs covered 99.6% of the total variance presented in the training samples. This result agrees with our previous findings in chapter 4. When some landmarks were occluded, however, more than 8 PCs were needed to cover the same amount of data variance. The first 19, 21, and 24 PCs were needed to cover the variance when 5%, 8%, and 12% of the landmarks were occluded, respectively. These results indicate that the handling of the missing data problem by the mean imputation method does introduce artificial biases in the data statistics. These artificial biases are then coded in the additional PCs, increasing the number of PCs required to cover the full pose variations.

Lastly, we investigate how the above artificial biases introduced by our missing data handling influence the accuracy of the PWLM system. Figure 7.8 compares the pose generalization errors of the pose estimation and shape synthesis processes of the PWLM system with and without the occlusion of landmarks. Average angular and position errors are plotted against the 50 different shape model sizes. In the figure, the down-triangles denote the errors by the PWLM system whose missing data is handled by the mean imputation method. The occluding plane parameter c is set to 0.1, resulting in 5% of landmarks missing. This occlusion percentage is similar to that of the training samples derived from the ATR 3D face database described in chapter 5. On the other hand, the broken lines denote the errors without any occlusion by setting the occluding plane parameter c to -1.0. For the pose estimation, the minimum error of 0.5 degrees was reached for the no occlusion case when the first 8 PCs were included to the shape model. When the occlusion was imposed, the system with the first 8 PCs resulted in 0.7 degrees error. The errors with the occlusion continued to decrease slightly by adding more shape PCs to the model. The minimum error of 0.6 degrees was reached when roughly 20 shape PCs were included, which agrees with our findings in the previous section. For the shape synthesis, the first 6 shape PCs resulted in the minimum error of 1.1 pixels, both with and without occlusion. By adding further PCs, the errors with the occlusion increased slightly to 1.2 pixels. For both processes, the error differences with and without occlusion were very small. This supports the feasibility of our missing data handling by the mean imputation method. For optimal accuracy, however, the first 20 PCs rather than 8 were required.

Evaluation of the Pose Estimation by Gradient-Descent

In the previous three evaluations, we used the pose estimation process defined in (6.2) with the ground-truth 3D angle vectors. In section 6.3, we have argued that this process is infeasible because the right-hand-side of the weight function includes the estimated 3D angles which should not be available as input. Section 6.3 has introduced a gradient-descent algorithm which overcomes this shortcoming. The purpose of this section is to numerically evaluate the feasibility of this gradient-descent pose estimation and shape synthesis. For this purpose, we conducted only generalization tests. According to the results in the previous sections, the trigonometric functional transformation $\mathcal{K}$ was fixed to the type B and only integer accuracy was used for this evaluation. σ_k was also made equal to the sample standard deviation of the 3D angle vectors for each local model LM_k by setting p in the equation (6.5) to 1. The occluding plane parameter c was set to 0.1, resulting in 5% missing components in the training sample vectors. The mean imputation method (equations (6.14) and (6.15)) described in section 6.4.3 was used for handling the missing components. We iterated the gradient-descent loop 500 times and set the learning rate η to 0.01 throughout the following experiments.

The left plot of figure 7.9 shows results of the generalization tests for the two different pose estimation processes of our PWLM system. The average angular errors for the different shape model sizes are plotted by a dotted line for the one-shot system in (6.2) and by a solid line with triangles for the gradient-descent iterative system. The errors for the one-shot and gradient-descent systems were

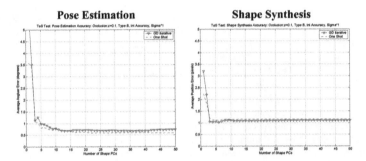

| Pose Estimation | Shape Synthesis |

Figure 7.9: Pose Estimation and Shape Synthesis Accuracy by Gradient Descent PWLM

0.7 and 0.8 degrees with the first 8 shape PCs, and 0.6 and 0.7 degrees with the first 20 PCs, respectively. This result shows that the accuracy of our PWLM system is slightly decreased in the gradient-descent system. However, the average error was still acceptable which is much lower than 1 degree, and the error difference between the two systems was at most 0.1 degrees.

The right plot of figure 7.9 shows results of the generalization tests for the two shape synthesis processes of our PWLM system. Because the gradient-descent pose estimation process simultaneously estimates the angle and shape vectors at each iteration step, the algorithm can also be seen as an iterative shape synthesis process. Although the original shape synthesis process defined in (6.3) is valid without modification, it gives an alternative way to synthesize a shape from 3D head angles. In this plot, the average position errors for the different shape model sizes are also plotted by a dotted line for the one-shot system in (6.3) and by a solid line with triangles for the gradient-descent system. The errors for the one-shot and gradient-descent systems were 1.1 and 1.0 pixels with the first 6 shape PCs, and 1.2 and 1.1 pixels with the first 20 PCs, respectively. Note that the accuracy of the gradient-descent system is slightly better than the one-shot system. These results, which show only a small error difference between the two systems, support the feasibility of the gradient-descent algorithm of our PWLM system, even with missing shape vector components due to the occlusion of landmarks.

154

7.2 Numerical Experiments with 3D Cyberware Scanner Data

In this section, we evaluate the PWLM system with the samples derived from the 3D facial data used in section 5.3. Our aim is to numerically test the performance of our system with more realistic data and with more individuals. For comparison, we used all the training samples for local models to construct also a single LPCMAP model and compare its performance with the PWLM system for different tasks.

7.2.1 Data Set

In these experiments, we use 2D samples generated from 3D facial models randomly picked from the ATR-Database of which examples are shown in figure 5.7. The same pose distributions used in the previous section (see figures 7.1 and 7.2 for the sketches of the distributions) are also used to create 7 sets of the training samples for the 7 different model centers and a set of test samples, for the 20 individuals. Therefore, for each individual, there are 2821 training and 804 test samples. Each training set includes 403 samples whose poses are within a range of ± 15 degrees around each model center. The test samples cover a pose range of ± 50 degrees around the origin of the 3D angle space. For each sample, the 3D head angles and the 20 facial landmarks defined in figure 4.9 are directly derived from the explicit rotation of the 3D facial models by manner described in section 4.2.1. The self-occlusion information is also derived from the rendering system and stored in the occlusion vectors described in section 6.4.3.

7.2.2 Systems

We built a **PWLM system** which consists of 7 local models with the training samples described in the previous section. 20 PWLM systems are trained separately for the 20 different individuals. For comparison, we construct a single LPCMAP system which is trained with all the 2821 training samples available for a single person. This system, therefore, lets a single model globally capture the wide range of the pose variations between ± 55 degrees along each axis, while the PWLM system allocates 7 local models to cover the same pose range. In order to prove the effectiveness of our PWLM system for solving the pose range limitation problem discussed in section 4.3, we need to show that the PWLM system largely improves the performance of this LPCMAP system when tested by samples with large pose variations. Hereafter, we refer to this single LPCMAP system as **GLOBAL system**. Figure 7.10 illustrates the PWLM and GLOBAL systems

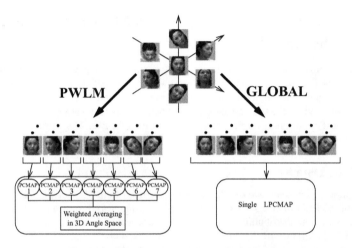

Figure 7.10: Sketches of PWLM and GLOBAL Systems

schematically.

For both the PWLM and GLOBAL systems, the type B transformation $\mathcal{K}$ is used. For the PWLM system, σ_k is set equal to the sample standard deviation according to our previous results with artificial data. In order to consider more realistic scenarios, the pose processing part of the PWLM system utilizes gradient-descent instead of the simple one-shot process in (6.2). In the gradient-descent, η is set to 0.01 and 500 iterations are performed for each test sample.

In the training data set used in this section, 5 to 10% of the total number of landmarks were self-occluded in each local training set. According to the previous results with artificial data, we use the mean imputation method described in section 6.4 for handling missing data due to self-occlusion. Using this data, we compared the three missing data handling methods the same way as illustrated in figure 7.6. Also in this pilot study the mean imputation method performed best, confirming our finding in section 7.1.2.

7.2.3 Analysis and Synthesis Performance

In this section, we numerically evaluate the analysis and synthesis processes of the PWLM system. We compare the performance of the PWLM and GLOBAL systems by the accuracy and generalization tests in the same manner as in the previous chapters. The same tests for the PWLM and GLOBAL systems are con-

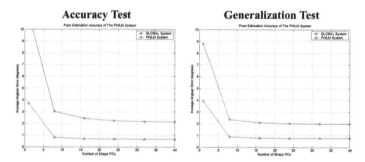

Accuracy Test

Generalization Test

Figure 7.11: Pose Estimation Errors of the PWLM System

ducted for the 20 individuals. The errors and similarities for each test are averaged over these 20 people.

Pose Analysis

Figure 7.11 shows results of the accuracy and generalization tests for the analysis process of our systems. Average angular errors of pose estimates by the PWLM and GLOBAL systems for 6 different sizes of the shape model (1,8,16,24,32,40) are plotted by up-triangles and down-triangles, respectively. For the accuracy test, the average errors with the 8 shape PCs for the PWLM and GLOBAL systems were 0.8 and 3.0 degrees, respectively. Standard deviation of the errors and the worst error were 0.6 and 5.6 degrees for the PWLM system and 2.4 and 18.9 degrees for the GLOBAL system. For the generalization test, the errors for the same systems were 0.9 and 2.4 degrees. The standard deviation and the worst error were 0.6 and 4.5 degrees for the PWLM system and 1.4 and 10.2 degrees for the GLOBAL system. The results for both tests show that the PWLM system largely decreases the average error of the GLOBAL system, indicating that the PWLM system greatly improves the pose estimation accuracy. The average errors of the PWLM system were very similar between the accuracy and generalization tests. This result suggests that the PWLM system successfully maintains good generalization capability to unknown poses. In comparison to the similar test with artificial data shown in figure 7.9, the errors of the PWLM system was slightly increased with more realistic facial data. This slight decrease in accuracy is due to the inhomogeneous depth variations at different landmarks which are intrinsic properties of faces. That the increase of the error is small indicates that these variational factors in the realistic data do not greatly influence the performance of our systems. For the GLOBAL system, the average errors for the generalization

157

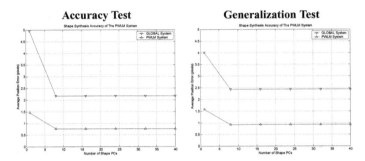

Accuracy Test **Generalization Test**

Figure 7.12: Shape Synthesis Errors of the PWLM System

test were lower than that for the accuracy test. This is perhaps due to the fact that the training samples include a wider range of pose variations (± 55 degrees) than the test samples (± 50 degrees). This again indicates that the LPCMAP model is very sensitive to the pose range in samples. The results also show that our systems with the first 8 PCs do not reach the minimum error. This is due to the missing data problem described in section 7.1.

Shape Synthesis

Figure 7.12 shows results of the accuracy and generalization tests for the shape synthesis process of our systems. Average position errors of synthesized shapes in pixels are plotted for the 6 different sizes of the PWLM and GLOBAL systems. The average errors of both systems in both tests reached their minimum with the first 8 shape PCs. For the accuracy test, the average errors with the 8 PCs were 0.8 and 2.2 pixels for the PWLM and GLOBAL systems, respectively. Standard deviation of the errors and the worst error were 0.4 and 3.0 pixels for the PWLM system and 1.2 and 7.6 pixels for the GLOBAL system. For the generalization test, the errors were 0.9 and 2.4 pixels for the two systems, respectively. The standard deviation and the worst error were 0.4 and 2.7 pixels for the PWLM system and 0.7 and 5.6 pixels for the GLOBAL system. Again, the PWLM system greatly improved the accuracy over the GLOBAL system. The difference of errors by the PWLM system between the accuracy and generalization tests were again small, indicating good generalization capability of the PWLM system to unknown poses. In comparison to a similar test with artificial data shown in figure 7.9, the errors of the PWLM system with the more realistic facial data was equivalent to those with artificial data. This result again indicates that the aforementioned variational factors in the realistic data do not greatly influence the performance of

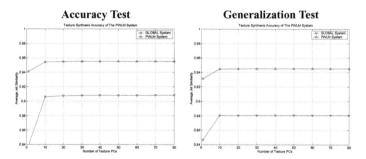

Accuracy Test

Generalization Test

Figure 7.13: Texture Synthesis Similarities of the PWLM System

our systems. The error decrease of the GLOBAL system in the generalization tests observed for our pose analysis experiments was not found in these experiments. The influence of the missing data problem was not observed in this case.

Texture Synthesis

Figure 7.13 shows results of the accuracy and generalization tests for the texture synthesis process of our systems. Average jet similarities of synthesized texture by the PWLM and GLOBAL systems are plotted by up-triangles and down-triangles, respectively. These average similarities are computed for 9 different sizes of the texture model (1,10,20,30,40,50,60,70,80) for each case. These similarities reached their maximum with the first 20 texture PCs. For the accuracy test, the average similarity value with the 20 PCs was 0.955 and 0.91 for the PWLM and GLOBAL systems, respectively. Standard deviation of the similarities and the worst similarity value were 0.03 and 0.81 for the PWLM system and 0.04 and 0.73 for the GLOBAL system. For the generalization test, the similarity value was 0.945 and 0.88 for the PWLM and GLOBAL systems, respectively. The standard deviation and the worst similarity value were 0.03 and 0.82 for the PWLM system and 0.03 and 0.77 for the GLOBAL system. See figure 4.24 for a reference of the similarity value range. Again, the PWLM system greatly improved the accuracy of the GLOBAL system especially for the generalization tests, suggesting the effectiveness of the system. The similarity difference between the accuracy and generalization tests of the PWLM system was again small, indicating good generalization of the PWLM system to unknown poses.

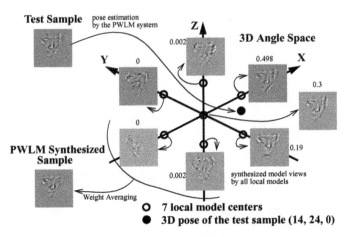

Figure 7.14: An Example of Sample Synthesis by PWLM System

7.2.4 Synthesized Samples

In this section, we qualitatively evaluate reconstructed images or model views of synthesized samples by the PWLM system. The same data and system settings in the previous error analysis are also used in this section. In order to reconstruct model views from synthesized samples, we used the same reconstruction method used in section 4.2.4.

Figure 7.14 illustrates the analysis-synthesis chain of our PWLM system. A test sample shown in the top-left corner of the figure is first subjected to the analysis process of the system, resulting in a 3D pose estimate denoted by a black dot. This estimate is then used as an input of the sample (shape and texture) synthesis processes by 7 local models whose centers are denoted by circles. Model views of these 7 locally synthesized samples are shown close to each model center in the figure. These samples are then subjected to a weighted averaging process with weights based on the distance of the estimated test pose and each model center. Numbers shown next to the local model views denote the weights. This weighted averaging results in a final synthesized sample shown in the bottom-left corner of the figure. Note that the local model views become more distorted as their model centers become farther from the input pose. This is because of the pose range limitation of local linear models. However, these largely distorted local samples do not greatly influence quality of the final sample because their contribution is strongly inhibited by very low weight values.

160

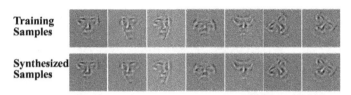

Figure 7.15: Synthesized Training Samples by PWLM System

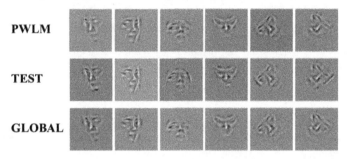

Figure 7.16: Synthesized Test Samples by PWLM and GLOBAL Systems (Large Angle)

Figure 7.15 displays model views of the 7 synthesized training samples by our PWLM system. The first and second rows of the figure show model views of the training samples used as tests and their corresponding synthesized samples, respectively. A sample of the left most column is with a frontal pose which corresponds to the origin of the 3D angle space. The rest of samples in this figure are with head poses which are rotated ±45 degrees along only one axis. As mentioned in section 4.2.4, the model view is not a perfect reconstruction of the original image because of the information loss by the coarse landmark and frequency samplings. However, this figure shows that the model views of the synthesized samples by our PWLM system are almost identical to their corresponding test samples, indicating the accuracy of the PWLM system. Note also that the PWLM system accurately covers a much wider pose range (±45 degrees) than that single LPCMAP model can deal with. For comparison, see figure 4.25 in section 4.2.4.

Figures 7.16 and 7.17 compare model views of the synthesized test samples by the PWLM and GLOBAL systems. The middle row of the two figures show test samples used as inputs to the analysis-synthesis chain process of both systems. The top and bottom rows of the figures show model views of their corresponding

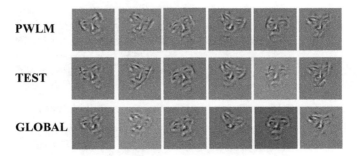

PWLM

TEST

GLOBAL

Figure 7.17: Synthesized Test Samples by PWLM and GLOBAL Systems (Far from Center)

synthesized samples by the PWLM and GLOBAL systems, respectively.

Figure 7.16 includes test samples in which one of their 3D pose angles is ±45 degrees while the rest of the angles are also non-zero. Thus, these test samples use 3D head poses which are not included in the training samples and are largely rotated along one axis. The model views by the PWLM system are almost identical to their corresponding reconstructed images of the test samples. This indicates that the PWLM system maintains its generalization capability to unknown poses even with the very wide pose range. There are no clear difference between the model views by the PWLM and GLOBAL systems. Our visual perception is insensitive to the difference which is, however, clearly shown in the average error difference of figures 7.12 and 7.13. Figure 7.17, on the other hand, includes test samples in which two of their 3D pose angles have large values. Thus, these test samples use head poses which are very far from any of the poses given as training samples. The figure shows that model views by the PWLM system are fairly accurate in comparison to their corresponding test samples. It also shows that model views by the GLOBAL system are slightly more distorted than those by the PWLM systems. These results suggest that the PWLM system improves the generalization capability to unknown poses from the GLOBAL system, indicating again the effectiveness of the PWLM system in comparison to the GLOBAL system based on a single LPCMAP model.

7.2.5 Facial Identification Performance

Lastly, we compared the PWLM and GLOBAL systems for the task of facial identification. We test two facial identification systems with a gallery of 20 known persons. Both systems are based on the basic concept of the LPCMAP recognition

Mapping Type	PWLM Sys (%)	GLOBAL Sys (%)	Improv. (Δ%)
SH-PO-SH-TX	98.7	91.6	+7.1
PO-SH-TX	99.3	92.4	+6.9

Table 7.1: Percentages of Correct Identifications by PWLM and GLOBAL Systems

system described in chapter 5. The only difference is that each known person is represented by either a PWLM or GLOBAL (single LPCMAP) system trained for the person. We call an identification system based on the PWLM system a **PWLM recognition system** and one based on the GLOBAL system a **GLOBAL recognition system**. The same parameters used in the previous experiments in this chapter are also used for building these two recognition systems. Namely, the type B transformation $\mathcal{K}$ is used and the shape and texture models include 8 shape and 21 texture PCs in both systems. For the PWLM recognition system, the 7 local models are created for the 7 model centers shown in figure 7.1. The σ_k for each local model is set equal to the sample standard deviation. The pose processing part of the PWLM system utilizes the gradient-descent algorithm. In the gradient-descent, η is set to 0.01 and 500 iterations are performed for each test sample.

Table 7.1 compares the percentages of correct identifications by the PWLM and GLOBAL recognition systems. We tested two different configurations of our systems, *SH-PO-SH-TX* and *PO-SH-TX*, whose results are shown in the first and second rows of the table, respectively. The SH-PO-SH-TX configuration of our systems corresponds to the most general recognition setting where head poses of arbitrary test samples are not previously known so that our systems need to estimate them. It utilizes the analysis-synthesis chain of the PWLM or LPCMAP systems in order to synthesizes a model view whose head pose is aligned to a test sample. This chain process consisting of shape-pose-shape-texture mappings (*SH-PO-SH-TX*) is applied to the 20 individual systems stored in the known-persons gallery, resulting in a pose-aligned model view for each known person. The PO-SH-TX configuration corresponds to a case where the head pose of every test sample is already known. It utilizes the shape and texture synthesis or animation process of our systems in order to align the head poses of 20 model views to each test sample. The process consists of pose-shape-texture mappings (*PO-SH-TX*). For both configurations of the two recognition systems, PWLM and GLOBAL systems for each known person are trained with 2821 samples described in section 7.2.1. Both recognition systems are tested with the same 16080 samples (804 samples x 20 individuals) also described in the section. Note that these samples include a much wider range of pose variations (± 55 degrees for training

163

Mapping Type	PWLM Sys (%)	GLOBAL Sys (%)	Improv. (Δ%)
SH-PO-SH-TX	96.2	81.7	+14.5
PO-SH-TX	97.9	82.2	+15.7

Table 7.2: Percentages of Correct Identifications by PWLM and GLOBAL Systems with Difficult Test Set

and ± 50 degrees for test samples) in comparison to the data set used in chapter 5. Therefore, results of these experiments should depict more clearly how well our face recognition system performs under pose variation. The results show that the PWLM recognition system improves the correct-identification rate of the GLOBAL system by 7% in each system configuration. The performance of the PWLM system was almost perfect, indicating its effectiveness. The performance increase by the PWLM system was fairly large although the correct-identification rate by the GLOBAL system was already fairly high.

In order to bring out the difference even better, we next prepared more difficult test samples. For this purpose, we use a subset of the 804 test samples for each individual such that a number of samples with easy head poses are removed. As shown in figure 7.2, there are two types of test samples. Samples of one type are spread out along the long vertical and horizontal thin lines in the figure, while samples of the other type lie along the lines forming diagonal crosses. The samples of the first type should be more accurately processed than the second type samples because they are relatively closer to one of the 7 model centers. Moreover, first-type samples are either within a cluster of training samples or between 2 clusters. Second-type samples are, however, between more than 3 clusters, which makes the interpolation of the PWLM system more difficult potentially. According to these observations, we prepared a set of 5280 test samples which consists of the 264 second-type samples for 20 known persons. The system configuration remains the same from the experiments shown in the previous table. Table 7.2 presents the correct-identification rates with the difficult test samples. It shows that the PWLM recognition system greatly improves the identification performance of the GLOBAL system. The correct-identification rates of the PWLM system were as high as those with the easy test samples shown in table 7.1, while the rates of the GLOBAL system are sharply reduced. The improvement of the correct-identification rate by the PWLM system was about 15%, which is very large. Also these results illustrate the effectiveness of the PWLM system.

7.3 Discussion

This chapter presented the results of numerical experiments for evaluating the performance of the PWLM system with two different types of data set. Our experimental results with artificial shape data empirically proved the correctness of the proposed system and supported the feasibility of missing data handling by the mean imputation method and of the gradient-descent pose estimation process. They also suggested that the Gaussian width for computing the local model's weights should be set equal to the standard deviation of the training 3D angle vectors. A very small difference of average errors between the accuracy and generalization tests supported a good generalization capability of the analysis and synthesis processes of the PWLM system to unknown poses.

The difference in terms of average errors between the tests with artificial and more realistic data was also very small. This indicates a robustness of our system against variational factors specific to faces. This result relates to the system's robustness against measurement errors. As discussed in chapter 2, automatically finding locations of facial landmarks is a very difficult task and is not usually sufficiently accurate. Low precision of the landmark locations often leads to poor accuracy in pose processing of a landmark-based system. Since our system is also based on facial landmark locations, the above robustness shown by the experiments is favorable and helps to avoid a potential performance decrease by such measurement errors.

The experimental results with the Cyberware-scanned faces showed that the PWLM system largely improves the performance of the LPCMAP model in all aspects of pose processings: pose estimation, sample synthesis, and facial identification. This indicates that the PWLM system effectively solves the pose range limitation problem of the LPCMAP model discussed in section 4.3.

The identification performance of the PWLM recognition system was very high even with faces that are largely rotated. As already mentioned in chapter 5, the absolute values of the high correct-identification rates, however, need to be interpreted cautiously because the number of known persons used in our experiments was twenty which is relatively small and our facial samples derived from 3D Cyberware-scanned data contain artifacts (i.e., constant incident light distribution, reflexes and shadows) that artificially distinguish them. These two factors may superfluously increase correct-identification rates. However, the improvement based on the relative identification performance between the PWLM and GLOBAL recognition systems should not be strongly influenced by the size of the known person gallery nor the artifacts in our data. Moreover, the data artifacts influence only texture information so that they do not concern our system's pose-invariant nature which is based on shape information. Therefore, our experimental results still suggest the feasibility of the proposed face recognition system with the PWLM system used as a known-persons gallery entry.

Despite the fact that the performance may have been artificially increased, the correct-identification rates do not reach 100%. This is because of the innate difficulty in achieving pose-invariance for face recognition. The FERET competition (Phillips et al. [157, 155]) has proven this point by showing that the best system in the tests could only result in 60% correct-identification rate with a much easier pose variation, roughly ±25 degrees along only one depth-rotation axis.

Chapter 8

Interpersonal Generalization of the Pose Estimation Process

In this chapter, we further extend the pose estimation process of the piecewise linear model (PWLM) system, described in chapter 6, in order to generalize it over shape variations of different individuals (**interpersonal generalization**). Section 8.1 introduces our motivation for this interpersonal generalization of the pose estimation. In section 8.2, we propose two different approaches for achieving interpersonal generalization in our framework. The rest of the sections numerically evaluate the proposed methods with various experimental settings.

8.1 Why is Interpersonal Generalization Desirable?

In chapters 5 and 7 we have evaluated our LPCMAP and PWLM systems for their generalization capability to unknown poses in the 3D angle space. In order to concentrate on investigating this generalization capability, each LPCMAP and PWLM model was learned for a specific individual by using training samples only from that specific person. Interpersonal generalization is another type of model property, in which a model is generalized over variations due to different appearances of individuals so that it performs equally well for arbitrary individuals without explicit knowledge of them. Our studies in the previous chapters have not addressed this issue.

In the previous chapters, we have unified the analysis and synthesis processes of human faces with pose variations in the single framework of the LPCMAP or PWLM model. In the context of interpersonal generalization, however, these two processes differ in nature. The nature of the synthesis process does not involve interpersonal generalization. Each single model based on a continuous-transformation is supposed to be tuned to the specific and detailed appearance of a particular person. Therefore, interpersonal generalization is not necessary for our synthesis process. On the other hand, the analysis process of our systems can benefit from interpersonal generalization. Although the pose analysis process tuned to a specific person might be a sensible way to achieve the best possible accuracy, it is more natural for the pose analysis process to be generalized over interpersonal variations.

Our common knowledge of human's visual perception supports this argument. There is no doubt that our brain performs the pose estimation of human faces since such information is extremely important for our social communication (Perrett et al. [150]). This ability is not compromised by a lack of identity information; we are fully capable of perceiving the head directions of unknown persons. Without interpersonal generalization, we could not achieve this ability.

Interpersonal generalization is also needed for automating the visual learning process of our systems. The LPCMAP and PWLM models proposed in this dissertation perform supervised learning of mappings between the vector spaces of single-view representations and physical parameters of 3D head angles. This form of learning requires explicit knowledge of the angle parameters for each training sample as **ground-truth**. In our previous experiments, such ground-truth is either measured by an external physical device or obtained *a priori* by creating an artificial data set. These methods for obtaining the physical parameters prevent the learning process from being fully automated and self-contained. Pose estimation or analysis with interpersonal generalization can be used to replace the external device by providing the head pose information of arbitrary faces. One might compare the pose derived from an external device to the head orientation information derived from our motor-feedback. In human learning, this feedback provides the ground-truth pose information by associating information on self-movement to the resulting view variations. Although this argument provides a rationale for the use of an external device, it is still preferable to use a vision-based system so that we can build a purely visual on-line learning system requiring only a stream of 2D images from a single camera.

A number of previous studies have addressed the issue of the interpersonal generalization for processing pose information. We have already reviewed these studies in section 2.2. For example, the linear class theory by Poggio provided a solution to this problem. However, these previous studies were severely restricted because they are based on the *discrete-transformation* and raw-image-based *pictorial* single-view representations.

Our goal in this chapter is to present a solution to this problem of interpersonal generalization in the pose estimation process which also overcomes the shortcomings of these previous studies. By using our LPCMAP and PWLM models, we provide a solution with the *continuous-transformation* which improves the pose estimation accuracy by continuously covering the 3D angle space. Our choice of the shape representation for processing the pose information is also important in this respect. Interpersonal variation affects a representation based on *geometrical* information much less than one based on *pictorial* information. Given the high similarity of facial shapes across different individuals, our systems based on geometrical information for extracting pose are expected to improve the performance over these previous systems based directly on pictorial information.

8.2 Two Approaches to Interpersonal Generalization of Pose Estimation

Our LPCMAP and PWLM systems are designed to accurately represent pose variations of a single person. In this chapter, however, we aim to extend our systems to also accommodate interpersonal variations while maintaining their ability to capture pose variations. For realizing this extension, knowledge of the intrinsic relationship between the two types of variation is needed. The two types of variation in our shape representation are *correlated*, because the way the landmark configuration changes with rotation depends on the 3D structure of the individual face. On the other hand, these variations could also be treated as approximately *independent* because the influence of interpersonal variations on pose-dependent variations is small. These observations lead to an important question:

Question: Could these two types of variation be treated as if they were independent, or is it necessary to explicitly accommodate correlations in the model structures?

In order to answer this question, we propose two different approaches, which correspond to the two situations illustrated in the question,

The Single-Model Approach: a single model accounts for both pose and interpersonal variation, and

The Multiple-Model Approach: the system consists of a set of models, each specific to one person, and it interpolates between models in order to deal with a given unknown person.

The single-model approach can be realized by training a single LPCMAP or PWLM system by using samples with different poses and identities. This realization treats the two types of variation equally in that it does not distinguish one variation from another. Moreover, there is no need for structural extension of our previous systems to accommodate the interpersonal variations; we only need to prepare samples of multiple individuals for constructing a single model. A key assumption for this approach is independence of the two types of variation, so that a subspace model in a LPCMAP model can separate the two types of variation in different sets of PCs. When this assumption fails in that single PCs turn out to be sensitive to both types of variation, the pose estimation accuracy of a system of this type is expected to become worsened because of the confused influence from interpersonal variations.

The multiple-model approach, on the other hand, can be realized by weighted averaging of the pose estimates of a set of PWLM systems, each of which is trained for a specific individual. This realization treats the two types of variation differently; individual pose variations are solely captured by each single system while interpersonal variations are represented in separate systems. This approach introduces an explicit hierarchical structure in our system where the two types of variation are captured on different levels. Therefore, this approach requires a structural extension of our PWLM system in order to accommodate interpersonal variations. The relationship between the variations is also a key for this approach. A multiple-model system is expected to perform better than the single-model system when the correlation between the two types of variation is not negligible and they are not linearly separable. Similar to our PWLM approach described in chapter 6, the feasibility of this approach depends on the choice of a weight function in order to capture interpersonal variations correctly.

In the following sections, we will present implementations of these two approaches. We will investigate the points raised in this section by comparing these implemented systems by a series of numerical experiments.

8.3 Numerical Experiments for the LPCMAP System

In this section, we investigate the interpersonal generalization capability of a system based on the single-model approach using the LPCMAP model. We conduct numerical experiments with different test conditions in order to evaluate this system. Because a LPCMAP model is a local component of the PWLM system, the experimental results in this section should provide useful insights for extending the PWLM system to this approach in the next section.

8.3.1 Single-LPCMAP System

In this section we rely on a single LPCMAP model, the type described in chapter 3. We call a single LPCMAP model trained for multiple poses and persons a

Single-LPCMAP System

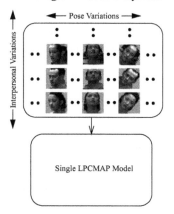

Figure 8.1: Sketches of Single-LPCMAP System

single-LPCMAP system, illustrated in figure 8.1. The system utilizes the type B transformation $\mathcal{K}$ according to our experimental results in chapter 4.

8.3.2 Data Set and Test Conditions

We evaluate pose estimation with the same real face data set used in section 4.2. It consists of 2D image samples derived from video sequences of continuously rotating faces. 3D head angles for each sample are also measured by a magnetic sensor, as described in section 4.2.1. Examples of the 2D facial image samples and corresponding 3D head angles are shown in figures 4.7 and 4.8, respectively. The real facial samples are used for assessing the system in the most realistic condition of sample acquisition.

For each person, a total of 1600 sample images are recorded. For three quarters (1200) of them, pose is rotated along only one 3D rotation axis at a time. We refer to these samples as *training samples*. For the remaining quarter (400), pose is rotated freely. These samples are called *test samples*. A single-LPCMAP system is trained with the 3600 training samples from 3 individuals. This system is tested in three conditions with different test sets,

Multi-Personal Accuracy Test (Type 1) test samples are the same 3600 samples used for training,

171

Interpersonal Interpolation Test(Type 2) test samples are 1200 test samples for the 3 individuals,

Interpersonal Extrapolation Test(Type 3) test samples are 1600 samples of an individual which is not included in the training samples.

The multi-personal accuracy and interpersonal interpolation tests are the same as the accuracy and (pose) generalization tests which have been used in the previous chapters. They only differ in that training and test samples are taken from several persons.

The multi-personal accuracy test evaluates the feasibility of the system. Poor results of this test will indicate that the single-model approach is infeasible. It means that the correlation between pose and interpersonal variations is large enough to prevent the system from correctly capturing pose variations. On the other hand, good results with low average errors are expected should the correlation be negligible.

The interpersonal interpolation test assesses the ability of generalizing over unknown poses in the presence of interpersonal variations. Its results give insights for whether pose generalization is influenced by the correlation between pose and interpersonal variations. It is interpreted as estimating head poses of *known persons*.

The interpersonal extrapolation test assesses the ability of generalizing over unknown poses and persons simultaneously. Good results will indicate that the single-model approach can generalize over interpersonal variation while maintaining its pose generalization capability. This test is the most general condition, requiring extrapolation of individuality for describing unknown persons.

8.3.3   Experimental Results

Figure 8.2 shows results of the 3 different test conditions. Average angular errors of estimated poses in the 3 conditions are plotted against the number of PCs included in the shape model. Down-triangles, up-triangles, and crosses denote results of the multi-personal accuracy, interpersonal interpolation, and interpersonal extrapolation tests, respectively. This figure shows that the best balance between accuracy and generalization are achieved when only the first 10 PCs are used. With the 10 PCs, the average error for the 3 conditions were 2.0, 2,2, and 2.5 degrees, respectively.

The result of the multi-personal accuracy test indicates the feasibility of the single-LPCMAP system. The average error with the 10 PCs was about 1 degree lower than best reported pose estimation error (3 degrees) in the literature. And the error was only slightly higher (0.3 degrees) than the error of the

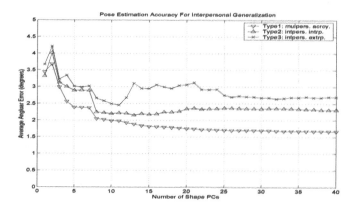

Figure 8.2: Pose Est. Errors by the Single-LPCMAP System for 3 Conditions

single-personal accuracy test shown in table 4.1. The result of the interpersonal interpolation test also shows good pose generalization in the presence of the interpersonal variations. Similar to the result of the multi-personal accuracy test, the error increase was very small (0.35 degrees) when comparing this result with the single-personal accuracy test shown in table 4.2. The result of the interpersonal extrapolation test supports a fair interpersonal generalization capability of the system. The accuracy of the system again exceeds the best pose estimation accuracy reported in the literature. Moreover, the average error difference between the 3 test conditions was also small (roughly 0.3 degrees).

The increase and the absolute values of the errors were small enough to suggest fair pose and interpersonal generalization capabilities of the single-LPCMAP system. This seems to suggest feasibility of the single-model approach and speaks for relative independence of the two types of variation. However, a definitive conclusion about the correlation structure between the two types of variation cannot be drawn solely from these results because the number of individuals used in these tests was not sufficient and the error increase in each case is not zero or negligibly small.

Interesting insights can be drawn from the way the average errors vary with the size of the shape model. For all 3 tests, the errors significantly dropped when the 8-th PCs are included in the model. This agrees with our previous finding for the LPCMAP model trained for a specific individual, in which a shape model with the first 8 PCs resulted in the best balance between accuracy and model size.

Unlike these previous results in chapter 4, however, the average errors of the two generalization tests first decreased slowly when adding a few more PCs and

173

next increased (rapidly for the results of the interpersonal extrapolation test) by including further PCs. The first error decrease indicates that more than the first 8 shape PCs coded statistical modes related to pose variations. However, the following error increase suggests that the shape variations caused by the pose and interpersonal variations seem to be coded separately in different PCs and that the pose variations are mainly coded in PCs with large variance while the interpersonal variations are coded in PCs with small variance. Therefore, truncating these PCs with small variances results in better pose estimation accuracy. This observation supports the single-model approach, in which the two types of variation were assumed to be independent.

This result is again inconclusive because the first error decrease with more than 8 PCs implies a cross-talk between the two variation sources although its influence appears to be benign. The small number of individuals in these experiments also requires a cautious interpretation of the above arguments. However, our results indicate that our system is accurate and is able to generalize over pose and person for practical purpose. We expect the pose estimation accuracy to improve further for the interpersonal generalization cases when a sufficiently large number of individuals are included in the training.

8.4 Numerical Experiments for the PWLM system

In this section, we propose two systems for extending the PWLM approach to accommodate interpersonal variations and compare their performance. The two extensions, single-PWLM and multiple-PWLM systems, correspond to the single-model and multiple-model approaches, described in section 8.2, respectively. By comparing the experimental results of these two systems, we investigate not only interpersonal generalization but also the relationship between the pose and interpersonal variations discussed in section 8.2. In this section, we first describe the two systems. A data set used for the numerical experiments and their test conditions is described next. Lastly, the results of the experiments are reported and discussed.

8.4.1 Single-PWLM and Multiple-PWLM Systems

Figure 8.3 illustrates the two systems which implement the single-model and multiple-model approaches by extending the PWLM systems.

The single-PWLM system is based on the single-model approach. Therefore, this extension does not involve a structural modification of the PWLM system, but

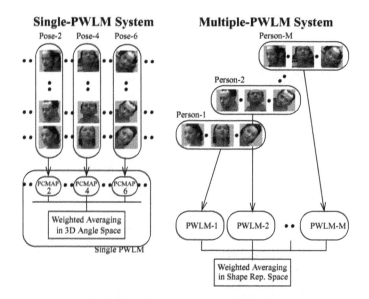

Single-PWLM System

Pose-2   Pose-4   Pose-6

Multiple-PWLM System

Person-M

Person-2

Person-1

PCMAP 2 • • PCMAP 4 • • PCMAP 6

Weighted Averaging in 3D Angle Space

Single PWLM

PWLM-1   PWLM-2   • •   PWLM-M

Weighted Averaging in Shape Rep. Space

Figure 8.3: Sketches of Single-PWLM and Multiple-PWLM Systems

each local LPCMAP model of the system is trained with multi-personal training samples as shown in the figure. Given a single-PWLM system, PM, which is trained with pose and interpersonal variation, a 3D pose estimate of an arbitrary input shape $\vec{x}$ from an arbitrary person is directly given by an output $\hat{\vec{\theta}}$ of the gradient-descent pose estimation process, equations (6.6) through (6.10), of the PM.

The multiple-PWLM system, on the other hand, is based on a set of the PWLM systems, each of which is trained for a specific person, and it interpolates them in order to account for interpersonal variations. Therefore, each single PWLM system trained for a specific person, an **individual system**, is equivalent to the PWLM system studied in chapter 6. The extension of the PWLM system for this multiple-PWLM system, however, requires a method to realize the interpolation of the set of individual systems. For this purpose, we propose to use a weighted averaging of 3D head poses estimated by a set of the individual systems, similar to our treatment in the plain PWLM system for piecing together a set of localized linear models.

Suppose a multiple-PWLM system consists of a number of K PWLM systems,

175

each of which is trained for one of the K different persons,

$$\{PM_1, .., PM_k, .., PM_K\}, \tag{8.1}$$

where each PM_k denotes an individual system.

The 3D head pose of an arbitrary input shape $\vec{x}$ of an arbitrary person is derived by averaging K 3D poses, estimated by the set of the K individual systems, with appropriate weights,

$$\tilde{\vec{\theta}} = \sum_{k=1}^{K} w_k \tilde{\vec{\theta}}_k \tag{8.2}$$

where $\tilde{\vec{\theta}}$ denotes the pose estimate by the multiple-PWLM system, w_k is a weight for the k-th individual system PM_k, and $\tilde{\vec{\theta}}_k$ is a pose estimate of the input shape $\vec{x}$ by the PM_k.

A weight function for the multiple-PWLM system needs to be different from our previous function (6.4) in the plain PWLM system. For the plain PWLM system, our task was to merge local models, which captures the pose variations around different points (model centers) in the 3D angle space. Therefore, the interpolation took place in the 3D angle space by computing the weights as a function of the distance between the input's head pose and each model center. However, a weight function for the multiple-PWLM system should be characterized by facial shape variations instead of the pose variations because the interpersonal variations appear in the facial shapes but not in their poses. Therefore, the interpolation for this system takes place in the shape representation space by computing the weights as a function of the distance between the input and estimated shape representations.

Let $(\tilde{\vec{\theta}}_k, \tilde{\vec{x}}_k)$ denote a pair of 3D pose and facial shape estimated by the gradient-descent algorithm of the k-th individual system PM_k. We define the weight function for the multiple-PWLM system as a normalized Gaussian function *but* in the shape representation space,

$$w_k(\vec{x}) = \frac{\rho_k(\vec{x} - \tilde{\vec{x}}_k)}{\sum_{k=1}^{K} \rho_k(\vec{x} - \tilde{\vec{x}}_k)}, \text{ where } \rho_k(\vec{x}) = \frac{1}{\sqrt{2\pi}\sigma_k^{sh}} \exp(-\frac{\|\vec{x}\|^2}{2(\sigma_k^{sh})^2}), \tag{8.3}$$

and σ_k^{sh} controls the width of the Gaussian.

Given an input shape $\vec{x}$, the multiple-PWLM system first results in K pose estimates $(\tilde{\vec{\theta}}_1, .., \tilde{\vec{\theta}}_K)$ by the K individual systems. Using the plain PWLM system's shape synthesis process (6.3), the system next results in K synthesized shapes $(\tilde{\vec{x}}_1, .., \tilde{\vec{x}}_K)$ from these K estimated poses. [1] The weight function (8.3) for this

---

[1]The gradient-descent pose estimation process actually performs these two steps simultaneously.

system is a function of distances between an input and the K *synthesized* shapes derived from each individual system. Because the synthesis process of each individual system captures intrinsic shape of the learned face with arbitrary poses, the distances between the input and synthesized shapes, whose head poses are aligned, can approximate a similarity of the input face to a number of faces learned in the system. Therefore, a function based on this shape distance can be used to determine an amount of contribution from each individual system to the average output $\tilde{\theta}$ of the multiple-PWLM system.

This function performs differently from the function (6.4) for the plain PWLM system, although these functions resemble each other in their form. A main difference is the model knowledge used for computing the distances. The function (8.3) in the multiple-PWLM system utilizes *implicit* model knowledge of each individual system by using the synthesized outputs for comparison, while the function (6.4) in the plain PWLM system utilizes *explicit* model knowledge of each local linear model by using the model centers stored by a learning process. Therefore, the behavior of the function (8.3) is influenced by the accuracy of both the pose estimation and shape synthesis of the individual systems. This influence actually helps to make a distribution of the input's similarities to the K individuals more distinct. An identity mismatch between an input and individual system will lead to a poorly synthesized shape due to the estimation error, resulting in lower similarity value than an intrinsic facial similarity of the input. This error propagation amplifies the dissimilarities of the input to the mismatched individual systems, making the range of the similarity values larger.

For both the single-PWLM and multiple-PWLM systems, the trigonometric functional transformation $\mathcal{K}$ is set to type B (1st-order). The σ_k in (6.4) for each individual system is set equal to the sample standard deviation of the training 3D angle vectors. For the gradient-descent of the individual systems, the learning rate η is set to 0.01 and 500 iterations are performed.

8.4.2 Data Set and Test Conditions

In these experiments, we use the same 2D samples as in section 7.2, which is generated from the 3D facial models of the ATR-Database shown in figure 5.7. Equivalent to the experiments in chapter 6, 2821 training and 804 test samples are created for the 20 different individuals. The number of individuals is increased from our experiments in the previous section, so that multi-personal statistics of our analysis will become more meaningful. 7 sets of training samples for the 7 different model centers shown in figure 7.1 and a set of test samples shown in figure 7.2 are created for each individual. Each training set consists of samples whose poses are within a range of ± 15 degrees around model centers. Therefore, the training samples as a total cover a pose range of ± 55 degrees around the origin of the 3D angle space. On the other hand, the test set consists of samples within a pose range of ± 50 degrees around the origin. For each sample, the 3D head angles and the 20 facial landmarks defined in figure 4.9 are directly derived from the explicit rotation of the 3D facial models. We use two test conditions, interpersonal interpolation and interpersonal extrapolation tests, described in section 8.3.2.

For the interpolation (known persons) test, each system is trained with all the 56420 training samples. A single-PWLM system is trained with all the samples while each individual system of a multiple-PWLM system is trained with 2821 samples for a specific person. These two systems are then tested with the same 16080 test samples from the 20 individuals. For the extrapolation (unknown persons) test, each system is trained with 53599 training samples of 19 individuals, excluding training samples referring to the person in the test set, so that the system does not contain knowledge of testing faces. The two systems are trained in the same way as the interpolation test and tested with the same 16080 test samples.

8.4.3 Experimental Results

Evaluations of the Shape Distance-Based Weight Function

This section presents results of numerical experiments which evaluate the feasibility of the shape distance-based weight function (8.3) for achieving interpersonal generalization.

This function is defined as a normalized Gaussian inverse distance function in the shape representation. The size of each Gaussian, controlled by a parameter σ_k^{sh}, represents the range within which an individual system contributes to the average output of the multiple-PWLM system. The larger the size of a Gaussian, the more neighboring systems (in terms of shape vector distance) influence the average output. Note also that weighted averaging with this function approximates the nearest-neighbor (or winner-takes-all) approach as the size of a Gaussian becomes very small.

First, we study the influence of the σ_k^{sh} value on the behavior of the shape distance-based weight function. For simplicity, we do not vary the parameter value for different individual models therefore we refer to the parameter by σ^{sh}. Note that the parameter is not associated with the sample standard deviation, unlike the case in equation (6.4). Figure 8.4 shows the pose estimation accuracy of the multiple-PWLM system with various σ^{sh} values in the two test conditions. Average angular errors are plotted against different sigma values ranging from 1 to 20. Results for the interpolation and extrapolation tests are shown by plots with up-triangles and down-triangles, respectively. For the extrapolation test, the best accuracy of 2.3 degrees error was achieved when the σ^{sh} is set to 7. On the other

178

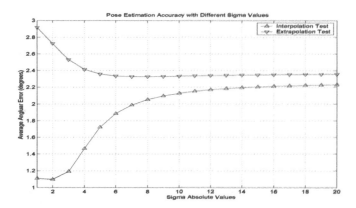

Figure 8.4: Different Sigma Values in the Shape Distance-based Weight Function

hand, for the interpolation test, the best accuracy of 1.1 degrees error was achieved when the σ^{sh} is set to 1 or 2. The results show that the multi-PWLM system behaves quite differently for the two conditions depending on σ^{sh}. Smaller σ^{sh} gives better accuracy of the system in the interpolation condition, while larger σ^{sh} gives better accuracy in the extrapolation condition. By increasing σ^{sh} beyond the optimal value, the average errors slowly increase for both conditions. The optimal σ^{sh} for the interpolation condition resulted in very high accuracy, while the optimal accuracy for the extrapolation condition was not too high. These results indicate that we cannot find a single value for the σ^{sh} which gives the best performance of the system in both conditions.

Next, we compare the performance of the multiple-PWLM system using either a constant or the shape distance-based weight function, in order to evaluate the effectiveness of the latter. A constant function assigns a constant value to each individual system without using any similarity information between an input and each learned individual. Interpolation with this function is equivalent to computing an arithmetic mean of pose estimates of all the individual systems. Therefore, a system with this weight function provides an unbiased base-line performance. In order to show the feasibility of the shape distance-based weight function, we need to show that a system with this function improves the base-line performance.

Figure 8.5 shows results of the interpolation and extrapolation tests, comparing systems with the two functions. In both tests, average angular errors of the multiple-PWLM system are plotted against 6 different sizes of the shape model. Up- and down-triangles correspond to the errors with the shape distance-based and constant weight function, respectively. The results for the two tests indicate

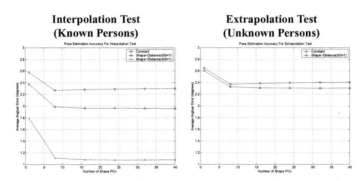

Figure 8.5: Constant and Shape Distance-based Weight Functions

that the pose estimation accuracy of our multiple-PWLM system is improved by using the shape distance-based function from the base-line, indicating the effectiveness of the function. With 8 shape PCs and σ^{sh} set to 7, the average error was 2.0 and 2.3 degrees for the interpolation and extrapolation tests, respectively. Standard deviation of the errors and the worst error were 0.8 and 5.1 degrees for the interpolation test and 0.9 and 5.5 degrees for the extrapolation test.

The improvement of the pose estimation accuracy was more obvious in the interpolation test than the extrapolation test. Moreover, for the interpolation test, a much larger improvement (more than 1 degree) of the average errors from the base-line was observed when σ^{sh} was set to the optimal value 1. In this condition with 8 shape PCs, the average error, the standard deviation, and the worst error were 1.1, 1.0, and 6.4 degrees, respectively. These results indicate that the weight function is more effective in the interpolation condition than the extrapolation condition.

Comparisons of the Single-PWLM and Multiple-PWLM Systems

Finally, we compare the pose estimation accuracy of the single-PWLM and multiple-PWLM systems, with both interpolation and extrapolation tests. Figures 8.6 and 8.7 show results of these tests. As a reference, both figures include pose estimation errors averaged over the 20 plain PWLM systems trained as individual systems for the 20 different persons, using the same data. Down-triangles denote the average angular errors of the single-PWLM system and up-triangles denote those of the multiple-PWLM system with σ^{sh} set to 7. The reference average errors of the individual systems are denoted by a solid line without markers.

180

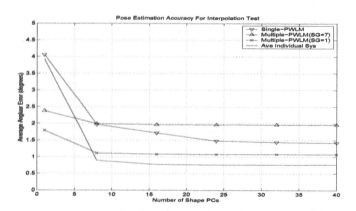

Figure 8.6: Interpolation Test of Single-PWLM and Multiple-PWLM Systems

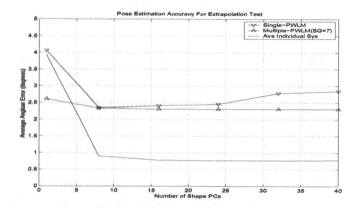

Figure 8.7: Extrapolation Test of Single-PWLM and Multiple-PWLM Systems

Note that the σ^{sh} value of 7 is found to be optimal for the extrapolation condition while the interpolation condition provides different optimal value. Therefore, results of interpolation tests of the multiple-PWLM system are also provided with the σ^{sh} set to the optimal 1 for the interpolation condition. The average errors of this case in the interpolation condition is denoted by crosses. These errors of each case are plotted against 6 different sizes of the shape model.

When σ^{sh} is set optimally for the extrapolation condition, the average errors of the single-PWLM and multiple-PWLM systems were very similar for both interpolation and extrapolation tests. With the first 8 shape PCs, the errors of the two systems were the same: 2.0 and 2.3 degrees for the interpolation and extrapolation tests. For the interpolation test, standard deviation of the errors and the worst error were 0.9 and 5.5 degrees for the single-PWLM system and 0.8 and 5.1 degrees for the multiple-PWLM system. For the extrapolation test, the standard deviation and the worst error were 0.9 and 5.9 degrees for the single-PWLM system and 0.9 and 5.5 degrees for the multiple-PWLM system. With more PCs included in the systems, the single-PWLM system performed better in the interpolation test and the multiple-PWLM system performed better in the extrapolation test. For both tests, the average errors of the two systems are roughly 1 to 1.5 degrees larger than the reference average errors with the 20 plain PWLM systems. When σ^{sh} is set optimally for the interpolation condition as shown in figure 8.5, the multiple-PWLM system clearly outperformed the single-PWLM system, improving the average errors by roughly 1 degree. Moreover, the error difference between the multiple-PWLM and reference systems became very small (roughly 0.2 degrees).

These results suggest that the single-PWLM and multiple-PWLM systems perform equally in the extrapolation condition while the multiple-PWLM system outperforms the single-PWLM system in the interpolation condition. Moreover, the multiple-PWLM system in the interpolation condition is very accurate when σ^{sh} is set correctly, indicating the effectiveness of the multiple-PWLM system. However this effectiveness is limited only to the interpolation condition; the best accuracy of the two systems in the extrapolation condition does not reach as high as the multiple-PWLM system in the interpolation condition. The implications of these results will be discussed in the next section.

8.5 Discussion

In this chapter, we have proposed two methods, single-PWLM and multiple-PWLM systems, for extending the pose estimation process in our linear framework to generalize over interpersonal variations. The single-PWLM system is based on training the plain PWLM system described in the previous chapter by multi-personal samples without modifications of the model structure. On the other hand, the multiple-PWLM system interpolates a number of the plain PWLM systems trained as individual systems for different persons. The interpolation is realized by weighted averaging of pose estimates by the individual systems with weights computed as a function of shape vector distance between inputs and each learned person.

Our experimental results indicate that both systems are fairly accurate, indicating the feasibility of our linear approach to generalize over for different persons. Even in the extrapolation condition (or pose estimation of unknown persons) which is the most general and difficult, the average accuracy of roughly 2 degrees error by our systems beats the best reported pose estimation accuracy (3 degrees) in the literature. The usage of the artificially rotated 3D facial models in our experiments should not compromise this result since our pose estimation process is based on shape information which is free from artificial effects due to the texture mapping used for creating the samples. In a pure vision scenario, the landmark locations and head angle measurements will naturally include some errors while the data used in our experiments were free from such errors. However, we expect that the pose estimation accuracy of our systems will not greatly decrease with such measurement errors because of its robustness against them due to our linear system design, as suggested by our experimental results in chapter 7.

The nature of the correlation between the pose and interpersonal variations, discussed in section 8.2, was another important issue we investigated in this chapter. In one case, the correlation is negligible such that we can assume independence of the two types of variation and, thereby, statistical analysis in our system can separate the two types of variation from mixed samples. In the other, the correlation is too large to be negligible so that extending our systems (designed to handle the pose variations) to accommodate the interpersonal variations in a different level helps to improve its accuracy. In order to evaluate these two possibilities, we have proposed the two generalization approaches, single- and multiple-model approaches, which are implemented as the single- and multiple-PWLM systems, respectively.

Our numerical experiments in section 8.4 probed this issue by comparing the pose estimation accuracy of the two systems. The results in the extrapolation condition, which corresponds to pose estimation of *unknown persons*, indicated that the correlation seems to be negligible, since the performance of the single-PWLM system was not deteriorated in comparison with the multiple-PWLM system.

However, this interpretation should be treated with caution because the single-PWLM system does not outperform the multiple-PWLM system, which would have strongly supported the independence of the two types of variation. Instead, the two systems performed equally and their performance was acceptable if not too accurate. This is perhaps due to either an insufficient number of individuals used to form the multiple-PWLM system, or is due to poor behavior of the shape distance-based weight function. Too few individuals in the model may lead to poor accuracy of cross-person pose estimation because it is more likely that a system does not include knowledge of faces whose shape is similar to the test sample. This lack of matching shape in the model knowledge can also affect the behavior of our weight function due to shape synthesis errors of the system, possibly decreasing the accuracy especially in the extrapolation condition. The experimental results do not provide a conclusive evidence as to which reason (or both) is responsible. Therefore, this issue still remains unresolved as one of our future topics.

The experimental results in the interpolation condition, which corresponds to pose estimation of *known persons*, showed that the multiple-PWLM system outperforms the single-PWLM system. This indicates the effectiveness of the multiple-PWLM system with the shape distance-based weight function when the system does not know the identity of test faces but its model knowledge always includes the knowledge of tested individuals.

Note also that the optimal accuracy of the system in this condition was achieved when σ^{sh} is set to a very small value. As we discussed earlier, the behavior of a system with such a small σ^{sh} becomes similar to **winner-takes-all**. This winner-takes-all method with a number of individual systems can be interpreted as a perceptual paradigm, which assumes that an identity of a given input is known prior to head pose estimation, the approach used for the reference baseline accuracy in figures 8.6 and 8.7. Therefore, the performance of the multiple-PWLM system with the small σ^{sh} needs to agree with the reference accuracy if our weight function is correct and effective so that each individual PWLM system effectively estimates the 3D head pose for one learned person. Our experimental results showed that this was indeed the case. These results, however, do not provide good insight into the correlation structure of the two types of variation because this reference condition imposes more constraints on the interpersonal variations than the pose variations, preventing an unbiased comparison with the results in the extrapolation condition.

Chapter 9

Conclusion

This chapter presents the concluding remarks of this dissertation. We first summarize the contributions of our studies. Next, we discuss the findings of our studies comparing them with psychological and biological studies which addressed similar issues. Lastly, as our future work, we describe the issues which are related to our studies but not addressed or solved in this dissertation.

9.1 Summary of Contributions

This dissertation presented a novel method for processing 2D facial images with 3D pose variation, which is compact, generalizable, data-driven, flexible, and parameterized explicitly by pose angles. The explicit parameterization in terms of pose makes it possible to realize the two complimentary processes, analysis (pose estimation) and synthesis (shape and texture synthesis), within a single framework. The PWLM system uses the piecewise linear model approach and consists of a number of localized linear models (LPCMAP models), each of which describes the pose variation within a region of the viewing sphere. These local models are interpolated in order to cover a wide and continuous range of poses. Because of its data-driven and flexible nature, our simple and general method possesses a least possible variation-specificity, which facilitates an extension of the method to other types of variation than pose.

9.1.1 Systematic Advantages

The proposed method is capable of accurately processing a wide range of arbitrary 3D head poses, which were inaccessible to the previously published methods as they considered only specific rotation dimensions or a limited pose range. It simultaneously improves accuracy and extends pose range and number of the rotation axes, instead of imposing a trade-off between them. Using training samples with a pose variation within ± 55 degree rotations along each 3D rotation dimension, we demonstrated that our system achieved sub-degree and sub-pixel accuracy for the pose estimation and shape synthesis processes, respectively.

The proposed method also generalizes well to unknown poses. This was demonstrated by showing that the average errors with test views of unknown pose were similar to the errors of test views of known pose. This characteristic enables our system to learn continuous pose variations from a small number of training samples and to synthesize a novel view of a learned face. Related to this generalization capability, our system can also be seen as a method for compressing the facial knowledge contained in the training samples. We showed that the size of our model/system was compressed by a factor of 60, although further systematic evaluation is still needed.

The proposed method handles the missing data problem caused by self-occlusion of facial landmarks by the mean imputation method. It is necessary for a system dealing with pose variation to solve this problem because it occurs naturally and frequently due to the nature of the variation, especially in a wide pose range. We demonstrated that the simple sample manipulation-based method successfully suppressed the missing data influence, resulting in virtually uninfluenced accuracy of the analysis and synthesis processes within the ± 55 degrees pose range.

9.1.2 Linear Parametric Eigenspace

The proposed system consists of a combination of linear systems. The LPCMAP model is based on the PC-based subspace model and linear mapping function, both of which are linear, while the PWLM system pieces together a number of the LPCMAP models used as spatially distributed local linear models.

This linear nature endows our system with a number of advantages which include 1) the ease of learning avoiding an expensive iterative process, 2) accurate generalization accuracy avoiding overfitting, and 3) the re-usability to other problems due to minimal reliance on problem-specific *a priori* knowledge. Unfortunately, the linearity assumption imposes pose range limitations, jeopardizing key criteria of our method, data-drivenness and flexibility. The PWLM system as an extension of the LPCMAP model was proposed to solve this problem while keeping the virtues of linearity. Our studies demonstrated that this extension effectively solves the problem.

We incorporated a non-linear process in our proposed system for transforming the pose parameters from 3D head angles. This transformation is derived from the explicit analytical knowledge of the Euclidean 3D rotation rather than an *ad hoc* choice from various functions. However, it does not influence a functional form of the mapping function which are kept linear. We empirically showed that this process helped to improve processing accuracy while not imposing the common pitfalls of non-linear learning such as variation-specificity, overfitting, time-consuming iterative learning, and complicated model selection.

The proposed system explicitly parameterizes our system by learning a continuous-transformation from sample statistics. The continuous-transformation, which maps between two vector spaces of facial representation and 3D head angles, is more appropriate for modeling continuous pose variation than the discrete-transformation, which maps between the facial representations for merely two fixed poses. The continuous-transformation, which covers the pose range continuously and smoothly, is a natural basis for high accuracy and powerful generalization to unknown poses.

The parametric eigenspace by Murase and Nayar is another solution of our problem using similar techniques. It non-linearly parameterizes pose- and illumination-manifolds in a PC-based subspace, which however necessitates an extensive search during pose estimation. Our method removes this shortcoming by treating the task as a function approximation so that the head pose results directly from the learned function without extensive search.

9.1.3 Experimental Emphases and Results

Our study emphasizes a thorough numerical analysis of our method. Especially, the generalization capability of our system was investigated rigorously. We conducted our numerical experiments with minimal constraints, namely with fully three-dimensional rotations, a wide pose range, and fine pose resolution, while none of the previous studies presented experiments with these conditions. Therefore, the results of these experiments provide better understanding of our problems which assists in avoiding *ad hoc* solutions and offers insights toward more practical and realistic applications.

Another aspect of our method is a separation of the shape and texture information into different representations. Our correlation and error analyses provided evidence that the shape information represented by the point-distributions of facial landmarks is more suitable for pose processing than the texture information, and that the correlations between the shape and texture representations can be utilized to linearly synthesize the Gabor jet-based texture representation from the corresponding shape representation.

9.1.4 Examples of Practical Applications

This dissertation demonstrated two applications of our method; pose-invariant facial identification and interpersonal pose estimation.

We proposed a novel face identification method which is robust against a wide rage of arbitrary 3D pose variation. In this method, each known person is represented by a PWLM system, which aligns the 3D head pose of the known persons' model views to an arbitrary pose of an input by the analysis-synthesis chain. This method improves the multiple-view-based method (e.g., Beymer) by reducing the size of a known-person database by using our compact representation model, and by reducing the search space for the nearest-neighbor identification process by using an input's pose information. We demonstrated that our method achieved 95–99% correct-identification rate with a database of 20 known persons with ±55 degrees pose variation.

We proposed two pose estimation methods to generalize for different people. One method consists of a single PWLM system which is trained for both pose and interpersonal variation, while the other describes an arbitrary person by a linear combination of a set of PWLM systems, each of which is trained for pose variation of a specific person. We demonstrated that both methods were fairly accurate for estimating head poses of unknown persons, achieving an average error of about 2 degrees, and that the latter method was very accurate for known persons, achieving about 1 degree average error.

There are a number of characteristics of our method which potentially leads to attractive applications.

The explicit parameterization of our compact system by 3D head angles provides an appropriate basis for realizing low-bandwidth and content-based communication, in which only the economical pose parameters, instead of a continuous video stream, are transmitted via a communication channel by using the analysis and synthesis processes of our system as an encoder and decoder, respectively. This type of visual communication will only be useful if changes in facial shape caused by gesturing are also parameterized and transmitted. This problem has been already solved by a method which is closely related to ours (Hong [92]).

Our method realizes a data-driven system whose model knowledge uses minimal *a priori* assumptions and can be learned from the statistics of uncontrolled samples. Such a system makes economical sample collection for creating an experimental database possible by requiring no subject cooperation and little operator assistance. This advantage also helps to realize an automatic on-line learning system which could be of practical and theoretical significance.

Lastly, it is worth mentioning that the proposed method should be applicable to different classes of objects other than faces. Although we did not investigate our method's applicability to non-face objects, it does not impose any constraints which limit its usage to only faces. This advantage extends our proposed method to a much wider range of application scenarios.

9.2 Discussion: Comparison to Biological Systems

Although our study did not explicitly include biological plausibility as a constraint on system design, it is useful to compare our proposed computer vision system to its biological counterpart in humans (or other primates), which is the best face recognition system known so far. For this purpose, this section presents a brief discussion of our studies in comparison to related psychological and biological studies.

9.2.1 Systematic Viewpoints

The most obvious biological plausibility of our system is its usage of the orientation- and scale-sensitive Gabor filter responses as texture representation. The rationale of this argument can be found elsewhere in the literature. For example, see Jones and Palmer [103] and Daugman [50, 51] about their similarity to responses of V1 hyper-column cells, and see Biederman and Kalocsai [20], Hancock et al. [85], and Bruce et al. [27] about the similarity of a face recognition system based on the Gabor jet representation (Lades et al. [111], Wiskott et al. [214], and Okada et al. [141]) to psychophysical results on human face perception. Recently, von der Malsburg and Shams [207] explored the Gabor filter response-based object representation associating the magnitudes of the complex-valued coefficients to the responses of V1 complex cells, which are insensitive to the phase of spatial gratings. This Gabor magnitude representation is also used in our facial identification system described in chapter 5.

Also the structure of our representation model has a certain degree of biological plausibility because of its continuous-transformation and function approximation features. These aspects enable us to interpret our model as a three-layer feed-forward neural network which was originally inspired by the substrata of the brain's information processing (Rumelhart and McClelland [170]). The learning process of the PC-based subspace models can be realized by using a two-layer linear feed-forward network (e.g., Oja [137], Xu [219]) or the same network with additional lateral inhibitory connections of the output neurons (e.g., Földiák [68]) together with an anti-Hebbian unsupervised learning rule which performs decorrelation of the input variance. Furthermore, the linear mapping function between the model and pose parameters together with the trigonometric functional transformation $\mathcal{K}$ can be realized by using a two-layer feed-forward non-linear network trained by supervised learning based on the delta rule. We did not, however, utilize these iterative learning solutions of our problems, for the more accurate and stable analytical solutions were available.

189

9.2.2   Studies on Human Faces with Pose Variations

This section discusses psychophysical and neurophysiological studies closely related to ours.

Psychophysical Studies

In past two decades, the psychology of human facial perception has been rigorously investigated, resulting in a number of functional and computational models (e.g., Bruce et al. [26], Burton et al. [35], Biederman and Kalocsai [20]). These models have facilitated our understanding of how faces are perceived in the brain.

Studies by Biederman and Kalocsai [104, 20, 21] have addressed issues of how the face recognition performance of humans is influenced by pose variation. Their experimental results showed that the human performance of a 2-way matching task in terms of both reaction time and error rates was significantly reduced, when there was pose difference (maximum 60 degrees along one depth-rotation axis) between the two facial pictures. When humans have only one picture as training sample or *model* of a person, human performance of face recognition becomes very sensitive to pose variation. This compares well with the property of the LPCMAP model whose valid pose range is limited.

A study by Troje and Bülthoff [192] is one of the recent studies which focused on face recognition tasks involving changes in head pose. This study provided a thorough investigation of the influences of pose variation on the recognition performance of human subjects. They conducted separate studies for the influences of the pose variation in the training and test samples and for those in shape and texture information, and statistically analyzed their cross-relations. Facial images used in their experiments were generated from Cyberware-scanned 3D heads similar to our study. They used faces with only shadings without their corresponding pigmentation as shape stimuli, while fully textured faces were used as texture stimuli. Their experimental results indicated that face recognition performance (error rates) was significantly influenced by pose variation in the training views, while the rate was independent of pose variation in the test views. This result agrees with a postulation of our PWLM-based face recognition system, which suggests that the recognition performance depends on the amount of previous experiences of the known objects. A recognition of a known person whose representation model is only trained with a limited range of views becomes naturally difficult because the model will fail to synthesize an accurate model view of unknown poses, reducing the chance of correct recognition. They also reported that the mean error rates with the shape stimuli showed more dependency on pose variation than the texture stimuli, and that the results with the shape stimuli were facilitated by symmetrical view pairs (the bilateral symmetry effect). This result

190

also supports our design choice of associating pose variation only to the shape representation. However, we need to treat these interpretations with care because their experiments used a very coarse pose resolution (9 poses along 1D depth-rotation) and the facial shape was treated in a different manner from our study.

Neurophysiological Studies

In the early 1970s, neurophysiological studies by Gross and his colleagues [82] revealed that some cells in the inferior temporal (IT) cortex of macaque monkeys selectively respond to a visual presentation of faces. Since this discovery, these so-called **face-cells** were further investigated in the various cytoarchitectonic areas of the IT cortex including, TE and STS (the superior temporal sulcus). These IT areas are located at the end of the ventral stream of the cortical visual processing (V1, V2, V4, TEO, and TE). Anatomically, STS receives forward projections from TE but also gives backward projections to these areas. STS is also multimodal, while the above five areas are dominated by visual inputs. An STS area, TPO, which has a high density of the face-cells, is reported to have both forward and backward projections with the parietal cortex. See reviews by Desimone [53] and Gross [81] for detailed properties of face-cells in the various areas.

The face-cells in TE and STS exhibit different response properties. The TE face-cells show more sensitivity to the identity of faces, while the STS face-cells show more sensitivity to the gaze direction, movement, and facial expression that are often hypothesized as carrying the **social attention** information (e.g., Perrett et al. [150]). Moreover, the majority of the STS face-cells are **view-sensitive** (sensitive to a specific pose of faces), while the **view-insensitive** (responding to faces in general regardless of their pose) face-cells are more likely to be found in the TE areas.

Perrett et al. [150] reported that the activities of these STS face-cells were modulated by eye and head gaze directions, which implies the processing of pose information may be carried out in this area. Their physiological results suggest that these cells were statistically more selective to a number of specific charac-teristic views instead of equally selective to arbitrary pose varying views. This finding agrees with the concept of our piecewise linear model approach which covers the viewing sphere by a few number of linear models distributed sparsely in the pose space. They also showed that the STS face-cells exhibited **broad view tuning**, in which the cells respond to a wide pose range. This again agrees with the continuous nature of the single LPCMAP model used as the local linear model of the PWLM system. However, these analogies need to be treated with caution because we have not established a basis of comparing the cell response activities and our system's numerical weights or errors.

For the face-cells in TE, Rolls [167] reported that the response properties of cells which are sensitive to facial identity are modified by exposure to novel faces. This finding suggests that these cells may play a role in the learning process of facial information. In general, IT cells are known to exhibit properties of **population coding**, which may be an analogy to our multivariate vector representation of faces. The fact that the view-sensitive and view-insensitive face-cells coexist in the same IT region may support a theory that the view-insensitive cells are built by convergence of the view-sensitive cells that code different views of the same person. Although the exact functional relationships between these two types of cell are not understood yet, this hypothesis supports the computational property of our system, in which view-independent representations of faces are built by associating the view-dependent 2D training samples by a three-layer network.

Studies of prosopagnosia patients have provided another tool for investigating the cortical nervous system related to facial processing. Prosopagnosia is the impairment of face recognition abilities due to brain damage. A number of reports are available in the psychology literature (e.g., Farah [66] and Young [222]). Heywood and Cowey [91] reported that bilateral ablation of STS of a macaque monkey resulted in an impairment of perceiving the gaze directions but did not exhibit the prosopagnosiaic impairment of facial identification ability of the monkey. These results confirmed the earlier findings of the STS face-cell properties and provided a link between the psychological studies of prosopagnosia patients and electrophysiological studies.

The existence of the forward and backward projections between the STS and parietal cortex is another interesting point. The parietal cortex interfaces the sensory and motor nervous systems and is involved in the dorsal stream of visual processing, which is strongly related to spatial awareness and attention. The pose information of objects is naturally relevant to spatial awareness and motor control, which justifies the connectivity between the two cortical regions.

A series of studies by Andersen and his colleagues (e.g., Andersen et al. [5], Snyder et al. [183], and Reed and Siegel [166]) have revealed interesting characteristics of the cells in the posterior parietal cortex such as the lateral intraparietal (LIP) and the medial superior temporal (MST) areas. They found that the LIP cells are retinotopically organized but their response activities are gain-modulated by the eye and head positions. This modulation by the gaze directions, or **gain field**, provides a mechanism for the coordinate frame transformation from retinal (eye-centered) to spatial (head- and body-centered) coordinates. This finding justifies our model's usage of an object-centered shape representation and the assumption of the availability of the ground truth 3D head pose information during the learning stage. Their multimodal studies of these LIP cells also indicated that auditory signals are represented in eye-centered coordinates, suggesting that the visual gain field is used as a common reference frame for spatial awareness and movement planning. This result suggests the possibility that a common reference frame of

3D object rotations may also exist. Such a common pose reference frame is useful for realizing a multimodal sensorimotor interface and justifies our model's usage of the global 3D rotation angle space as a reference frame of the pose variation.

These cortical systems for processing facial information revealed by neuroanatomical and neurophysiological studies provide an interesting parallel to our computational studies. However, our understanding of the nervous system is still too incomplete to allow a detailed comparison. A number of studies have reported that various cortical areas that have monosynaptic connections with IT, such as STP (the superior temporal polysensory area), the amygdala, the ventral putamen, and the ventrolateral frontal lobe, were found to include face-cells [81]. These findings indicate the existence of a complex array of structures for facial information processing involving a number of multimodal cortical functionalities. However, their intricate functional relationships are still not understood. Further investigations of these cortical systems are required for developing not only a better understanding of our cognitive processes but also a better computational theory of object recognition.

9.3   Future Work

In this section, we discuss a number of issues which were not addressed in this dissertation, and are substance for future work.

9.3.1   Extension to Other Types of Variation

While this dissertation concentrated mainly on pose variation, our long-term goal is to realize a representation model which accommodates all kinds of environmental and object variations presented in 2D object views. Therefore, our proposed system needs to be extended to other types of variation such as shape and illumination. Fortunately, our system design with data-driven and flexible criterion provides an appropriate framework for this extension. The extension to the shape deformations caused by various facial expressions should be tractable because the expression variation is best characterized by the shape information similar to our case. Challenges are due to the non-linearity and subtlety of the variation. Our recent in-house study (Hong [92]) using more elaborate shape representation indeed demonstrated the extendability of our method to facial expression. The extension to illumination variations may also be possible because the scene radiance of objects is described as a function of the 3D structure of the objects. Therefore, illumination parameters such as the 3D location of point light sources can be associated with the texture representation, while the texture is associated with the corresponding shape representation, as shown in our study. We expect that an attempt to learn these different variations by a single system would likely be confronted by the curse of dimensionality which makes the learning difficult, and by intensive labor for collecting enormous number of training samples. However, the nature of our system can mitigate these problems because of its intrinsic capability for generalization which mitigates the curse of dimensionality problem and its data-driven nature which reduces labor during sample collection. For realizing these extension, we must know more about these variations. Unlike our case of pose, intrinsic properties of facial expression and illumination variations in 2D images are not fully understood yet. Further understanding of these variations would be the natural next step towards our aforementioned goal.

9.3.2 Non-Linear PCA

The performance of principal component analysis (PCA) as feature extractor is limited because it can only derive orthogonal linear component vectors. This was the reason that our system needed 8 shape PCs to describe the variation of 3 degrees of freedom, although we empirically show that the additional PCs do not compromise the processing accuracy of our method. A feature extractor which could find non-linear basis whose number of components corresponds to the innate degrees of freedom of a given variation would provide a number of advantages including 1) the reduction of the number of components (which mitigates the curse of dimensionality), 2) the facilitation of the linear mapping between the model and physical parameters (which potentially leads to a better generalization), and 3) another solution to the pose range limitation of the linear model which replaces our PWLM solution by a single compact system. Despite these advantages, the currently available non-linear feature extractors such as kernel PCA have a number of shortcomings as described in chapter 2, which prevented us from using them for our system. Therefore, this extension with a non-linear feature extractor remains for future work.

9.3.3 Extrapolation of Our Representation Model

The PWLM system was proposed to cover a wide range of pose variation by interpolating a set of spatially distributed local linear models. When we further increase the variation range and the number of dimensions, the system becomes less compact requiring a large number of local models because of this interpolation nature. An obvious solution is to seek an extrapolation capability in our method. However, our current system is not capable of extrapolation because of the nature of our model design and of the targeted variation. We are currently investigating a new method based on a second-order transformation law for extrapolating a representation model which maps the physical variations to the representation space.

194

A mapping realized by our linear model can be treated as first-order derivatives of our vector representation with respect to the physical parameters. Therefore, the transformation law of this mapping can be described as second-order derivatives of them. In the case of 3D pose variation, these second-order derivatives become constant with respect to each local tangent coordinate frame. This property may be used to realize the extrapolation of a learned model to an arbitrary point in the parameter space. We plan to further investigate this method in the near future.

9.3.4 Towards On-Line Incremental Learning

In section 9.1 we have argued the advantages of our method which help to realize an on-line incremental learning system. However, a number of difficult problems still need to be solved to achieve this goal. One problem is an on-line clustering of a video input stream into sets of training samples, each of which is used to construct a local model. A solution of this clustering problem needs to possess an on-line nature in order to learn from a continuous video stream. Moreover, the **resource allocation problem** needs to be addressed for incrementally distributing the local models in the most effective way within a 3D angle space. Another problem is related to incremental learning. For automatically learning a known-person database whose entry is represented by a PWLM system, each unknown person appearing in the input stream needs to be detected and added into the database as a new entry. Also for incrementally improving the learned models, a new appearance of a known person can be consolidated to a PWLM system representing the known person. This operation can be realized by either a simple addition of a new local model to the corresponding PWLM system or an incremental learning of the PC-based subspace models. The latter is a difficult problem because the order of the PCs are sensitive to a specific set of training samples so that the correspondences of the PCs between two subspaces cannot be easily determined. The problem of the **knowledge transfer** addresses issues of additively training a system while conserving the knowledge acquired from previous learning. This problem also needs to be solved for realizing the incremental learning of the subspace model.

9.3.5 Towards Pose-Invariant Landmark Finding

The automation of our proposed system requires a reliable landmark finding system for preprocessing each training and test sample. For this purpose, our study in section 4.2 demonstrated a successful automatic preprocess by using a tracking-based on-line landmark finder developed by Maurer and von der Malsburg. One of the main constraints of this system, however, is that, for each tracking session, a frontal view needs to be presented for initializing the landmark locations. Although this can be tolerable for many application scenarios, it is highly desirable to remove this constraint such that facial landmarks in any 3D pose can be reliably found using only single view statistics without referencing previous views. For example, our proposed pose-invariant face identification system looses attractiveness when a frontal view of each input face is always available. In such a situation as postulated by the usage of the tracking-based landmark finder, there would be much simpler well-known solutions for identifying frontal views of faces. This observation motivates us to investigate a method for realizing a pose-invariant landmark finder. An iterative application of the pose analysis and shape synthesis processes of our system may provide a core of such a method. Note, however, that this is an ill-posed circular problem because the landmark locations and 3D head poses depend on each other in our formulation. A clever method of finding an appropriate initial condition for arbitrary head poses and/or of utilizing the co-dependency as a boot-strapping force is required to solve this problem.

9.3.6 Further Investigation for the Learning Process of Our Model

The following two questions related to the learning process of our system were not investigated in this dissertation and should be answered in the near future. One question is the minimum number of training samples required for learning an accurate representation model. Assuming a homogeneous density of a data-cloud of training samples in the 3D angle space, it is interesting to see how far the sample distribution can be sparsified while maintaining the pose processing accuracy. The more sparsified the sample distribution, the less training samples a model learns from. Therefore, an answer to this question gives us further insights about our system's ability to learn from a few number of samples and its data-compression capability. Another more general question is the effectiveness of the learning process against various distributions of training samples in the 3D angle space. In a purely data-driven learning scenario, a training data-cloud in parameter space can have arbitrary shape, size, and density. Although we studied the different sizes of the data-cloud, we did not thoroughly investigate how various shapes and distributions of the data-cloud would influence our system's performance. Designing numerical experiments for investigating this question is difficult because the number of all possible data-cloud shapes and densities is enormous. However, this question should be answered to give insights for realizing an on-line learning system as mentioned earlier.

9.3.7 Relationship between the Pose and Interpersonal Variations

Our investigation in chapter 8 did not provide a conclusive answer for the relationship between pose and interpersonal variations. Our error analysis implied that these two types of variation should be fairly independent because the single-PWLM system, which treats the two types of variation equally, resulted in relatively good accuracy. However, this question remains unresolved as a future topic because of the inconclusiveness of our experimental results. The comparison of the single- and multiple-PWLM systems for the interpersonal pose estimation indicated that the former performed best for known faces while the latter won for unknown faces. This result implies a need of separate mechanisms for processing familiar or unfamiliar faces. Another issue is the modulatory relationship of pose and interpersonal variations. This issue addresses the question of which variation is processed before the other. The pose-invariant facial identification method proposed in this dissertation assumes a perceptual paradigm in which the variational analysis, such as pose estimation, takes place before the identification process. However, a paradigm with a reverse relationship of the variations has been used in successful object recognition systems such as the parametric eigenspace system by Murase and Nayar and may be equally valid. Which modulatory relationship is correct or whether both paradigms should coexist remains another future topic.

9.3.8 The Missing Data Problem

Our handling of the missing shape vector components due to self-occlusion of landmarks was based on a simple sample manipulation-based mean imputation method. Although we empirically showed that our system with this method performed accurately within the ± 55 degrees 3D pose range, this method is expected to be suboptimal when much larger pose variations are considered because artificial biases introduced by these sample manipulation-based methods become non-negligible. Therefore, we need to revisit this problem in order to apply our system to a specific scenario which requires coverage of a much wider pose range while maintaining high accuracy. We are currently considering a number of methods to solve this problem. As mentioned in chapter 7, the EM algorithm for solving a maximum likelihood estimation problem has been claimed as a solution for the general missing data problem [120]. Another approach is to extend a linear neural network implementation of the PCA based on the constrained gradient-descent approach (e.g., Oja [136, 137], Oja and Karhunen [138], Földiák [68], Chauvin [37], Xu [219], Plumbley [159, 160], and Baldi and Hornik [7]). We plan to further investigate this approach in the near future.

Bibliography

[1] H. Abdi, D. Valentin, and A. J. O'Toole. A generalized autoassociator model for face processing and sex categorization: From principal components to multivariate analysis. In *Optimality in Biological and Artificial Networks*, pages 317–337. Erlbaum, Mahwah, N.J., 1997.

[2] S. T. Acton and A. C. Bovik. Piecewise and local image models for regularized image restoration using cross-validation. *IEEE Transaction of Image Processing*, 8(5):652, May 1999.

[3] K. Aizawa, H. Harashima, and T. Saito. Model-based analysis synthesis image coding (MBASIC) system for a person's face. *Signal Processing: Image Communication*, 1:139–152, 1989.

[4] S. Amari, A. Cichocki, and H. H. Yang. A new learning algorithm for blind signal separation. In *Advances in Neural Information Processing Systems*, volume 8. MIT Press, 1996.

[5] R. A. Andersen, L. H. Snyder, D. C. Bradley, and J. Xing. Multimodal representation of space in the posterior parietal cortex and its use in planning movements. *Annual Revue of Neuroscience*, 20:303–330, 1997.

[6] J. L. Arbuckle. Full information estimation in the presence of incomplete data. In *Advanced Structural Equation Modeling: Issues and Techniques*, pages 243–278. Lawrence Erlbaum Associates, 1996.

[7] P. Baldi and K. Hornik. Learning in linear neural networks: A survey. *IEEE Transactions on Neural Networks*, 6:837–858, 1995.

[8] M. S. Bartlett, M. Lades, and T. J. Sejnowski. Independent component representations for face recognition. In *Proceedings of the SPIE Symposium on Electronic Imaging: Science and Technology; Conference on Human Vision and Electronic Imaging III*, pages 528–539, San Jose, USA, 1998.

[9] M. S. Bartlett and T. J. Sejnowski. Independent components of face images: A representation for face recognition. In *Proceedings of the Fourth Annual Joint Symposium on Neural Computation*, Paris, 1997.

[10] M. S. Bartlett and T. J. Sejnowski. Viewpoint invariant face recognition using independent component analysis and attractor networks. In *Neural Information Processing Systems: Natural and Synthetic*, volume 9, pages 817–823. MIT Press, 1997.

[11] R. Basri. Recognition by prototypes. Technical Report A.I. Memo, No. 1391, Artificial Intelligence Laboratory, M.I.T., 1992.

[12] L. A. Belanche Buñoz. *Heterogeneous Neural Networks: Theory and Applications*. PhD thesis, Universitat Politecnica de Catalunya, 2000.

[13] A. J. Bell and T. Sejnowski. An information maximization approach to blind separation and blind deconvolution. *Neural Network*, 7:1129–1159, 1995.

[14] A. J. Bell and T. J. Sejnowski. The independent components of natural scenes are edge filters. *Vision Research*, 37(23):3327–3338, 1997.

[15] D. Beymer. Face recognition under varying pose. Technical Report A.I. Memo, No. 1461, Artificial Intelligence Laboratory, M.I.T., 1993.

[16] D. Beymer and T. Poggio. Face recognition from one example view. Technical Report A.I. Memo, No. 1536, Artificial Intelligence Laboratory, M.I.T., 1995.

[17] D. Beymer, A. Shashua, and T. Poggio. Example based image analysis and synthesis. Technical Report A.I. Memo, No. 1431, Artificial Intelligence Laboratory, M.I.T., 1993.

[18] M. Bichsel and A. Pentland. Automatic interpretation of human head movements. Technical Report Technical Report No. 186, MIT Media Laboratory, Vision and Modeling Group, 1993.

[19] I. Biederman. Visual object recognition. In *An Invitation of Cognitive Science*, pages 121–165. MIT Press, 1995.

[20] I. Biederman and P. Kalocsai. Neurocomputational bases of object and face recognition. *Philosophical Transactions of the Royal Society: Biological Sciences*, 352, 1997. 1203–1219.

[21] I. Biederman and P. Kalocsai. Neural and psychophysical analysis of object and face recognition. In *Face Recognition: From Theory to Applications*, pages 3–25. Springer-Verlag, 1998.

[22] C. M. Bishop. *Neural Networks for Pattern Recognition*. Oxford University Press, New York, 1995.

[23] M. J. Black and Y. Yacoob. Recognizing facial expressions under rigid and non-rigid facial motions. In *Proceedings of the International Workshop on Automatic Face and Gesture Recognition*, pages 12–17, Zurich, 1995.

[24] V. Blanz and T. Vetter. A morphable model for the synthesis of 3D faces. In *Proceedings of Siggraph*, pages 187–194, 1999.

[25] V. L. Brailovsky and Y. Kempner. Application of piece-wise regression to detecting internal structure of signal. *Pattern Recognition*, 25:1361–1370, 1992.

[26] V. Bruce, A. M. Burton, and I. Craw. Modeling face recognition. *Philosophical Transactions of the Royal Society of London*, 335:121–128, 1992.

[27] V. Bruce, P. J. B. Hancock, and A. M. Burton. Comparisons between human and computer recognition of faces. In *Proceedings of the International Conference on Face and Gesture Recognition*, pages 408–413, 1998.

[28] V. Bruce and G. W. Humphreys. Recognizing objects and faces. *Visual Cognition*, 1:141–180, 1994.

[29] V. Bruce and A. Young. Understanding face recognition. *British Journal of Psychology*, 77:305–327, 1986.

[30] R. Brunelli. Estimation of pose and illuminant direction for face processing. Technical Report A.I. Memo, No. 1499, Artificial Intelligence Laboratory, M.I.T., 1994.

[31] R. Brunelli and T. Poggio. Face recognition through geometrical features. In *Proceedings of the Second European Conference on Computer Vision*, volume 588, pages 792–800, 1992.

[32] R. Brunelli and T. Poggio. Caricatural effects in automated face perception. *Biological Cybernetics*, 69:235–241, 1993.

[33] R. Brunelli and T. Poggio. Face recognition: Features versus templates. *IEEE Transactions on Pattern Analysis and Machine Intelligence*, 15:1042–1052, 1993.

[34] R. Brunelli and T. Poggio. Template matching: Matched spatial filters and beyond. Technical Report A.I. Memo, No. 1549, Artificial Intelligence Laboratory, M.I.T., 1995.

[35] A. M. Burton, V. Bruce, and R. A. Johnston. Understanding face recognition with an interactive activation model. *British Journal of Psychology*, 81:361–380, 1990.

[36] B. B. Chai, T. Huang, X. H. Zhuang, Y. X. Zhao, and J. Sklansky. Piecewise-linear classifiers using binary-tree structure and genetic algorithm. *Pattern Recognition*, 29(11):1905–1917, November 1996.

[37] Y. Chauvin. Principal component analysis by gradient descent on a constrained linear Hebbian cell. In *Processings of the Joint International Conference on Neural Networks*, volume 1, pages 373–380, 1989.

[38] R. Chellappa, C. L. Wilson, and S. Sirohey. Human and machine recognition of faces: A survey. *Proceedings of the IEEE*, 83(5):705–740, 1995.

[39] Q. Chen, H. Wu, T. Fukumoto, and M. Yachida. 3D head pose estimation without feature tracking. In *Proceedings of the International Workshop on Automatic Face and Gesture Recognition*, pages 88–93, Nara, 1998.

[40] J. B. Cheng and H. M. Hang. Adaptive piecewise-linear bits estimation model for mpeg based video coding. *Journal of Visual Communication and Image Representation*, 8(1):51–67, March 1997.

[41] K. N. Choi, M. Carcassoni, and E. R. Hancock. Estimating 3D facial pose using the EM algorithm. In *Face Recognition: From Theory to Applications*, pages 412–423. Springer-Verlag, 1998.

[42] P. Common. Independent component analysis, a new concept. *Signal Processing*, 36:287–314, 1994.

[43] T. F. Cootes, A. Hill, C. J. Taylor, and J. Haslam. The use of active shape models for locating structures in medical images. *Image and Vision Computing*, 12:355–366, 1994.

[44] N. Costen, I. Craw, G. Robertson, and S. Akamatsu. Automatic face recognition: What representation? Technical report, Department of Mathematical Sciences, University of Aberdeen, 1996.

[45] G. W. Cottrell and P. Munro. Principal components analysis of images via back propagation. In *Proceedings of the Society of Photo-Optical Instrumentation Engineers*, pages 1070–1077, 1988.

[46] I. Craw. Machine coding of human faces. Technical report, Department of Mathematical Sciences, University of Aberdeen, 1996.

[47] I. Craw and P. Cameron. Face recognition by computer. In *Proceedings of British Machine Vision Conference*, pages 489–507, 1992.

[48] I. Craw, N. Costen, and T. Kato. How should we represent faces for automatic recognition? submitted to IEEE Transactions on Pattern Analysis and Machine Intelligence, 1997.

[49] I. Craw, N. Costen, T. Kato, G. Robertson, and S. Akamatsu. Automatic face recognition: Combining configuration and texture. In *Proceedings of the International Workshop on Automatic Face and Gesture Recognition*, pages 53–58, Zurich, 1995.

[50] J. G. Daugman. Complete discrete 2-D Gabor transforms by neural networks for image analysis and compression. *IEEE Transactions on Acoustics, Speech, and Signal Processing*, 36:1169–1179, 1988.

[51] J. G. Daugman. Non-orthogonal wavelet representations in relaxation networks: image encoding and analysis with biological visual primitives. In *New Developments in Neural Computing*, pages 233–250. Institute of Physics Press, 1989.

[52] P. Demartines and J. Herault. Curvilinear component analysis: a self-organizing neural network for nonlinear mapping of data sets. *IEEE Transactions on Neural Networks*, 8:148–154, 1997.

[53] R. Desimone. Face-selective cells in the temporal cortex of monkeys. *Journal of Cognitive Neuroscience*, 3:1–8, 1991.

[54] G. Donato, M. S. Bartlett, J. C. Hager, P. Ekman, and T. J. Sejnowski. Classifying facial actions. *IEEE Transactions on Pattern Analysis and Machine Intelligence*, 21(10):974–988, 1999.

[55] R. O. Duda and P. E. Hart. *Pattern Classification and Scene Analysis*. Wiley, New York, 1973.

[56] S. Duvdevani-Bar and S. Edelman. Visual recognition and categorization on the basis of similarities to multiple class prototypes. in preparation, 1998.

[57] S. Duvdevani-Bar, S. Edelman, A. J. Howell, and H. Buxton. A similarity-based method for the generalization of face recognition over pose and expression. In *Proceedings of the International Workshop on Automatic Face and Gesture Recognition*, pages 118–123, Nara, 1998.

[58] S. Edelman, F. Cutzu, and S. Duvdevani-Bar. Similarity to reference shapes as a basis for shape representation. In *Proceedings of Eighteenth Annual Conference of the Cognitive Science Society*, pages 260–265, 1996.

[59] S. Edelman and S. Duvdevani-Bar. A model of visual recognition and categorization. *Philosophical Transactions of the Royal Society of London*, 1997. in press.

[60] S. Edelman and T. Poggio. Bringing the grandmother back into the picture: a memory-based view of object recognition. Technical Report A.I. Memo, No. 1181, Artificial Intelligence Laboratory, M.I.T., 1990.

[61] S. Edelman, D. Weinshall, and Y. Yeshurun. Learning to recognize faces from examples. In *Proceedings of the Second European Conference on Computer Vision*, volume 588, pages 787–791, 1992.

[62] G. J. Edwards, C. J. Taylor, and T. F. Cootes. Interpreting face images using active appearance models. In *Proceedings of the International Conference on Automatic Face and Gesture Recognition*, pages 300–305, Nara, Japan, 1998.

[63] G. J. Edwards, C. J. Taylor, and T. F. Cootes. Learning to identify and tracks faces in image sequences. In *Proceedings of the International Conference on Automatic Face and Gesture Recognition*, pages 260–265, Nara, Japan, 1998.

[64] E. Elagin, J. Steffens, and H. Neven. Bunch graph matching technology. In *Proceedings of the International Conference on Automatic Face and Gesture Recognition*, pages 136–141, Nara, Japan, 1998.

[65] I. A. Essa and A. Pentland. Facial expression recognition using visually extracted facial action parameters. In *Proceedings of the International Workshop on Automatic Face and Gesture Recognition*, pages 35–40, Zurich, 1995.

[66] M. J. Farah. *Visual Agnosia*. MIT Press, Cambridge, MA, 1990.

[67] J.-M. Fellous. Gender discrimination and prediction on the basis of facial metric information. *Vision Research*, 37:1961–1973, 1997.

[68] P. Földiák. Adaptive network for optimal linear feature extraction. In *Processings of the Joint International Conference on Neural Networks*, volume 1, pages 401–405, 1989.

[69] B. Fritzke. Incremental learning of local linear mappings. In *Proceedings of the International Conference on Artificial Neural Networks*, volume 2, pages 217–222, Paris, 1995.

[70] P. Fua. Regularized bundle-adjustment to model heads from images sequences without calibration data. *International Journal of Computer Vision*, 38(2):153–172, 2000.

[71] N. Futamura, K. Okada, S. Akamatsu, K. Mori, and Y. Suenaga. An ICA based representation of facial images and its application for face recognition systems. In *Proceedings of IEICE Workshop of Pattern Recognition and Media Understanding*, pages 21–28, Ehime, Japan, December 1999.

[72] S. Geman, E. Bienenstock, and R. Doursat. Neural networks and the bias/variance dilemma. *Neural Computation*, 4:1–58, 1992.

[73] A. S. Georghiades, P. N. Belhumeur, and D. J. Kriegman. From few to many: Generative models for recognition under variable pose and illumination. In *Proceedings of Fourth International Conference on Automatic Face and Gesture Recognition*, pages 277–284, Grenoble, France, 2000.

[74] Z. Ghahramani and M. I. Jordan. Learning from incomplete data. Technical Report A.I. Memo, No. 1509, Artificial Intelligence Laboratory, M.I.T., 1994.

[75] S. Gong, E. J. Ong, and S. McKenna. Learning to associate faces across views in vector space of similarities to prototypes. In *Proceedings of British Machine Vision Conference*, pages 54–63, 1998.

[76] G. G. Gordon. Face recognition based on depth and curvature features. In *Proceedings of the IEEE Computer Society Conference on Computer Vision and Pattern Recognition*, pages 108–110, 1992.

[77] G. G. Gordon. Face recognition from frontal and profile views. In *Proceedings of the International Workshop on Automatic Face and Gesture Recognition*, pages 47–52, Zurich, 1995.

[78] G. G. Gordon. 3D pose estimation of the face from video. In *Face Recognition: From Theory to Applications*, pages 433–455. Springer-Verlag, 1998.

[79] D. B. Graham and N. M. Allinson. Characterizing virtual eigensignatures for general purpose face recognition. In *Face Recognition: From Theory to Applications*, pages 446–456. Springer-Verlag, 1998.

[80] D. B. Graham and N. M. Allinson. Face recognition from unfamiliar views: Subspace methods and pose dependency. In *Proceedings of Third International Conference on Automatic Face and Gesture Recognition*, pages 348–353, 1998.

[81] C. G. Gross. Representation of visual stimuli in inferior temporal cortex. *Philosophical Transactions of the Royal Society of London*, 335:3–10, 1992.

[82] C. G. Gross, C. E. Rocha-Miranda, and D. B. Bender. Visual properties of neurons in inferotemporal cortex of the macaque. *Journal of Neurophysiology*, 35:96–111, 1972.

[83] B. Günter, C. Grimm, D. Wood, H. Malvar, and F. Pighin. Making faces. In *Proceedings of Siggraph*, pages 55–66, 1998.

[84] S. Gutta and H. Wechsler. Face recognition using hybrid classifiers. *Pattern Recognition*, 30(4):539–553, 1997.

[85] P. J. B. Hancock, V. Bruce, and A. M. Burton. A comparison of two computer-based face identification systems with human perceptions of faces. *Vision Research*, 1998. in press.

[86] R. M. Haralick and H. Joo. 2D-3D pose estimation. In *Proceedings of Nineth International Conference on Pattern Recognition*, pages 385–391, 1988.

[87] T. Hastie and W. Stuetzle. Principal curves. *Journal of the American Statistical Association*, 84:502–516, 1989.

[88] P. Havaldar and G. Medioni. Segmented shape descriptions from 3-view stereo. In *Proceedings of the International Conference on Computer Vision*, pages 102–108, Boston, 1995.

[89] J. Heinzmann and A. Zelinsky. 3D facial pose and gaze point estimation using a robust real-time tracking paradigm. In *Proceedings of the International Workshop on Automatic Face and Gesture Recognition*, pages 142–147, Nara, 1998.

[90] G. T. Herman and K. T. D. Yeung. On piecewise-linear classification. *IEEE Transaction of Pattern Analysis and Machine Intelligence*, 14(7):782–786, July 1992.

[91] C. A. Heywood and A. Cowey. The role of the 'face-cell' area in the discrimination and recognition of faces by monkeys. *Philosophical Transactions of the Royal Society of London*, 335:31–38, 1992.

[92] H. Hong. *Analysis, Recognition and Synthesis of Facial Gestures*. PhD thesis, University of Southern California, 2000.

[93] H. Hong, H. Neven, and C. von der Malsburg. Online facial expression recognition based on personalized gallery. In *Proceedings of the International Conference on Automatic Face and Gesture Recognition*, pages 354–359, Nara, Japan, 1998.

[94] B. K. P. Horn. *Robot Vision*. McGraw-Hill, Boston, USA, 1986.

[95] F. J. Huang, Z. Zhou, H. J. Zhang, and T. Chen. Pose invariant face recognition. In *Proceedings of Fourth International Conference on Automatic Face and Gesture Recognition*, pages 245–250, Grenoble, France, 2000.

[96] J. Huang, D. Ii, X. Shao, and H. Wechsler. Pose discrimination and eye detection using support vector machines (SVM). In *Face Recognition: From Theory to Applications*, pages 528–536. Springer-Verlag, 1998.

[97] D. H. Hubel and T. N. Wiesel. Receptive fields, binocular interaction and functional architecture in the cat's visual cortex. *Journal of Physiology*, 160:106–154, 1962.

[98] D. P. Huttenlocher and S. Ullman. Recognizing solid objects by alignment with an image. *International Journal of Computer Vision*, 5:195–212, 1990.

[99] A. Hyvärinen and E. Oja. Independent component analysis: A tutorial. http://www.cis.hut.fi/projects/ica/, 1999.

[100] H. Imaoka and S. Sakamoto. Pose-independent face recognition method. In *Proceedings of IEICE Workshop of Pattern Recognition and Media Understanding*, pages 51–58, June 1999.

[101] N. Intrator, D. Reisfeld, and Y. Yeshrun. Face recognition using a hybrid supervised/unsupervised neural network. In *Proceedings of the International Conference on Pattern Recognition*, pages 50–54, 1994.

[102] K. Isono and S. Akamatsu. A representation for 3D faces with better feature correspondence for image generation using PCA. Technical Report HIP96-17, The Institute of Electronics, Information and Communication Engineers, 1996.

[103] J. P. Jones and L. A. Palmer. An evaluation of the two-dimensional Gabor filter model of simple receptive fields in cat striate cortex. *Journal of Neurophysiology*, 58:1233–1258, 1987.

[104] P. Kalocsai, I. Biederman, and E. E. Cooper. To what extent can the recognition of unfamiliar faces be accounted for by a representation of the direct output of simple cells. In *Proceedings of Investigative Opthalmology & Visual Science*, volume 35, page 1627, 1998.

[105] P. Kalocsai, E. Elagin, I. Biederman, and W. Zhao. Face similarity space as perceived by humans and artificial systems. In *Proceedings of the International Conference on Face and Gesture Recognition*, pages 177–180, 1998.

[106] P. Kalocsai, C. von der Malsburg, and J. Horn. Face recognition by statistical analysis of feature detectors. *Image And Vision Computing*, 18:273–278, 2000.

[107] T. Kohonen. *Associative Memory: A System Theoretic Approach*. Springer-Verlag, Berlin, 1977.

[108] N. Krüger, M. Pötzsch, and C. von der Malsburg. Determination of face position and pose with a learned representation based on labeled graphs. Technical report, Institut für Neuroinformatik, Ruhr-Universität Bochum, 1996.

[109] Y. H. Kwon and N. V. Lobo. Face detection using templates. In *Proceedings of the International Conference on Pattern Recognition*, pages 764–767, 1994.

[110] M. Lades. *Invariant Object Recognition Based on Dynamical Links, Robust to Scaling. Rotation and Variation of Illumination*. PhD thesis, Ruhr-Universität Bochum, 1994.

[111] M. Lades, J. C. Vorbrüggen, J. Buhmann, J. Lange, C. von der Malsburg, R. P. Würtz, and W. Konen. Distortion invariant object recognition in the dynamic link architecture. *IEEE Transactions on Computers*, 42:300–311, 1993.

[112] M. Lando and S. Edelman. Generalization from a single view in face recognition. In *Proceedings of the International Workshop on Automatic Face and Gesture Recognition*, pages 80–85, Zurich, 1995.

[113] A. Lanitis, C. J. Taylor, and T. F. Cootes. Active shape models–their training and application. *Computer Vision Graphics and Image Understanding*, 61:38–59, 1995.

[114] A. Lanitis, C. J. Taylor, and T. F. Cootes. A unified approach to coding and interpreting face images. In *Proceedings of the Fifth International Conference on Computer Vision*, pages 368–373, Cambridge, USA, 1995.

[115] A. Lanitis, C. J. Taylor, and T. F. Cootes. Automatic interpretation and coding of face images using flexible models. *IEEE Transactions on Pattern Analysis and Machine Intelligence*, 19:743–755, 1997.

[116] A. Lanitis, C. J. Taylor, T. F. Cootes, and T. Ahmed. Automatic interpretation of human faces and hand gestures using flexible models. In *Proceedings of the International Workshop on Automatic Face and Gesture Recognition*, pages 98–103, Zurich, 1995.

[117] S. Lawrence, C. L. Giles, A. C. Tsoi, and A. D. Back. Face recognition: A hybrid neural network approach. Technical Report UMIACS-TR-96-16, Institute for Advanced Computer Studies, University of Maryland, 1996.

[118] R. Lengagne, O. Monga, and P. Fua. Using differential constraints to generate a 3D face model from stereo. In *Face Recognition: From Theory to Applications*, pages 556–567. Springer-Verlag, 1998.

[119] Y. Li, S. Gong, and H. Liddell. Support vector regression and classification based multi-view face detection and recognition. In *Proceedings of Fourth International Conference on Automatic Face and Gesture Recognition*, pages 300–305, Grenoble, France, 2000.

[120] R. J. A. Little and D. B. Rubin. *Statistical Analysis with Missing Data*. Wiley, New York, 1987.

[121] E. Mael. A hierarchical network for learning robust models of kinematic chains. In *Proceedings of the International Conference on Artificial Neural Networks*, pages 617–622, Bochum, 1996.

[122] S. Makeig, A. J. Bell, T. P. Jung, and T. J. Sejnowski. Independent component analysis of elecroencephalographic data. In *Advances in Neural Information Processing Systems*, volume 8, pages 145–151. MIT Press, 1996.

[123] D. Marr. *Vision: A Computational Investigation into the Human Representation and Processing of Visual Information.* Freeman, New York, 1982.

[124] K. Matsuno and S. Tsuji. Recognizing human facial expressions in a potential field. In *Proceedings of the International Conference on Pattern Recognition*, pages 44–49, 1994.

[125] T. Maurer and C. von der Malsburg. Learning features transformations to recognize faces rotated in depth. In *Proceedings of the International Conference on Artificial Neural Networks*, volume 1, pages 353–359, Paris, 1995.

[126] T. Maurer and C. von der Malsburg. Single-view based recognition of faces rotated in depth. In *Proceedings of the International Workshop on Automatic Face and Gesture Recognition*, pages 248–253, Zurich, 1995.

[127] T. Maurer and C. von der Malsburg. Tracking and learning graphs and pose on image sequences. In *Proceedings of the International Workshop on Automatic Face and Gesture Recognition*, pages 176–181, Vermont, 1996.

[128] S. J. McKenna and S. Gong. Real-time face pose estimation. *Real-Time Imaging*, 4:333–347, 1998.

[129] S. Mika, B. Schölkopf, A. Smola, K.-R. Müller, M. Scholz, and G. Rätsch. Kernel PCA and de-noising in feature spaces. In *Proceedings of Neural Information Processing Systems*, pages 39–43, 1998.

[130] J. Modayil, H. Cheng, and X. B. Li. Improved piecewise approximation algorithm for image compression. *Pattern Recognition*, 31(8):1179–1190, August 1998.

[131] B. Moghaddam and A. Pentland. An automatic system for model-based coding of faces. Technical report, M.I.T. Media Laboratory Perceptual Computing Section, 1995.

[132] B. Moghaddam, W. Wahid, and A. Pentland. Beyond eigenfaces: Probabilistic matching for face recognition. In *Proceedings of the International Conference on Face and Gesture Recognition*, pages 30–35, 1998.

[133] H. Murase and S. K. Nayar. Visual learning and recognition of 3-D objects from appearance. *International Journal of Computer Vision*, 14:5–24, 1995.

209

[134] U. Neumann, J. Li, R. Enciso, J.-Y. Noh, D. Fidaleo, and T.-Y. Kim. Constructing a realistic head animation mesh for a specific person. Technical Report 99-691, Computer Science Department, University of Southern California, 1999.

[135] J. Ng and S. Gong. Multi-view face detection and pose estimation using a composite support vector machine across the view sphere. In *Proceedings of the International Workshop on Recognition, Analysis and Tracking of Faces and Gestures in Real-Time Systems*, pages 14–21, 1999.

[136] E. Oja. A simplified neuron model as a principal component analyzer. *Journal of Mathematical Biology*, 15:267–273, 1982.

[137] E. Oja. Principal components, minor components, and linear neural networks. *Neural Networks*, 5:927–935, 1992.

[138] E. Oja and J. Karhunen. On stochastic approximation of the eigenvectors and eigenvalues of the expectation of a random matrix. *Journal of Mathematical Analysis and Applications*, 106:69–84, 1985.

[139] K. Okada. Development of an active range finder system and its application to human face recognition. Master's thesis, Nagoya University, Nagoya, Japan, 1994.

[140] K. Okada, S. Akamatsu, and C. von der Malsburg. Analysis and synthesis of pose variations of human faces by a linear pcmap model and its application for pose-invariant face recognition system. In *Proceedings of Fourth International Conference on Automatic Face and Gesture Recognition*, pages 142–149, Grenoble, France, 2000.

[141] K. Okada, J. Steffens, T. Maurer, H. Hong, E. Elagin, H. Neven, and C. von der Malsburg. The Bochum/USC face recognition system: And how it fared in the FERET phase III test. In *Face Recognition: From Theory to Applications*, pages 186–205. Springer-Verlag, 1998.

[142] K. Okada and C. von der Malsburg. Automatic video indexing with incremental gallery creation: Integration of recognition and knowledge acquisition. In *Proceedings of Third International Conference on Knowledge-Based Intelligent Information Engineering Systems*, pages 431–434, Adelaide, Australia, 1999.

[143] K. Okada, C. von der Malsburg, and S. Akamatsu. A pose-invariant face recognition system using linear pcmap model. In *Proceedings of IEICE*

Workshop of Human Information Processing, pages 7–12, Okinawa, Japan, November 1999.

[144] E. Osuna, R. Freund, and F. Girosi. Training support vector machines: an application to face detection. In *Proceedings of the IEEE Computer Society Conference on Computer Vision and Pattern Recognition*, pages 130–136, 1997.

[145] A. J. O'Toole, H. Abdi, K. A. Deffenbacher, and D. Valentin. Low-dimensional representation of faces in higher dimensions of the face space. *Journal of the Optical Society of America*, 10:405–411, 1993.

[146] A. J. O'Toole, S. Edelman, and H. H. Bülthoff. Stimulus-specific effects in face recognition over changes in viewpoint. *Vision Research*, 38:2351–2363, 1998.

[147] F. I. Parke. Computer generated animation of faces. In *Proceedings of the ACM Annual Conference*, 1972.

[148] J. S. Penev and J. J. Atick. Local feature analysis: a general statistical theory for object representation. *Network: Computation in Neural Systems*, 7:477–500, 1996.

[149] A. Pentland, B. Moghaddam, and T. Starner. View-based and modular eigenspaces for face recognition. Technical report, M.I.T. Media Laboratory Perceptual Computing Section, 1994.

[150] D. I. Perrett, J. K. Hietanen, M. W. Oram, and P. J. Benson. Organization and functions of cells responsive to faces in the temporal cortex. *Philosophical Transactions of the Royal Society of London*, 335:23–30, 1992.

[151] G. Peters and C. von der Malsburg. Interpolation of novel object views from two or three sample views. In *Proceedings of Engineering of Natural and Artificial Intelligent Systems*, 2001. accepted.

[152] P. J. Phillips, H. Moon, P. Rauss, and S. A. Rizvi. The FERET evaluation methodology for face-recognition algorithms. In *Proceedings of the IEEE Computer Society Conference on Computer Vision and Pattern Recognition*, pages 137–143, 1997.

[153] P. J. Phillips, H. Moon, P. Rauss, and S. A. Rizvi. The FERET september 1996 database and evaluation procedure. In *Proceedings of Audio- and Video-Based Person Authentication*, pages 395–402, Crans-Montana, Switzerland, 1997. Springer.

[154] P. J. Phillips, H. Moon, S. Rizvi, and P. Rauss. The FERET evaluation. In *Face Recognition: From Theory to Applications*, pages 244–261. Springer-Verlag, 1998.

[155] P. J. Phillips, H. Moon, S. A. Rizvi, and P. J. Rauss. The FERET evaluation methodology for face-recognition algorithms. *IEEE Transactions on Pattern Analysis and Machine Intelligence*, 22:1090–1104, 2000.

[156] P. J. Phillips and P. Rauss. Face recognition technology (FERET program). In *Office of National Drug Control Policy, CTAC International Technology Symposium*, Chicago, USA, August 1997. in press.

[157] P. J. Phillips, P. Rauss, and S. Z. Der. FERET (face recognition technology) recognition algorithm development and test results. Technical report, US Army Research Laboratory, 1996.

[158] F. Pighin, J. Hecker, D. Lischinski, R. Szeliski, and H. Salesin. Synthesizing realistic facial expressions from photographs. In *Proceedings of Siggraph*, pages 75–84, 1998.

[159] M. D. Plumbley. A Hebbian/anti-Hebbian network which optimizes information capacity by orthonormalizing the principal subspace. In *Processings of the IEE Artificial Neural Networks Conference*, pages 86–90, 1993.

[160] M. D. Plumbley. A network which performs orthonormalized principal subspace extraction. Technical Report Technical Report 94/06, Department of Computer Science, King's College London, 1994.

[161] T. Poggio and F. Girosi. A theory of networks for approximation and learning. Technical Report A.I. Memo, No. 1140, Artificial Intelligence Laboratory, M.I.T., 1989.

[162] T. Poggio and T. Vetter. Recognition and structure from one 2D model view: Observations on prototypes, object classes and symmetries. Technical Report A.I. Memo, No. 1347, Artificial Intelligence Laboratory, M.I.T., 1992.

[163] M. Pötzsch, T. Maurer, L. Wiskott, and C. von der Malsburg. Reconstruction from graphs labeled with responses of Gabor filters. In *Proceedings of the International Conference of Artificial Neural Networks*, pages 845–850, Bochum, 1996.

[164] W. H. Press, S. A. Teukolsky, W. T. Vetterling, and B. P. Flannery. *Numerical Recipes in C: The Art of Scientific Computing*. Cambridge University Press, New York, 1992.

[165] M. Proesmans and L. Van Gool. Getting facial features and gestures in 3D. In *Face Recognition: From Theory to Applications*, pages 287–309. Springer-Verlag, 1998.

[166] H. L. Reed and R. M. Siegel. Modulation of responses to optic flow in area 7a by retinotopic and oculomotor cues in monkey. *Cerebral Cortex*, 7:887–890, 1997.

[167] E. T. Rolls. Neurophysiological mechanisms underlying face processing within and beyond the temporal cortical visual areas. *Philosophical Transactions of the Royal Society of London*, 335:11–21, 1992.

[168] E. Rosch, C. B. Merwis, W. D. Gray, D. M. Johnson, and P. Boyes-Baräm. Basic objects in natural categories. *Cognitive Psychology*, 8:382–439, 1976.

[169] H. A. Rowley, S. Baluja, and T. Kanade. Human face detection in visual scenes. Technical Report CMU-CS-95-158, School of Computer Science, Carnegie Mellon University, 1995.

[170] D. E. Rumelhart and J. L. McClelland. *Parallel Distributed Processing*. MIT Press, Cambridge, MA, 1986.

[171] T. Sakai, M. Nagao, and T. Kanade. Computer analysis and classification of photographs of human faces. In *Proceedings of First USA-Japan Computer Conference*, pages 55–62, 1972.

[172] T. Sakai, M. Nagao, and T. Kanade. Computer analysis of photographs of human faces. *Denshi Tsushin Gakkai Ronbunshi*, 56D:226–233, 1973.

[173] A. Samal and P. A. Iyengar. Automatic recognition and analysis of human faces and facial expression: a survey. *Pattern Recognition*, 25:65–77, 1992.

[174] Y. Sato. Piecewise linear approximation of plane curves by perimeter optimization. *Pattern Recognition*, 25:1535–1543, 1992.

[175] Y. Sato and M. Otsuki. Three-dimensional shape reconstruction by active range finder. In *Proceedings of IEEE Computer Society Conference on Computer Vision and Pattern Recognition*, pages 142–147, New York, 1993.

[176] S. Schaal and C. G. Atkeson. Constructive incremental learning from only local information. *Neural Computing*, 10:2047–2084, 1998.

[177] B. Schölkopf, A. Smola, and K.-R. Müller. Nonlinear component analysis as a kernel eigenvalue problem. Technical Report TR44, Max-Plank-Institut fur Biologische Kybernetik, 1996.

[178] P. G. Schyns and H. H. Bülthoff. Conditions for viewpoint dependent face recognition. Technical Report A.I. Memo, No. 1432, Artificial Intelligence Laboratory, M.I.T., 1993.

[179] M. A. Shackleton and W. J. Welsh. Classification of facial features for recognition. In *Proceedings of the IEEE Conference on Computer Vision and Pattern Recognition*, pages 573–579, 1991.

[180] J. Sherrah and S. Gong. Fusion of 2D face alignment and 3D head pose estimation for robust and real-time performance. In *Proceedings of International Workshop on Recognition, Analysis and Tracking of Faces and Gestures in Real-Time Systems*, pages 26–27, 1999.

[181] I. Shimizu, Z. Zhang, S. Akamatsu, and K. Deguchi. Head pose determination from one image using a generic model. In *Proceedings of the International Workshop on Automatic Face and Gesture Recognition*, pages 100–105, Nara, 1998.

[182] L. Sirovich and M. Kirby. Low dimensional procedure for the characterisation of human faces. *Journal of the Optical Society of America*, 4:519–525, 1987.

[183] L. H. Snyder, K. L. Grieve, P. R. Brotchie, and R. A. Andersen. Separate body-and world-referenced representations of visual space in parietal cortex. *Nature*, 394:887–890, 1998.

[184] J. Steffens, E. Elagin, and H. Neven. Personspotter - fast and robust system for human detection, tracking and recognition. In *Proceedings of the International Conference on Face and Gesture Recognition*, pages 516–521, 1998.

[185] J. B. Tenenbaum. Mapping a manifold of perceptual observations. In *Advances in Neural Information Processing*, volume 10, pages 682–688, 1998.

[186] J. B. Tenenbaum, V. de Silva, and J. C. Langford. A global geometric framework for nonlinear dimensionality reduction. *Science*, 290:2319–2323, 2000.

[187] H. Tenmoto, M. Kudo, and M. Shimbo. Piecewise linear classifiers with an appropriate number of hyperplanes. *Pattern Recognition*, 31(11):1627–1634, November 1998.

[188] J.-C. Terrillon, M. N. Shirazi, M. Sadek, H. Fukamachi, and S. Akamatsu. Skin-color based segmentation and invariant detection of human faces in still scene images by use of support vector machines. In *Proceedings of IEICE Workshop of Human Information Processing*, pages 1–7, Okinawa, Japan, November 1999.

[189] M. E. Tipping and C. M. Bishop. Mixtures of probabilistic principal component analyzers. *Neural Computation*, 11:443–482, 1999.

[190] C. Tomasi and T. Kanade. Shape and motion from image streams under orthography: a factorization method. *International Journal of Computer Vision*, 9:137–154, 1992.

[191] V. Tresp and R. Hofmann. Nonlinear time-series prediction with missing and noisy data. *Neural Computation*, 10:731–747, 1998.

[192] N. F. Troje and H. H. Bülthoff. Face recognition under varying poses: The role of texture and shape. *Vision Research*, 36:1761–1771, 1996.

[193] N. F. Troje and H. H. Bülthoff. How is bilateral symmetry of human faces used for recognition of novel views? Technical Report TR38, Max-Plank-Institut fur Biologische Kybernetik, 1996.

[194] A. Tsukamoto, C.-W. Lee, and S. Tsuji. Detection and pose estimation of human face with synthesized image models. In *Proceedings of the International Conference on Pattern Recognition*, pages 754–757, 1994.

[195] M. Turk and A. Pentland. Eigenfaces for recognition. *Journal of Cognitive Neuroscience*, 3:71–86, 1991.

[196] S. Uchida and H. Sakoe. Piecewise linear two-dimensional warping. In *Proceedings of International Conference on Pattern Recognition*, pages Vol III: 538–541, 2000.

[197] S. Ullman and R. Basri. Recognition by linear combinations of models. *IEEE Transactions on Pattern Analysis and Machine Intelligence*, 13:992–1006, 1991.

[198] D. Valentin, H. Abdi, and A. J. O'Toole. Categorization and identification of human face images by neural networks: A review of the linear autoassociative and principal component approaches. *Journal of Biological Systems*, 2:413–429, 1994.

[199] D. Valentin, H. Abdi, A. J. O'Toole, and G. W. Cottrell. Connectionist models of face processing: a survey. *Pattern Recognition*, 27:1209–1230, 1994.

[200] V. Vapnik. *The Nature of Statistical Learning Theory*. Springer-Verlag, New York, 1995.

[201] K. Venkataraman and T. Poston. Piece-wise linear morphing and rendering with 3D textures. *Computer Networks and ISDN Systems*, 29:1625–1633, 1997.

[202] T. Vetter and V. Blanz. Generalization to novel views from a single face image. In *Face Recognition: From Theory to Applications*, pages 310–326. Springer-Verlag, 1998.

[203] T. Vetter, M. J. Jones, and T. Poggio. A bootstrapping algorithm for learning linear models of object classes. In *Proceedings of the IEEE Computer Society Conference on Computer Vision and Pattern Recognition*, pages 40–46, 1997.

[204] T. Vetter and T. Poggio. Linear object classes and image synthesis from a single example image. *IEEE Transactions on Pattern Analysis and Machine Intelligence*, 19:733–742, 1997.

[205] T. Vetter and N. Troje. A separated linear shape and texture space for modeling two-dimensional images of human faces. Technical Report TR15, Max-Plank-Institut fur Biologische Kybernetik, 1995.

[206] S. Vijayakumar and S. Schaal. Local adaptive subspace regression. *Neural Processing Letters*, 7:139–149, 1998.

[207] C. von der Malsburg and L. Shams. Making sense of complex cells. submitted to Nature, 2000.

[208] M. Vriesenga and J. Sklansky. Neural modeling of piecewise linear classifiers. In *Proceedings of International Conference on Pattern Recognition*, pages 281–285, 1996.

[209] J. Walter. *Rapid Learning in Robotics*. PhD thesis, University of Bielefeld, 1996.

216

[210] J. Wieghardt and C. von der Malsburg. Pose-independent object representation by 2-D views. In *Proceedings of IEEE International Workshop on Biologically Motivated Computer Vision*, May 2000. submitted.

[211] L. Wiskott. *Labeled Graphs and Dynamic Link Matching for Face Recognition and Scene Analysis*. PhD thesis, Ruhr-Universität Bochum, 1995.

[212] L. Wiskott. Phantom faces for face analysis. In *Proceedings of the Third Joint Symposium on Neural Computation*, volume 6, pages 46–52, Pasadena, CA, 1996.

[213] L. Wiskott, J.-M. Fellous, N. Krüger, and C. von der Malsburg. Face recognition and gender determination. In *Proceedings of the International Workshop on Automatic Face and Gesture Recognition*, pages 92–97, Zurich, 1995.

[214] L. Wiskott, J.-M. Fellous, N. Krüger, and C. von der Malsburg. Face recognition by elastic bunch graph matching. Technical Report IR-INI 96-08, Institut für Neuroinformatik, Ruhr-Universität Bochum, 1997.

[215] L. Wiskott, J.-M. Fellous, N. Krüger, and C. von der Malsburg. Face recognition by elastic bunch graph matching. *IEEE Transactions on Pattern Analysis and Machine Intelligence*, 19:775–779, 1997.

[216] W. Wothke. Longitudinal and multi-group modeling with missing data. In *Modeling Longitudinal and Multiple Group Data: Practical Issues, Applied Approaches and Specific Examples*. Lawrence Erlbaum Associates, 1998. in press.

[217] Y. Wu and K. Toyama. Wide-range, person- and illumination-insensitive head orientation estimation. In *Proceedings of Fourth International Conference on Automatic Face and Gesture Recognition*, pages 183–188, Grenoble, France, 2000.

[218] R. P. Würtz. *Multilayer Dynamical Link Networks for Establishing Image Point Correspondences and Visual Objects Recognition*. PhD thesis, Ruhr-Universität Bochum, 1994.

[219] L. Xu. Least mean square error reconstruction principle for self-organizing neural nets. *Neural Networks*, 6:627–648, 1993.

[220] M. Xu and T. Akatsuka. Detecting head pose from stereo image sequence for active face recognition. In *Proceedings of the International Workshop on Automatic Face and Gesture Recognition*, pages 82–87, Nara, 1998.

[221] Y. Yacoob, H.-M. Lam, and L. S. Davis. Recognizing faces showing expressions. In *Proceedings of the International Conference on Pattern Recognition*, pages 747–749, 1994.

[222] A. W. Young. Face recognition impairments. *Philosophical Transactions of the Royal Society of London*, 335:47–54, 1992.

[223] W. Y. Zhao and R. Chellappa. SFS based view synthesis for robust face recognition. In *Proceedings of Fourth International Conference on Automatic Face and Gesture Recognition*, pages 285–292, Grenoble, France, 2000.

[224] W. Y. Zhao, R. Chellappa, and A. Krishnaswamy. Discriminant analysis of principal components for face recognition. In *Proceedings of the International Conference on Face and Gesture Recognition*, pages 336–341, 1998.

www.ingramcontent.com/pod-product-compliance
Lightning Source LLC
LaVergne TN
LVHW042333060326
832902LV00006B/146